Riding with the Comanches

Riding with the Comanches

The 35th Battalion Virginia Cavalry, Confederate
Army During the American Civil War

ILLUSTRATED

The Comanches

Frank M. Myers

Service With the Laurel Brigade

William N. McDonald

LEONAUR

Riding with the Comanches
The 35th Battalion Virginia Cavalry, Confederate Army During the American Civil War
The Comanches
by Frank M. Myers
Service With the Laurel Brigade
William N. McDonald

ILLUSTRATED

FIRST EDITION

Leonaur is an imprint of Oakpast Ltd
Copyright in this form © 2023 Oakpast Ltd

ISBN: 978-1-915234-98-8 (hardcover)
ISBN: 978-1-915234-99-5 (softcover)

http://www.leonaur.com

Publisher's Notes

The views expressed in this book are not necessarily
those of the publisher.

Contents

Exeter, Loudoun Co., Va., Dec. 2, 1870.

Captain F. M. Myers:

Dear Sir,—We, the undersigned, officers of the Thirty-Fifth Battalion, Virginia Cavalry, C.S.A., having examined the MSS. of your history of the same, do most heartily endorse the said history, and must congratulate you upon the graphic manner in which you have related the story of their deeds of daring, their trials and sufferings for the "Lost Cause."

Most respectfully, your old comrades and companions in arms,

Elijah V. White,
Late Lieut.-Col. Thirty-Fifth Va. Cav.

J. R. Crown,
Late First Lieut. Co. B, White's Bat.

Benj. F. Conrad,
Late Second Lieut. Co. A, Thirty-Fifth Va. Cav.

Geo. W. Chiswell,
Late Captain Co. B, White's Battalion.

Ed. J. Chiswell,
Late Second Lieut. Co. B, Thirty-Fifth Va. Cav.

Wm. F. Barrett,
Late First Lieut. Co. A, White's Battalion.

Wm. F. Dowdell,
Late Captain Co. C, Thirty-Fifth Va. Cav.

J. Mort. Kilgour,
Late Capt. and A.Q.M., Thirty-Fifth Va. Cav.

Preface

To the Members of the Thirty-Fifth Virginia Cavalry:

The following pages have been prepared under many and great difficulties, and while they exhibit the history of the command, we were so proud of in the dark days of the war for States Rights and the old Constitution, they are very far from presenting a *full* history of our battalion.

Almost all the papers relating to the operations of the "Comanches," whether belonging to the field and staff or to company officers, were lost at the surrender of the army, in consequence of which I have been compelled to draw nearly all that is recorded from my own memory, assisted materially by Col. White, in the account of the "Battle of Brandy Station," and of the raids in Fairfax and Loudoun in 1863.

To Mr. John O. Crown I am under obligations for the use of his MSS., giving an account of the operations in the autumn of 1862, and of the last winter of the war, and to Lieuts. J. R. Crown and E. J. Chiswell for much that is interesting in the history of Company B; to the former especially, for a report of his fight with Cole's battalion in Maryland, and of his capture by the same command in 1863.

The lists of killed and wounded for Company B were prepared by Lieut. Chiswell; for Company C, by Capt. Dowdell; for Company E, Lieut. Strickler, and for Company A, by myself.

From Company F, I regret exceedingly that I have not been able to obtain any information whatever.

As for the *manner* of the work, while I am free to confess that the story is by no means well told, yet, the men of the battalion who, by education and talent, were well qualified for the task of preparing it, would not, and it has thus fallen to my lot to write this history; and, such as it is, I submit it to your judgment for approval or not, as you may decide; but among its faults I claim that violations of the "historian's religion"—truth—will not be laid to its charge; and the thoughts, feelings, and impressions, unbiassed by the warpings of after events, have been presented as far as possible.

It is a story altogether of the past, and, as soldiers of the "Lost Cause," we have nothing to do with the efforts of politicians, North or South, to galvanise the Confederacy into spasmodic action, and then cry—

There's life in the old land yet.

There is no attempt either to conceal or parade the grief we, as Confederate soldiers, felt at the furling of the "conquered banner."

For though conquered, we adore it,
Love the cold, dead hands that bore it.

But while we do love so dearly the battle-flag of "Dixie," we regard it only as the emblem of the "storm-cradled nation that fell," and as the winding-sheet of its dead and buried glory, over whose gloomy tomb the brave, true-hearted men of the southland have raised a monument of noble deeds, which will defy malice, oppression, and time.

We know that the Southern Confederacy is dead, and all its mourning lovers ask is permission to bury their dead reverently.

Hushed is the roll of the Rebel drum,
The sabres are sheathed, and the cannon are dumb,
And fate with pitiless hand has furled,
The flag that once challenged the gaze of the world.

But the fame of its soldiers deserves to live on the pages of history, and, if I have aided in rescuing from oblivion the story of the gallant deeds performed by the men that followed Col. Elijah V. White through the bloody years of that desolating war, I am satisfied.

F. M. Myers.

Loudoun County. Va., Nov. 27, 1870.

1: The Early Career of Elijah V. White

In commencing the story of the brave deeds performed during the dark days of the great civil war in America by the gallant band known as "White's Battalion," it will be proper to give a short sketch of the man who, as chief of the "Comanches," gave to the Thirty-Fifth Battalion, Virginia Cavalry, its existence, and led it through so many campaigns, battles and raids, to occupy a place in the history of the war second to no command of its numbers, and distinguished under the special notice of such men as "Stonewall" Jackson, Richard S. Ewell, J. E. B. Stuart, William E. Jones, Thomas L. Rosser and the gallant Butler of South Carolina; besides receiving the highest encomiums from the greatest cavalry commander since the days when Murat led the squadrons of Napoleon—General Wade Hampton—and of Robert E. Lee, before whose fame the most splendid garlands of glory that wreathe the brows of the noblest men of earth in all time, pale as does the silver moon-beam before the radiant rays of the noon-day sun.

Elijah V. White was born near Poolsville, Montgomery County, Maryland, on the 29th of August, 1832, and continued at his father's home until he was sixteen years of age, when he was sent to Lima Seminary, Livingston Co., N.Y., to be educated. Here he remained for two years, at the expiration of which he attended Granville College, in Licking Co., Ohio, for two more years, when he returned to his home in Maryland.

During the war in Kansas, in 1855 or '56, he went to that territory, and joining a company from Missouri, took an active part in the troubles that then threatened to overthrow the pillars of the old Constitution in the terrible maelstrom of abolitionism that afterwards swept away their foundations.

After the Kansas war closed, young White came home, and shortly afterwards bought a farm on the south bank of the Potomac, in Loudoun County, Virginia, where he took up his residence in 1857, and on the 9th of December of the same year married Miss Sarah Elizabeth Gott.

GENERAL WADE HAMPTON

At the first signal of war, given by John Brown at Harper's Ferry, in October, 1859, White was a corporal in the Loudoun Cavalry, a company then commanded by Capt. Dan. T. Shreve, with which he took part in the scenes of excitement that followed this mad attempt of Northern fanaticism to sweep the twin scourges of fire and blood over the South. At the breaking out of the war in 1861, White was still a member of this company; but owing to a change of its officers, which, to a great extent, damaged its efficiency, he left it and attached himself to the company of Capt. Frank Mason, in Ashby's Legion, with which he served until the autumn of that year, being engaged principally in scouting, much of which he did under the orders of Col. Eppa Hunton, who, during the summer, commanded in Loudoun County.

On one of his scouts for Col. Hunton, in Maryland, he captured the first Yankee prisoner of the war in the person of one Costine, of Gen. McCall's staff. When Gen. Evans took command in Leesburg, "Lige White," as he was familiarly known, reported to him, and the night before the fight at Bolivar, the general asked "Lige" "if he didn't want some fun," at the same time informing him that Ashby intended to attack Geary on the following morning; whereupon "Lige" started at 9 o'clock, reaching Ashby's camp just as that commander was marching out to make his demonstration on Harper's Ferry.

In this brilliant affair he bore his full share, and when it was over returned on a furlough, to Loudoun, to make necessary arrangements for leaving his family in as comfortable circumstances as possible, while he followed the fortunes of the battle flag of Dixie. Early on the morning of the 21st of October, while driving to Leesburg from Mr. Henry Ball's, in a buggy, with Miss Kate Ball, he heard the firing of the opening fight at Ball's Bluff, and hastily returning to Mr. Ball's, he mounted his horse and reported at once to General Evans for duty.

The general, who was somewhat the worse for whiskey, gruffly asked him what he could do; to which "Lige" replied that he could scout, could carry dispatches, or could go into the ranks and fight. After a few moments of study, Evans exclaimed, "Well, sir, go to the front and fight like hell and damnation;" and "Lige" rode off and reported to Col. Hunton, who was the actual commander in this battle.

The colonel requested White to remain with him and scout for him during the day; and shortly after, when returning from a scout to the left to learn if the enemy was attempting any movement on the flank, he found fully one-third of the 8th Virginia Regiment in utter rout, caused by a misunderstanding of an order for that part of the regiment, which had been considerably advanced, to retire on the main line, and they taking it to be an order to retreat. With great difficulty the order was explained and the men rallied and brought back to the line, when Col. Hunton ordered an advance of his regiment which vigorously attacked the enemy, driving his whole right wing back to the woods bordering on the bluff, and capturing two brass howitzers, but the left of his line stood firm, and White was ordered by Col. Burt, of the 18th Mississippi, to go into the woods and bring up two companies of his regiment that had been stationed on the extreme right of the Confederate line to guard against a flank attack in that quarter, and form them on the right of the 17th.

As soon as this order had been executed, Col. Burt ordered his regiment to advance, which it did, the colonel and White riding in rear of the line, and when in about fifty yards of a skirt of timber that grew along a ravine in the old field, the enemy, who till that moment had lain concealed, raised up and poured a most terribly destructive volley into the Mississippi line, by which about one hundred and thirty men were killed and wounded; in fact, by far the largest part of the Confederate loss on that day was caused by this one murderous fire. Col. Burt was mortally wounded by White's side and the latter represents himself as being terribly frightened but untouched, and says the men of the 18th stood unflinchingly in the storm and soon drove the enemy from his position. Col. Burt, who was held on his horse by two of his men, asked White to ride to Col. Jenifer and inform him that he (Burt) was mortally wounded and must leave the field.

On his return he found Col. Hunton in front of the 18th Regiment instructing its major to advance through the woods upon the enemy, but the major objected, saying he did not know the ground; when Hunton said, "Come on, I'll lead you;" to which the major replied, "No, sir; I can lead my own men, all I want is a guide;" and Col. Hunton turned to White, saying, "Lige, my boy, won't you go with them?" which settled the question of a guide, and "Lige" rode forward in front of the Mississippians, soon finding himself between two fires, the foe in front and friends behind; but the Yankees soon gave way, leaving a splendid brass 24-pounder rifle gun as a trophy to the gallantry of the noble 18th Mississippi.

This closed the battle, and Col. Hunton again sent "Lige" on a scout to the left to see what the enemy was doing in that direction. It was now dark and White had not gone far before he was halted by a voice which he knew to belong to a Yankee, and replying in a low

COLONEL E. V. WHITE COMMANDER 35TH BATTALION

J E B Stuart

tone, "halted;" the man asked who he was; "Lige" answering by asking the same question, and the fellow replied—"I belong to the New York Tammany Regiment."

White, still speaking very low, called out excitedly, "You do! Come to me, come to me!" and the Yankee advanced close to him with gun at a charge bayonet, when White said to him, "Surrender, or you are a dead man;" at the same time levelling his pistol on him, but the Yankee was pluck, and exclaiming, "Never, to any man!" stepped back to bayonet his foe, and "Lige" at the same moment drew trigger but his pistol missed fire; hastily cocking it again he was just in time, and sent a bullet crashing through the Yankee's brain just as he was in the act of driving his bayonet through him.

"Lige" now satisfied himself that the enemy had retired all along the line, and returned to Col. Hunton, who now marched his people back to their camp, ordering White to remain with Lieut. Chas. Berkeley, who with fifteen men was to remain on picket near the river during the night. The ladies of Leesburg had sent a kingly supper to the soldiers, and after satisfying their appetites, which had been sharp-set by a day of fasting and fighting, White proposed to Lieut. Berkeley that they take a scout to the river, for, strange as it may appear, not a single Confederate had been *to* the bluff, although they had fought to within a few yards of its edge.

To this Lieut. B. readily agreed, and passing quietly along over the dead and dying, they reached the river, and soon heard a boat crossing over from the opposite bank. In a few minutes it struck the Virginia shore, and leaving Berkeley and his men, White walked up to the landing place where he found himself among a great crowd of Yankees, all eager to get aboard the one *gondola*, and terribly excited. To return to the lieutenant and report was the next move, and "Lige" declared that he believed there were 800 to 1,000 Yankees down under the bluff, and asked Berkeley what they were to do, to which he replied, "We will capture the whole of them."

White agreed to it, provided the fifteen would all promise to carry it through or die trying, when one of the men said to him that Lieut. B. was a rash man and he, for one, was not willing to follow him, as he feared they would all be killed; upon which "Lige" started to the camp of the 8th Virginia for reinforcements. On arriving there he found Lt.-Col. Tebbs in command, who said that if any of the men chose to do so they might go, but advised them to let the enterprise alone. On telling his story and asking for volunteers, Captain W. N. Berkeley said,

"I'll follow you," and at once some of Capt. B's men responded with, "Yes, and we'll follow *you*."

So that in a short time quite a force had volunteered, composed as follows:—Captains, W. N. and Edmund Berkeley; Lieutenants, R. H. Tyler, L. B. Stephenson and R. Coe; Sergeants, F. Wilson, J. O. Adams and ——— Gochnauer; Corporals Aye, B. Hurst, W. Fleshler, B. Hutchison and Wm. Thomas; and Privates, A. S. Adams, J. W. Adams, F. A. Boyer, J. L. Chin, G. Creel, R. S. Downs, W. Donnelly, G. Insor, C. R. Griffin, John George, D. L. Hixson, T. W. Hutchison, J. F. Ish, R. I. Smith, W. C. Thomas, J. W. Tavenner, J. M. McVeigh, L. W. Luckett, C. D. Luckett, M. H. Luckett, A. M. O'Bannon, Rev. Chas. Linthicum, R. O. Carter, George Roach, E. Nails, Howard Trussell, D. Rourke, Thomas E. Tavenner, P. Gochnauer, F. Tinsman, T. H. Benton, T. Kidwell, C. Fox, V. R. Costello, Will. Moore, J. Ellis, William McCarty, J. McClanahan, E. Herrington and R. Julian.

With this force White started back to the river, where he had left Lieut. Berkeley watching the enemy, and on reaching it, after an absence of nearly two hours, found the situation unchanged, except that the number of the enemy was perceptibly lessened, the gondola having made several trips. Hastily arranging his forces, "Lige" posted Lieut. Berkeley on top of the bluff, just over the Yankees, while he moved the remainder down to the edge of the river and charged at once upon the enemy, firing and yelling like demons, when at the same moment Lieut. B. opened fire from the bluff with his party. The consternation was terrible among the Yankees, some leaping into the river and drowning themselves, some wading out in the water as far as they could, some running up the river bank, and some, too much paralyzed with fear to act at all, just fell down and screamed.

Very soon an Irish captain, a gallant fellow, appeared and called a parley, when the firing ceased and the captain asked who was in command, to which Capt. William Berkeley replied, "Gen. White," and the captain at once asked upon what terms his men would be allowed to surrender, and when told they should be treated kindly as prisoners of war, he called them up from their hiding places, saying, "the general assures me you shall be kindly treated; come out and give yourselves up." This had the desired effect and they all came up, to the number of 320, and surrendered to the "brigade of General White."

A few days after this, a recommendation was drawn up and signed by the regimental commanders, asking that White be commissioned in the Regular Army of the Confederate States, for meritorious conduct at the battle of Leesburg. This was approved by Gen. Evans, and cordially endorsed by Gen. Beauregard, but when "Lige" presented it to the Secretary of War, he was informed that no commissions in the Regular Army were being granted then, but that his name should be registered for the first vacancy.

This did not suit him and learning that his old friend, Col. Hunton, was in Richmond, called upon him, and was advised by that officer to apply for permission to organise an independent company for service on the border, which he did, and through Col. Hunton's influence succeeded without any difficulty in getting the appointment of Captain in the Provisional Army, with the authority to raise a company as proposed, and he now returned to Leesburg where he opened a recruiting office under very favourable auspices, the militia of the county having been called to that point by Gen. D. H. Hill, (who succeeded Evans in command of the department soon after the battle,) to work on the fortifications in course of construction there, and it was natural to suppose that many of them would prefer ranging service on the border to wielding the shovel and the hoe in the breast-works.

2: White's Scouting Company

In the last days of December, 1861, Captain Elijah V. White, for such was his rank now, reported to General Hill, with fifteen men for duty, and was ordered by that officer to establish a line of couriers between Leesburg and Winchester, which he did on the 29th, stationing Ben. F. Conrad and James W. Harper at Leesburg, Richard Harding and William H. Luckett at Hamilton, Peter J. Kabrich and Frank. M. Myers at Round Hill, C. C. Wenner and R. W. Washington at Castleman's Ferry, Joseph E. Conner and W. T. Cruzen at Berryville, and Richard Ferro at Winchester, with Gip. Peter in command at that end of the line, while the captain himself remained at Leesburg.

The company was thus employed until the 14th of January following, when an order was passed along the line calling all the men to assemble in Leesburg, and on reaching that point the captain found he had about twenty-five men, whom he marched to Waterford and established in winter quarters at that place. Maj. Win. F. Barrett, of the 57th Regiment Virginia Militia, acted as orderly sergeant and quartermaster, and with the captain formed the board of officers of the company. The Madison Cavalry, under Capt. Graves, was also stationed at Waterford and picketed the Potomac from the Point of Rocks to

Berlin, and Capt. White proposed to co-operate with these men in scouting, and guarding the line of river all the way to Harper's Ferry; and here commenced the active duty of what was afterwards to be the famous battalion, now not having enough men to entitle it to a company organisation, but whose rolls afterwards bore nearly 700 names.

About this time an officer was sent by Gen. Hill to muster the company regularly into the military service of the Confederate States, and this duty performed, the men considered themselves tied fast and were perfectly satisfied with their lot.

Among the first duties required of the company was that of executing an order of Gen. Hill, to collect the delinquent Militia of the 56th Virginia Regiment, and take them to their comrades who were at work on the fortifications around Leesburg, but this was no easy matter, many of them having crossed the Potomac—some to take service in the army of Abraham I, and others to escape doing any kind of military duty in the Confederacy—while a large portion of those who remained were Quakers, who, according to the tenets of their religion, could not perform such duty, and paid their exemption fines.

Another order of the general's required Capt. White to go into south Loudoun and upper Fauquier, and impress into the service all the wagons, teams and negroes that could be spared from that section, and take them to Leesburg.

The execution of this order was entrusted to Henry K. Moore, who, finding the citizens exceeding loth to give over their property to the tender mercies of the C. S. A., took their excuses instead, and returned to camp with sundry promises on the part of the people to send the required articles at a "more convenient season."

On making his report to the captain, the latter expressed decided disapprobation of that style of executing a military order, and to show what he considered the proper mode, he only allowed Henry and his detail time enough to feed their horses, when he had them in the saddle again, and taking charge of the expedition himself, he sallied forth among the reluctant citizens of the favoured region named in Gen. Hill's order. And this time the wagons and contrabands came; but he left a very bitter memory among the people whom he visited, for they were just congratulating themselves that they had so easily escaped the fulfilment of the order which Henry had shown them, when White swooped down upon them and executed it promptly and to the letter.

It was the custom of Capt. White to leave his quarters about dark, on those long winter nights, and striking the Potomac at some one of the fords or ferries along that stream, lie quiet and watch for the Federals to come over, and also to look out for the people, who, loyal to the Lincoln dynasty but traitors to their State, would cross over, some to carry news to the Yankees and return with their blood money to gather more, and some to escape being called into the military service in Virginia.

Not the least however of his care, was to stop the exodus of the negro population who, on the border, were constantly being decoyed by Yankee emissaries away from their masters and their homes.

On one of these occasions, he was accompanied by the Rev. Mr. ———, an Old School Baptist preacher, who, with his shot gun on his shoulder, agreed to act as pilot for the command in a little scout to the river opposite the Point of Rocks.

It was Sunday night and very cold, but a faithful negro had given information to the captain that a party of his coloured brethren had made an arrangement to run away that night, and that some Yankees were to meet them with a boat at the mouth of the Catocton Creek.

On getting near the ground the men dismounted and tying their horses, walked to the position, when the captain placed one man in the bridge over the creek at that place, and posted the others at the boat landing. The one man was to watch for the negroes and give quiet notice of their approach, while the others were to capture the party that brought over the boats.

Unfortunately the reverend gentleman remained with the picket in the bridge, and just when the boats were heard approaching, the poles grating on the river bottom and plainly heard; for the night was too dark to see anything on the water; the contrabands approached the bridge, and, instead of quietly retiring with the information, the picket ordered them to halt, whereupon they commenced to run, and in great excitement the preacher sprang forward, and, firing his piece, called upon them in language far more emphatic than elegant to halt.

At this the boats hastily put back and a volley of bullets from the Yankee side came whizzing over the river, the great signal lights on the point at the same time beginning to swing to and fro, giving a weird and ghostly gleaming to the wild scene. The captain and his party at once rushed to the bridge, hoping at least to catch some of the negroes, but they were gone, not even a wounded one left as the result of the preacher's shot.

The company then returned to camp, and that was, I believe, the last, as well as the first, expedition ever made by the parson as a scout.

One night the captain ordered the company to saddle up, and taking with him his negro boy "Baz," went down near Harper's Ferry, in search of news from "over the water." Here he passed himself and people for Yankees, and had a very pleasant time among the loyal (coloured) folks of that region; but his information, although very abundant, was not of much value; so after making free with the cherry-bounce, and frightening the little niggers at "old Taps" until their eyes were a great deal too large for their faces, he started "Baz" to a house near the crossing of the Shenandoah, just opposite the town, to try if he couldn't get them to take him over, he representing himself as a runaway, and it being pretty generally understood that the family there was engaged in that business.

It so happened, however, that none of the men were at home, and "Baz" was persuaded by the ladies to wait till morning; but after some time he concluded to put off his trip, and returned to the company, about fifteen of whom were waiting for "Baz"—as part of his programme was to make arrangements for crossing, then return for a couple of friends who were going with him—and he had been so long about it that White, fearing he had got into trouble, or perhaps had turned the thing into earnest and gone over literally, had started to the house and met "Baz" a very short distance from it.

His men at once surrounded the cabin, and Ferro, going on the porch, commenced to inquire of the women—who were still standing there—the news, but no sooner did he speak, than, apparently for the first time comprehending the situation, they threw themselves on the floor and began to scream—"Rebels, rebels; oh, my friends, come over here!—come quick!" &c., and the sentinels on the other side fired their muskets. At once the drums commenced to roll and very soon the troops were in line, when White ordered his party to retire, which they did at once; but the women kept on screaming, and the Yankees opened a fire which rendered the retreat of the scouts a very interesting operation until they reached the point where the grade turns the mountain. And thinking they had heard enough for one night they mounted their horses, and going up the valley to the residence of a good citizen, above Neersville, turned in until morning.

Although returning empty-handed from his scouts, operations of this kind had a good effect on the border, for the reason that they diminished greatly, and at some points stopped the communications entirely, with the other side of the river.

In this manner January and February passed away, but during the latter part of February the business became a great deal more particular, and one Sunday evening the captain returned to camp from Leesburg with an order to cross Goose Creek and make a scout into Fairfax. Leaving the camp at dark, as usual, the command marched through Leesburg, and on reaching the burnt bridge found the creek very high; in fact, some of the horses had to swim; but all crossed safely, and passing down the pike reached Dranesville, when the captain turned to the right, and bivouacked his men in the house of a citizen. Here they slept until morning, and continuing the scout, met Lt.-Col. Munford, with a party of the 2nd Virginia Cavalry, also on the hunt of the enemy; but nothing came of it, and White returned to his camp, with his men pretty badly used up.

Soon after this, Col. Geary of the 28th Pennsylvania, began to pay attention to the Loudoun side of the river, and needed a great deal of looking after on the part of our scouting company. One day the captain, with a party, went up to the Loudoun Heights, and from the old blockhouses there, discovered that a pontoon bridge was nearly completed over the Shenandoah, which evidently showed an intention to cross the river. After staying there for an hour or two, in easy gunshot of the workmen, the captain concluded to go across to the Short Hill and from the Eagle Rock take a look at Sandy Hook and the Rail Road generally. Just as he reached his observatory some of the men looked over at the blockhouses, which they had left a short while ago, and discovered that a detachment of the enemy was in possession of them, having gone up the mountain by one path while White's command was coming down by another. This was decidedly interesting, and the next day the captain took his boys up to the Short Hill again, to have another look at them.

Pretty soon after reaching the top of the mountain one of the boys saw a man in a blue coat lying behind some rocks, and showing him to the captain he called upon him to come out and surrender, which he did, and just at that moment one of the boys, farther out on the mountain, slipped from a rock and accidentally discharged his gun. This created quite a panic, the scouts imagining that they were beleaguered by Yankees, and be it known not many of them had ever seen a Yankee except with the Potomac between them.

The trouble was soon over though, and the prisoner, who proved to be a lieutenant in Co. D, 28th Pennsylvania, explained that he was one of a party that had crossed the hill there on the way to Lovettsville, and by stopping at a house for something to eat he had got behind, and as a consequence fallen into the hands of those whom he termed "guerrillas."

No boy was ever prouder of his first pantaloons than White's boys were of their first prisoner, and rapidly retiring from the mountain they made their best time down the country towards Leesburg, to show him, but great was their astonishment to see the citizens fly from their approach as if they had been a tribe of wild cats.

They couldn't understand it all until, on reaching Wheatland, they met Major Peyton, of Gen. Beauregard's staff, who informed the captain that the people had heard he and his men were all captured, and they thought the party were Yankees coming to devour them.

Capt. White, with his prisoner, and some of his men, went with Major P. to Mr. Braden's, and the others stopped at Mr. Orrison's, where they got supper, and related their marvellous exploit, as they then considered it, and so scrupulously chivalrous were they towards the captured officer that the men took turns at walking in order that he might ride the whole way, and although he was provided with canteen, gum-cloth and haversack, everything in fact that a completely equipped soldier needs, they took nothing from him but his pistol.

The lieutenant informed them that he and all his men were fighting for the Union, and not to set the negroes free; that if he thought for one moment the latter was the object of the war, he would quit the army at once and either go home and stay there, or come South and join the Confederates.

After supper the company united and marched for Leesburg, but on reaching Clark's Gap found that the men who had been left in camp, alarmed at the rumours they had heard, had loaded the wagons and moved everything from Waterford to the turnpike, and had the teams still hitched up ready to move further. Leaving the company here, Capt. W. took the prisoner to Gen. Hill, and in the morning came up and moved his wagons back to Waterford. This was Sunday morning, and a company of Michigan Cavalry came down to about one and a-half miles of the town, when White got his men in the saddle to meet them, but they were only on a scout, and after getting a look at the Southern pickets returned to their camp. The next day the captain took his men again to the mountain, this time to capture the blockhouses on Loudoun Heights.

After reaching the top of the mountain, about two and a-half miles from the object of his expedition, he dismounted five men, to wit: T. S. Grubb, John Tribbey, R. Ferro, C. Cooper, and F. M. Myers, and putting the last named in command, sent them forward along the backbone of the Blue Ridge, as a forlorn hope, with instructions to get as close as possible without being perceived by the enemy, and then to fire and dash upon the houses, telling them that he would support them with the balance of the company, which now numbered about thirty-five men—and boys. The advance guard moved off, thinking that whatever their captain said was all right, and that his orders must be obeyed at every hazard.

They were deployed as skirmishers, the commander keeping as near the line of the mountain summit as possible, while on the right and left were two men, the first ten steps from the leader and the second the same distance beyond the first. In this manner they moved quietly along, with the understanding that as a signal their leading man, in case of need, should whistle once to cause them to lie down, and two notes from the natural bugle meant forward again. While on the way, Cooper asked to be allowed to shoot at the first Yankee he saw and as soon as he saw him, to which Myers objected, but finally agreed that if he was near enough to see the white of his eye he might shoot.

Almost before they knew it they were at the edge of the clearing around the blockhouses, and the Yankees were close by them, upon which the leader whistled and all lay down to look at the situation; but soon a tramp was heard, and looking to the right they saw a sentry walking his beat, which would bring him within ten feet of the forlorn hope, if he kept on, and on looking at Cooper he was seen with his gun across a stump, cocked, ready to fire, and aiming at the Yankee, the white of whose eye was plainly visible certainly, and it required all the signs in his power to make for Myers to prevent him from shooting the sentry, who passed on unconscious of treading so close to the heads of five rebels. There were about eight hundred infantry and five pieces of artillery at the blockhouses, and three of the guns were pointing exactly in the direction of the scouts.

Here was a beautiful piece of work; thirty men to assault such a force as this; but they were going to do it, and the five only waited for the others to get in supporting distance, to commence the attack. It was not made, however, for while lying there they heard a shot in the rear, and crawling back through the bushes until out of sight of the enemy, they got up and travelled as fast as possible to the rear, and finally reached the captain, who only pointed with his hand down towards the valley, and wheeling his horse dashed away. Looking in that direction they saw a force of cavalry and infantry moving up the grade, and already they were beyond Neersville, while in their rear some forage wagons were going along the grade.

They at once conjectured that their captain was going to attack this party and hurried back faster than ever to get their horses, and as soon as all his people were together White dashed down the mountain and charged the foragers, but they were too fast for him, and after following them under the guns of the blockhouses he turned about and gave up the chase.

The company then returned to their quarters, and for several days did nothing but picket, the force being divided into two parties, one under Henry Moore and the other under Frank Myers, who would relieve each other every six hours.

This was soldiering with the gilding off, and many were the homesick boys, as during the stormy hours of those winter nights they sat on their horses peering through the dark for the enemy who threatened them always, but never came to drive them away, although their cavalry came near to us many times; on one occasion going to the old schoolhouse at Rehoboth, which had been occupied by the Southern cavalry as a shelter for their pickets, and burned it down, although they knew they were advancing and it could no longer be used for that purpose.

On another occasion some of them made a valiant descent upon Taylortown and captured "Stout" Williams' Mill at that place, carrying off his books and papers, along with his flour and almost everything else that was moveable about the premises.

However, the hard duty performed by the little garrison at Waterford was soon to change now, for matters drew to a crisis very rapidly after McClellan's army commenced to advance from the lines around Washington, and one evening Capt. White came up from Leesburg and informed his company that the time had come when the border would no longer be on the Potomac, for Generals Beauregard and Johnson were going to fall back from Manassas in order to draw McClellan into a battle away from his base.

The boys all thought the movement was a good one, and by midnight their wagons were loaded and everything in moving order, but all felt very sure they wouldn't be away more than a month at farthest, for one more battle would, in their opinion, about end the war.

About 2 o'clock in the morning the pickets were called in, and the wagons started for Leesburg, while the companies of White and Graves prepared to guard them.

This ended the pleasant experience of camping in Waterford, and closed the Winter campaign for 1861 and '2, the first in which Capt. White's company had been engaged, and from this time forth they were no longer to play soldier, but act it out in sober earnest.

3: A Gunfight and a Wound

On the morning of March 4th, 1862, Captain White marched from Waterford to Leesburg, and when they reached the top of Catocton Mountain they saw what desolation the retiring army was inflicting on the country, and knowing what would follow the Yankees in their advance, it did really appear that the people of their beloved and beautiful Loudoun must leave their homes or be burned with them, for all over the country could be seen the flames going up from the stack-yards and mills, and the morning air was dark and heavy with the gloom of the destruction which brooded over the land.

On arriving at Leesburg Gen. Hill's troops were seen marching away, the general and his staff being mounted, ready to leave the town when the last soldier had gone out. Hill ordered White to remain and act as he thought best, but to watch the enemy, and keep him advised of all movements along the border.

The captain remained in town until evening, when he went up among the Quakers and encamped for the night, and for several days hung around this section, watching for an opportunity to annoy the enemy, but they did not appear desirous of being annoyed by him, for it was almost two days after White left Waterford before the Michigan cavalry appeared in that place; but from here their march to Leesburg was rapid, and after that they remained very quiet for several days, being only engaged in arresting citizens and operating under the instigation of the tory citizens of the county who now flocked into the desolated land, and as far as their power went, destroyed every vestige of free will among the people, and turned loose the demon of political persecution upon those unfortunate people—whose only crime was loyalty to their old mother State.

The situation of the little company of scouts was now rather precarious, cut off from supplies from both directions—their homes and the army too—no regular organisation of their own, no quartermaster, and what rendered the matter worse, the men had made no preparation for a campaign out of reach of their homes, and their supply of clothing was very scanty. The captain bestirred himself to supply, as far as possible, all deficiencies, and made arrangements to get cloth from the factory at Waterloo; and pretty soon he learned that Lieut.-Col. Munford, with four companies of his regiment, had been left to operate along the border.

To this gallant officer and gentleman, he at once applied to have himself and people admitted into his command, which request was readily granted, and in the welcoming speech of the colonel he assured the little band of homeless wanderers that "the men of the mountains welcomed the boys of the Potomac, and would gladly share with them their blankets and their bread."

Here they had a temporary home, and very soon their ranks filled up to the number required by law for a company, and on the 19th of March, under Col. Munford's superintendence, the company was regularly organised, Capt. White being unanimously chosen to command it, with Frank M. Myers as 1st Lieutenant, Wm. F. Barrett 2nd Lieutenant, and R. C. Marlow 3rd Lieutenant.

Lieut. Marlow was placed in general charge of the quartermaster department, and Lieut. Barrett was sent to Culpeper on duty as a recruiting officer.

Col. Munford kept Geary's forces in constant fear and trembling, so that his cavalry never ventured out of hearing of the infantry; and it was no easy matter to make anything out of them.

On one occasion the colonel came from Salem to Rector's Cross Roads, where he found some of the enemy's pickets, and White, with about half a dozen men, tried to capture them, but with all speed they flew down the pike towards Middleburg, closely pursued by the Confederates. On reaching the town, White's party was in striking distance, and succeeded in killing one and wounding another; but here they ran into the 28th Pennsylvania, just in the act of forming their line of battle, and but for a citizen, the captain would have gotten into serious difficulty.

As it was, he turned quietly and rode back to Munford's people, who, by this time, were almost in town, and the whole force moved slowly back towards Rectortown. Capt. White halted about a mile from town and watched the enemy, who marched out a short distance and commenced rapid firing from infantry and artillery, but they were too far away to do any damage at all.

Geary magnified this exploit, in the newspapers, into one the of most terrible incidents of the war, reporting that he had surprised the camp of the rebel guerrilla White, which was in a mountain cave, and had captured a great quantity of war material besides about one hundred prisoners.

In the course of Geary's operations in Loudoun, he reported captures of White's men to the number of over six hundred, besides the killed and wounded.

After Geary got his command on the railroad, Capt. White, by permission of Col. Munford, made a raid in his rear at Salem, and driving off the guard, took possession of all the baggage of the entire 28th Pennsylvania, which he carried safely off with him; and Col. Munford, soon after, came down on his commissary stores at Piedmont, making a heavy capture of flour and many other articles, as well as some negroes whom the Pennsylvania hero had stolen away from their homes.

In the latter part of April, Munford was ordered to report to his regiment, then lying on the Rappahannock, near the O. and A. R. R., and White went with him, but soon after reaching the camp of the 2nd regiment, through Col. Munford's influence, he was ordered to report to Gen. Ewell, to act on scouting and courier duty for that officer; accordingly, he started at once for his new field of action, and reached Gen. Ewell's headquarters at Liberty Mills on the 1st of May. Soon after which the division marched to Jackson's department in the Valley, crossing the Blue-Ridge at Swift Run Gap and establishing camp at Auglebright's, in whose house Gen. Ewell had his headquarters.

The general was a stern, fierce old soldier, having been an officer of the old army and on duty among the Indians and on the frontier for many years. He was a rigid disciplinarian, and White's men were a great deal more afraid of him than of Yankees. One of his abominations was to receive "don't know" for an answer, and before very long every man detailed for duty at the general's headquarters went with fear and trembling, for there were a great many things which they really did not know, and when asked about them they couldn't say anything else.

It was an unfortunate time for such *greenhorns* as White's people were to go on such duty as this, for the general had reached the valley just at the moment when Jackson was starting on his McDowell expedition, and without any knowledge of the plans or intentions of his superior, Ewell was compelled to lie still in camp with his little army, while the troops of Banks gathered all around him, and he was rendered extremely cross and impatient thereby; but one day that peerless cavalier, Gen. Ashby, who had been with Jackson, rode up to Ewell's headquarters, and meeting the general, saluted him and inquired how

29

he did, to which Ewell replied, "I've been in hell for three days! been in hell for three days, Gen. Ashby. What's the news from Jackson?"

Ashby replied, "Gen. Jackson says the Lord has blessed our arms with another glorious victory," and then proceeded to give him the details of "Stonewall" and his army getting lost among the mountains, but being finally found by the Yankee generals, Milroy, Schenck and Co., to their great discomfort.

The recital brightened the spirits of our general to such an extent that the boys began to think there might be a warm place somewhere away down in his rugged, iceberg of a heart, and they decided that he wasn't such a savage old bear after all, but the change didn't amount to much, and it was finally given up that "old Ewell" didn't love but one thing on earth, and that one thing was "Friday," the ugliest, dirtiest and most aggravating and thievish little wretch of an Indian boy in the country.

However, his staff was composed of very clever gentlemen, especially Capt. Brown, his special *aide-de-camp*, who was very accommodating and pleasant, and all the boys liked him very much. Major Barbour, A. A. General, too, was a favourite; so was Major Snodgrass, the quartermaster. But some of the brigadiers were far from being admired; and not one of the men would have acted as courier for Gen. Dick Taylor, if they could have avoided it.

On one occasion a courier went into Ewell's headquarters to make some report, in the course of which he replied to one of the general's questions with the remark, "I passed Taylor's Brigade," upon which Taylor, who was present, exclaimed, "How dare you speak in that manner! I am *General* Taylor, sir;" but Gen. Ewell, with a glance of his fierce eye, remarked, "This is *my* courier, sir," and went on with his questions.

Taylor was undoubtedly a splendid officer, but he was proud as Lucifer, and therefore unpopular.

Gen. Elzey also commanded a brigade in the division at that time, and was rather popular with his couriers; but they were very fond of the good-natured Gen. Trimble, and it was never any trouble to get men to report to him for courier duty, provided Major Snodgrass was supplied, as the quartermaster's department was first choice always.

Gen. Ewell also had a small cavalry brigade, composed of the 2nd and 6th Virginia regiments, and commanded by Col. Munford, who had been promoted to the colonelcy of the 2nd regiment at the reorganisation of the army in April.

It was sometimes necessary to send couriers with Major Wheat, of the celebrated "Tiger Battalion," of Louisiana, who was very often on detached service in the Luray Valley, and was also a very popular man with White's people. While camping at this place, some of the boys determined to visit their homes, and accordingly four of them deserted and made their way back to Loudoun and Fairfax.

About the middle of May, the first heavy misfortune that befell the company occurred.

Gen. Ewell was always anxious to get the news from Banks' army in the Shenandoah Valley, and Capt. White was always ready to exchange camp life for the privilege of scouting. So, taking with him his first lieutenant, and Capt. Brown of the 16th Mississippi Infantry, with a small detail of his men, he left camp in the afternoon, and crossing the river at Miller's Bridge, they climbed the Massanutten mountains.

It was quite dark when the party reached the top, and the night was cold, making the bivouac very uncomfortable, for without blankets or overcoats, they had nothing but the rocky brow of the Massanutten for a bed; and to crown everything, they had brought nothing to eat—for, until arriving on the mountain top, it had not been the intention of the party to wait for daylight to do their scouting—so with fasting and freezing the weary night wore away, but from their observatory the scouts looked down upon the camp fires of the Federal Army, and the position of each regiment was clearly discerned.

When daylight came, which it did with a clear and bracing air to the men on the mountains—while yet the valley country was shrouded in mist and fog that fled from the day as the sun advanced, and rolling its huge masses up the gloomy mountain wall broke away and hid itself to wait again for the night to come down—the scouts bethought them of breakfast, as *supper* had occupied their waking hours during the darkness, and the captain sent them all back to camp except Capt. Brown, Lieut. Myers and Serg't Boyd Barrett, (recently transferred from Co. K, 6th Va. Cav., to White's Company,) who, leaving their horses, descended the mountain on foot, intending to try their fortune among the Yankee foragers.

Near the foot of the mountain the party halted at a cabin and asked for something to eat, which, after some difficulty and a good deal of rather impatient waiting, was finally obtained; and along with the rations the captain—by representing to the king of the wigwam that himself and comrades were Yankees—received some interesting information about the enemy, which he dispatched by Barrett to Gen.

Ewell.

The scouting party—now reduced to three—walked cautiously out into the open valley country and soon found themselves inside of the enemy's lines.

They saw several squads and companies of the blue-coated troopers, but did not come in contact with any, although several times they had to hide themselves while the enemy passed by them, and finally about noon reached the handsome residence of Mr. Rhodes, near Lacy's Spring, where they endeavoured to make themselves known in their true character as Confederates. This, however, was not so easily done, for their dress about as closely resembled one uniform as the other, and the "Jessie Scouts," of Fremont's hatching, were plentiful in the Valley; and besides this, the Yankee camp was less than half a mile distant, from which they were almost constantly receiving visitors; consequently, under all the circumstances, argument was thrown away, until, as a last resort, Lieut. Myers prevailed on one of the ladies to examine the Virginia buttons on his coat.

This, with Capt. White's elaborate argument, that "nobody but a Virginia soldier ever did wear a Virginia button," convinced the family, and their dangerous predicament outside of the house was exchanged for a place in the parlour, where, with closed blinds, they enjoyed a splendid dinner and heard Mr. Rhodes detail the valorous doings of the defenders of the "star spangled banner," in the way of making bloody assaults upon the hen-roosts, and fearless dashes into spring-houses and stables in the Valley Department.

Among other things he informed them of two cavalrymen who had spent the night at a house of rather doubtful repute, a short distance away, and whose horses had left them during the night, but as soon as morning came, they had gone off to replace them from some citizen's pasture, leaving their saddles and bridles at the house, and Mr. R. thought it probable they had returned with the stolen horses by that time. White and his comrades decided at once to attempt the capture of the gentlemen, and they set about it as soon as it was ascertained that they were still at Cook's.

Approaching the house, two fine horses, with full cavalry rig, were seen tied to the fence in front of the door, and White made for them immediately, leaving Brown and Myers to attend to the Yankees, one of whom, coming to the door to see what was wrong with the horses, was suddenly pounced upon by Capt. Brown and captured without difficulty; but Myers had more trouble with his man, who staid in the house

32

and made no answer to the order to surrender, although it was backed by the presentation of a big horse pistol, but commenced to draw his revolver, and Myers, feeling extremely doubtful about his horse pistol going the first time—a thing it had never done yet—stuck it hastily in his belt, and snatching the Yankee's half drawn revolver, twisted it out of his hand, with the remark, "Guess you'll surrender now, won't you?" to which the blue jacket replied, he "guessed he would."

The two captains then mounted the horses, and leaving Myers to follow with the prisoners, with instructions to wait on top of the mountain until they found their horses and brought them up, started back to their last night's camp, but were unable to find it, and after the party had got together again White proposed going on foot with the prisoners, to Dr. Hansberger's, while Brown and Myers should hunt up the horses and bring them down, saying he would have supper ready by the time they got there.

The arrangement was agreed to, and all started to put it into execution, but as White was going down the mountain he passed a house where several citizens were standing and inquired of them the road. They answered him and he pushed on, but as soon as he had passed, the citizens decided that it was a party of Yankees on a scout, and hastily arming themselves, five of their number followed, intending to capture them, and White, on seeing that he was pursued, thought at once that they were Union bushwhackers going to rescue the prisoners, and turning towards them he demanded why they were following him, to which they replied by asking, "What are you doing with those men?"

White then drew his pistol, and Sheetz, the leader of the citizens, raised his double-barrel gun. Both drew trigger at once and both weapons missed fire, but the captain was ready first, and just as the citizen's gun was raised again, White fired, his bullet breaking Sheetz's arm above the elbow. He immediately caught his gun with the other hand, and was in the act of firing when White's pistol exploded again and his remaining arm fell, shattered at the elbow precisely as the first one was. The other citizens all run but one who hid himself in the fence corner along the road, and White did the same, but after waiting some time, became impatient, and raising his head above the top rail to look for his assailants, the citizen fired at him with a small sporting rifle, the ball taking effect near the right eye.

This ended the fight, and when Brown and Myers rode up about half an hour later, they found the citizens in a terrible state of excitement over the result of their unfortunate attack, one of their number being stretched on the ground desperately wounded, while Capt. White sat in a fence corner almost dead, in fact all who saw him, supposed him to be dying. And the Yankee prisoners were expecting every moment to be immolated, for, said they, "If the rebels will treat each other in this manner, what won't they do with us?"

And no sooner did Lieut. Myers dismount from his horse than they ran to him for protection, and absolutely refused to leave him for a single moment, until he wanted one of them to bring some water from a spring nearby, and the lieutenant was compelled to actually drive him from him then. Capt. Brown rode immediately on to camp, to inform the company of the tragic winding up of the scout, and very shortly a considerable number of the boys, accompanied by their surgeon, Dr. William N. Lupton, with his ambulance, were on the march for the scene of conflict, and on their arrival, before learning the full particulars of the affair, it was all that Lieut. Myers could do to prevent them from killing all the citizens engaged in it.

Meantime the captain had been making "his will," and supposing he was soon to be in the land of spirits, gave to the lieutenant quite a number of messages to be delivered to his wife and child in Maryland, but his mind dwelt upon his company too, and every few minutes he would exclaim, "Tell the boys to do as I did—never surrender!"

Dr. Lupton examined the wound and pronounced it a dangerous one, but not necessarily fatal by any means, and soon after he was placed in the ambulance, and in great misery, moved to the house of a kind citizen a few miles nearer to camp, where he remained for two or three days, when his men carried him on a litter to the hospitable home of Dr. Miller, on the river bank, where he remained until he had sufficiently recovered to ride over to his friends at Charlottesville.

4: Cross Keys and Brown's Gap

The command of the company now devolved upon Lieut. Myers, and in a very few days Gen. Ewell marched his whole division to Columbian Bridge, about twenty-five miles lower down the river, where he halted for a time, and Myers and Barrett endeavoured to put the business of the company into shape, as there had not been a payroll made off, and only one muster roll since the company had been in the service, but on the 21st of May, General Ewell sent for Lieut. Myers, and giving him a bundle of dispatches, told him to mount the best horse he could find and carry them to General Jackson.

Now be it known, nobody had heard from that officer for a long while, and the lieutenant naturally desired to ask the question—"Where is Gen. Jackson?" but from former experience was afraid to venture it, and walked disconsolately from headquarters and the presence of the general, without any definite plan whatever in his mind, and sighing with the Psalmist for the "wings of a dove," but Major Barbour had noticed his elongated visage, and divining his trouble, met him in the yard, where he proceeded to explain to him the road to Jackson, but while thus engaged, Gen. Ewell stepped out and exclaimed in his quick, spiteful tone, "Lieutenant Myers, go to New Market and take the turnpike road to Harrisonburg; be quick now, I want to see you again today."

The lieutenant crossed the Massanutten and found some of Ashby's cavalry at New Market, who told him Jackson was coming down the pike, and a nine mile ride up the valley brought him to the marching army of "Stonewall," and very soon he met a party of officers riding among the infantry, when selecting one whom, for the plainness of his dress, he took for a courier, he asked him to show him Gen. Jackson, supposing, of course, to have one of the finely dressed officers pointed out to him, but the courier simply replied, "I am Gen. Jackson; where are you from, sir?"

After reading the dispatches, he wrote a few lines to Gen. Ewell, and cross-questioned the lieutenant a short time, when he sent him back, saying, "I'll see you at Luray tomorrow." On the way back to camp, the lieutenant met Gen. Ewell on the mountain, and on reaching the river found everything moving towards New Market, but this was soon changed, and the troops took the road to Luray, where, on the following morning they met Gen. Jackson and some of his people, and the two generals held a conference, after which Ewell pushed forward to Front Royal, reaching that place about 3 o'clock in the evening of the 23rd of May.

Here they found a force of the enemy, and a fierce battle ensued, at the beginning of which Gen. Ewell ordered Lieutenant Myers to remain near him with a party of his men, but after capturing Kenly's 1st Maryland, and driving the rest of the Yankees from town, a force appeared on the river hills and opened a heavy artillery fire upon the Confederates, during which the shells howled savagely around the general and his escort, when, looking around, the old fellow broke out on Myers with "What do you mean, sir, by making a target of me with these men!"

Upon which the lieutenant replied, "Why, general, you told me to stay near you, and I'm trying to do it."

"Clear out, sir, clear out," roared the general, "I didn't tell you to get all your men killed and me too," and that was the last time they troubled him that day, for the men deemed themselves discharged from further attendance upon him, and pitched in for plunder, every man doing his best to equip himself for service, they being as yet mostly armed with double-barrelled guns only, and riding citizen saddles brought with them from home. Many of them succeeded in securing sabres and pistols, and nearly all possessed themselves of gum cloths, canteens and other articles of great value to soldiers.

That night the whole force moved across the river on the Winchester road, passing, as they did so, the ground where the Southern cavalry fought so well, and where so many gallant men found bloody deaths in charging the Yankee infantry, among them Capt. George Baxter, of the Loudoun Cavalry, 6th Virginia regiment, Capt. George F. Sheetz, who was said by many to be a better officer than Ashby himself, and Capt. Fletcher, the gallant commander of Ashby's old company.

General Ewell, who had been an old cavalry officer, and knew how to appreciate the splendid display of valour, skill and devotion made by Ashby's troops at this point, worthy as it was of the "sons of the sires," whom Light Horse Harry had led in days as dark and stormy, long ago, and here on the field of Front Royal added another leaf to the Laurel Crown, which Fame, in "Auld Lang Syne," had woven for the honour of the cavaliers of the "Old Dominion," spoke of this charge as one of the most gallant affairs he had ever witnessed, and no higher praise could be given than to say they fought under the eye of General Richard S. Ewell, and won his warmest admiration, for, like Jackson, he never bestowed it unmerited, and he meant everything he said.

In the bivouac that night the general had his escort near his headquarters, and as his staff did not join him for a long time after, he called upon Lieut. Barrett to act as A. A. General for him, and kept the lieutenant busily engaged until a late hour in writing dispatches and reports for him, and the next morning he started the company on a scouting expedition, in which it was engaged all day, re-joining the general about dark, who was then marching towards Winchester with all his force.

The weather was raw and chilly, but the night was spent in making reconnaissances and marching for short distances, but no fires were kindled or noises made which might apprise General Banks of the proximity of the rebels until about 3 o'clock, when the enemy's pickets were found by Sergt. C. B. Barrett, who, with a squad, had been on detail at headquarters, and upon receipt of this information Gen. Ewell took a company of infantry and stirred up the Yankee picket lines by firing on their posts and driving them in. About an hour before daylight one of the couriers brought to Gen. Ewell a dispatch from "Stonewall," which the writer saw as Gen, E. opened it, and it was simply a sheet of paper upon which was delineated the roads, streams, woods, &c., around Winchester, and showing the disposition of the enemy's forces in Ewell's front, as well as Jackson's position on the Valley pike, and beneath the plan the words "attack at daylight" were written.

No other instructions were needed, and with the dawning of that bright and beautiful Sabbath morning in May the regiments moved forward to the battle. For some time everything went smoothly, and the enemy broke at every point, but by-and-by a large body of them were rallied and placed behind a stone fence, where they lay quietly and entirely unperceived by the 21st North Carolina infantry, which was moving over that part of the field, and when within twenty or thirty yards the Yankees raised up and poured a tremendous volley into their ranks, killing and wounding nearly one-third of the regiment, but the men were promptly rallied by their gallant colonel, who instantly ordered a bayonet charge, which was executed in splendid style, and the enemy retreated in great confusion before the brave North Carolinians, but their victory was dearly bought, for Col. Strickland fell dead at the fence, and his men lay thick around him.

From this time there was no rallying point for Banks' army except the Potomac, for just then Gen. Jackson bursted his column at Middletown, and with Ashby in their rear they rather flew than ran along the valley pike to the thirty miles distant river; but in one wild scene of disorder and cowardice they raced that distance at such a speed that not even Mameluke cavalry, though mounted on Arabia's choicest steeds, could have caught them, and just beyond Winchester "old Stonewall" halted his infantry and encamped his army.

Here White's company, which had been scattered in squads, scouting and fighting, and acting as escort and bodyguards for the different generals, re-united about sunset, and nearly every man was completely armed and equipped with sabres, revolvers, and everything necessary to fit them for service, including Yankee bridles and halters, and many saddles bearing the letters U. S., which letters also embellished the shoulders of many of their horses and all their blankets.

Next morning Gen. Ewell gave them a box containing twenty new carbines of the "Merrill" pattern, which he directed should always be carried by the scouting details, and then ordered Lieut. Myers to take twenty men and proceed to Charlestown to take charge of the Government stores at that place, instructing him to take an inventory of everything and send to him in order that he might send wagons to move them.

Myers pushed on to Charlestown and found a large quantity of stores, arms, and everything needed by an army, which the enemy had abandoned; and sending a messenger to the general with the necessary information, he encamped, and his men were taken by the citizens to their houses and regaled with the best of everything the land could afford. These people had been under Yankee rule for more than two months, and the change almost made them wild with joy, so much so that they were ready to worship Gen. Jackson and his men for relieving them of the hateful presence of their tyrannical conquerors who, during all these weeks, had lorded it over them in the approved Yankee style of domination over a helpless people and their desolated homes; whence had vanished the glory which their household gods were wont to shed around them, but in spite of it all they were not conquered, and the "quenchless spirits, hushed by force, in dauntless eye burned brightly."

While White's cavalrymen were enjoying the good things provided by the tried and true in Charlestown, Major John Shack. Green, of the 6th Virginia Cavalry, rode up with a detachment from his regiment, and proposed to encamp near the town, which was done, and the next morning a scout came in saying the Yankees were at Halltown and still advancing, upon which Major Green moved his command down the road, took a position on the right, while Myers' men formed to the left, and sending a little party to the front to look out for the enemy, they waited for events to determine their actions.

In half an hour the advance party was heard skirmishing with the enemy, and soon after a regiment of infantry appeared in the road, about half a mile away, and soon after two other regiments of infantry and one of cavalry appeared, escorting a battery of artillery.

The Confederates moved down and skirmished some, but very soon the battery opened fire, and Major Green retired slowly to a position beyond the town.

Myers kept his men in front for some time, until finding that the

Yankees wouldn't advance a step with a Confederate force of any size in gunshot range, and seeing also the shells from the battery were passing over his position and falling in the town, he fell back to the other end of the town, and in a short time a force of cavalry moved up the road, supported by the infantry and artillery, and set fire to the stores, which were still in the market-house, in the very centre of Charlestown, after which they retired rapidly towards Harper's Ferry, and Myers returned to Gen. Ewell to inform him that the necessity for sending wagons for the stores of which he had received an inventory, no longer existed, but he met Gens. Jackson and Ewell both marching, with a strong force, on Charlestown, and the next morning, after again enjoying the hospitality of the good citizens of Charlestown, Gen. Ewell ordered Lieut. Myers to dismount his company and find the force and position of the enemy in the direction of Halltown.

After moving about a mile, Ed. Oxley reported that he had found in a wheat field, the frying pans, blankets and other articles of the skirmish line. So halting the command, the lieutenant made a reconnaissance, in which he discovered about, as he thought, two thousand infantry and a regiment of cavalry, on the road, which he reported to the general, and was very much astonished that an advance was not made at once,.

But after waiting some time, and seeing the enemy retire slowly, he resolved to see where they went, and taking Ed. Wright with him, the pair got into the mill-race which passes into Halltown, and hid from view by the high banks and bushes, waded safely to the miller's house, which is right in town, and going to the upper windows had a full view of all the force there, which did not consist of over six hundred cavalry and a regiment of infantry; and, deeming this information of importance, they returned to Gen. Ewell and reported; finding both the generals, Ewell and Jackson, on a hill about half a mile from the town, and on the same position the enemy had occupied in the morning.

The officers both expressed themselves highly pleased with the information and the manner in which it was obtained, but Gen. Ewell thought it would have been better if the scouts had returned to him immediately on getting it, instead of stopping at the miller's house to eat a good dinner, which was on the table when they came down stairs; but it was too late then, for they had the dinner, and mentally resolved to do the same thing, when the opportunity presented itself, whether the general liked it or not, but they also resolved, in the same manner, not to tell him next time.

It appeared that General Jackson had no intention of making a fight here, but only to demonstrate upon the Yankees along the river until he could get his immense quantities of captured stores and baggage away from Winchester and the railroad, and he now had only a small force of infantry with a battery at Halltown.

While lying here watching the enemy, five of them came on the road, in good gunshot of the battery, and annoyed the men there very much, but were themselves perfectly safe, and, at the solicitation of Ed. Wright and Norman Smith, Lieut. Myers went to Gen. Ewell for permission to go and drive them away, which, for some time, he refused, but finally, on the third application, he rather testily exclaimed, "Yes; go on, go on; but you'll come back faster than you go;" and away went the three with their new carbines to try their luck.

They managed to get a good position unperceived by the sharpshooters, and as only one of them could be seen, and he very imperfectly, it was decided that Myers, who was supposed to be the best shot, should fire first, and Smith and Wright take theirs when the Yankees raised up. They were all successful, and left three of the boys lying on the ground, but no sooner had they done so than they found themselves in a perfect hornet's nest, for two companies of infantry, who had been lying all the while concealed among some trees on the hillside, just beyond the pike, opened a hot fire upon the three scouts, and they being now in an open clover field, had to run for their lives.

Smith and Wright ran to a hollow and escaped easily, but Myers started directly up the hill to the battery, and being dressed in a new red shirt, had a lively time of it, and would scarcely have escaped at all but for the general opening on them with his artillery; as it was his red shirt got three balls through it, and his fright was well-nigh mortal.

This affair brought on a heavy cannonade, which kept up nearly all the afternoon, and when night came the Confederates fell back, which they continued to do until they reached Winchester again, and the company of White had a long and hard scout to find Gen. Ewell's ordnance train, which by some means had got off the road at Smithfield; and during this scout they found a box of sabres at Stevenson's depot, which was sent back by a detail for the purpose, and the Yankees coming up about this time gave the boys carrying the arms a chase, in which several sabres were lost, but they boasted that all the scabbards were saved.

On reaching the division the train was found to have been in camp all the time, and now the fact that Fremont was coming down on one flank, and Shields on the other, both moving on lines that would unite them in Jackson's rear, impelled that commander to move up the Valley, not thinking it very desirable to form a junction with the generals named so far away from the Blue Ridge, which was always the great commander's wall of defence under his faith in the Great Jehovah.

Sunday morning, June 1st, 1862, the army reached Strasburg, and at this point Gen. Fremont attempted to flank "Stonewall," but the latter preferred not to be flanked, and to prevent it unlimbered his batteries and after an hour's conversation by the brazen lips of these interpreters, Gen. F. decided that if Jackson didn't want to be flanked, why he wouldn't do it, and gave up the job, but from now on the Yankees closely pressed the rear, and Ashby with his cavalry and Chew's battery fought them from every hill.

It was while on this march that Col. Sir Percy Wyndham bagged Ashby, an exploit by which he hoped to win a brigadier's commission, and undoubtedly would have done so if he had taken Ashby to Washington instead of allowing Ashby to take him to Richmond.

The couriers had extremely severe work on this march up the Valley pike, but the army encamped regularly every night, and never for one moment did the march take the appearance of a retreat, for the rear guard always held its positions as long as it was necessary.

On arriving at Mount Jackson, Gen. Ewell established headquarters, and pitched his tent at the end of the bridge and on the bank of the river, but during the night a tremendous storm of rain came down and the stream raised so rapidly that before headquarters knew what was going on it was on an island, with the water rising every moment, and no boat to get out in. Everything was soon in confusion, but Gen. Ewell mounted his old grey horse, "Rifle," and taking the little Indian, "Friday," behind him, plunged into the water without coat or hat and swam over to the camp of his cavalry, leaving the staff and wagon to get out as they could, but the company went to their assistance and soon had the whole business moved over.

Next morning Lieut. Barrett was ordered to New Market, with a detail from the company, to act as provost guard, and the division lay in camp all day just beyond the town. Here the news of the battle of Seven Pines was received and of the wounding of General Johnston, at that time Commander-in-Chief of the Virginia Army. There was a great deal of wonder and speculation as to who would succeed him, some thinking Beauregard would take command, while many of the men thought our own Stonewall was the man for the place, but nobody thought of Lee, until in reply to a question on the subject, we heard Gen. Ewell remark, "No, sir; I don't know who will be General Johnston's successor, but I shan't be scared at all if the choice falls on Lee."

This circulated from camp to camp, and many of the soldiers freely admitted that *they* would be scared, for they considered that Gen. Lee's Western Virginia campaign a failure, and if old Scott did say beware of Lee on an advance, they were afraid that the change from following the retreating Johnston to that of rallying under the banners of the advancing Lee wouldn't be very beneficial to the army or the country, and Gen. Beauregard always had whipped the Yankees without either an advance or a retreat.

These were only some of the many expressions of opinion on the subject of changing commanders, and only for the fact that for a short while they were lying quiet, with nothing to do, the subject would scarcely have had a place in the minds of Jackson's men, for soldiers soon learn to submit blindly to the powers that be, and obey, unquestioningly, the orders of their officers.

Theirs not to reason why,
Theirs not to make reply,
Theirs but to do and die.

While halted at New Market, an incident occurred which banished all thought of the Richmond Army from the minds of those who witnessed it, and filled each heart with pride, which claimed Virginia as its home, and that was the daring and almost miraculous escape of Gen. Ashby from the enemy, who attacked him at the bridge on the turnpike and chased him almost to town, killing his celebrated white stallion, but nearly every one of the seven pursuers were killed or wounded by Ashby and his single companion, although the general had no loads in his pistols and fought entirely with the sabre.

This was the last time we ever saw the great soldier on the war path, for he was killed the next day while leading an infantry regiment in the battle at Harrisonburg, (June 5th, 1862), and thus went down in a billow of blood the brilliant star of glory which promised to dazzle the astonished nations with the splendid blaze of chivalric light which now only blazons the fame of the knights of the olden time,

Whose bones are dust, whose swords are rust,
Whose souls are with the saints, we trust.

Whatever the world may say of the right or wrong of the "Lost Cause," it will never deny that many of those by whom it was upheld, and who crowned its banners with glory in carrying them so gallantly and so far, were inspired by motives as patriotic, as pure and bright as ever burned in the bosom of mortal man. They were brave men; they fought as brave men fight, and died as brave men die. Upon a hundred "stormy heights and carnage-covered fields," they attested their devotion to their cause, and among the truest and bravest of them all, the name of Gen. Turner Ashby shines with a radiant glory that will brighten still as it goes "sounding down the ages,"

The knightliest of the knightly race,
Who since the days of old
Have kept the lamp of chivalry
Alight in hearts of gold.

There was mourning in the camp that night, and every face wore a look of gloom as if in the calamity which had just befallen them, the soldiers felt that a harbinger of still greater desolation had been given them, and when Gen. Jackson appeared in the morning, all eyes looked eagerly to see how he felt the loss of the great cavalier, but in that calm and steady eye was an inscrutable look, and no man could form an idea of what were the feelings of the commander by the expression of the face that never changed, either in the glory of triumph or the gloom of defeat.

The army lay quiet all day, and the next moved towards Port Republic, encamping near the old Church at Cross Keys. Some of the men became very impatient at the constant and rapid marching, and one of them asked Gen. Jackson, as he passed along the column, where he was going to fight the Yankees. The general, with a half-smile, replied, "We'll fight them in Brown's Gap," and the soldiers at once became exceedingly interested in that place, continually asking each other how far it was to Brown's Gap. Would the Yankees follow them there?" &c., little imagining that the ground upon which they then stood was to be their battlefield for the morrow.

Sunday morning, June 8th, broke bright, clear and hot, and by 8 o'clock everyone knew that Ewell was going to match his division against the advancing columns of Fremont, for the cavalry, now commanded by Col. T. T. Munford, slowly retired before the Yankee infantry, and Gen. Ewell's brigades moved out quietly and formed their battle lines. The scouts and couriers now had plenty of work again, and Lieut. Barrett, with a part of the company, was ordered to act as provost guard again, while Gen. Ewell ordered Lieut. Myers and Ed. Wright to scout on the right, and let him know when the enemy made any demonstration in that direction. The remainder of the boys were on duty as couriers with the generals.

The battle opened with some artillery firing, but pretty soon Taylor's brigade met and whipped a line of Yankees that advanced upon Ewell's centre, and all was quiet again for an hour, when Elzey's men became engaged, and at the same time Myers and Wright discovered a heavy force moving by the flank to Ewell's right. Gen. Trimble was the first man they met on their return with this important information, and communicating it to him, that officer promptly moved his brigade forward, and attacking the flanking party in flank, they were very soon driven off with heavy loss in men and all their artillery. About the time Trimble's guns opened, General Taylor advanced, and for a while the battle raged with great fury, but General Trimble's movement exposed the enemy's left flank, and they fell back along the whole line.

This ended the Battle of Cross Keys, with the exception of some cannonading on the left about sundown, and although some horses of the couriers had been struck, only one of White's men was touched, and he very slightly, by a bouncing grape shot.

That night they slept upon the battlefield, but with the dawn everything moved rapidly towards Port Republic, for Shields, with his army, was moving up the river, and Gen. Jackson was going to "fight in Brown's Gap" again.

On Monday morning "Stonewall" crossed the bridge almost alone, and rode into the town, but on his return found a Yankee major with two pieces posted at the mouth of the bridge, and, without a moment's hesitation, rode up to the officer, saying, "Turn your guns, sir, turn your guns; the enemy is coming from that direction," pointing at the same time down the river, and without a question, the unsuspecting major had his pieces wheeled about, in order to command the approach of the enemy, which to him was no enemy at all, and without waiting to explain any further, Gen. Jackson dashed rapidly across the bridge to his own people, but he had not a moment to spare, for the baffled Yankee had his guns going on him before he cleared the bridge.

Jackson instantly ordered his artillery up, and very soon the enterprising "boys in blue" were compelled to change their position, thus leaving the bridge open to the Confederates, and General Jackson's old division crossed the river, followed slowly by that of Gen. Ewell, with whom White's cavalry moved.

Immediately on reaching the east bank, the line of battle was formed, and the fight commenced, and as soon as everything had crossed the bridge it was fired, cutting off Fremont's army from that of Shields, and with it a company of the 6th Va. Cavalry, which acted as rear guard and was compelled to swim the river.

Here was begun and carried through to complete success one of the most brilliant displays of generalship witnessed during the war, or, in fact, in any war of modern times.

"Stonewall" had not only eluded the superior force of Fremont, but had actually whipped him, almost in cannon shot of his colleague, on the 8th, and now, on the 9th of June, was massing all his troops and crushing the army of that colleague—(Gen. Shields)—while Fremont, with his troops formed in battle-ranks on the hillsides bordering the Shenandoah, was unable to do more than look at the battle and see the army of Shields annihilated; while, without a guard, and just in his front, moved the long train composed of all of Jackson's wagons, all of Ewell's and nearly every one of Banks', besides some of his own; and standing still in all the circumstance and panoply of war, the blazing bridge cutting off his last and only means of doing harm to his wily foe, the savage Gen. Fremont, in pitiful helplessness and vindictive vandalism, could only fire his guns upon the empty town of Port Republic.

By 10 o'clock the battle was over and Shields flying down the river with the scattered remnant of his army, which Gen. Jackson only followed for nine miles when he returned to look after his trains and captures.

The enemy had lost all of his artillery, consisting of about fifteen guns, all of his wagons and a great number of prisoners, besides many killed and wounded, for Shields fought with more obstinacy than Fremont, although the latter had considerably more force than his adversary—Gen. Ewell—while Shields had an inferior one to the combined troops of Jackson and Ewell.

The couriers had very warm and exciting work today, as is usual on the battlefield, but although many narrow escapes were made not one was wounded, and they captured a full company of Ohio infantry.

Lieut. Myers was sent by Gen. Jackson, during the heat of the battle, with a dispatch to Col. Munford to charge, with his cavalry, a battery which was doing heavy execution, and remained with the colonel until the enemy's lines broke up in full retreat, when he rejoined Gen.

Jackson and kept with him in the nine mile pursuit, which caused him to be the recipient of another scolding from Gen. Ewell, who informed him that he was no courier for Gen. Jackson, and that his business was to keep his (Ewell's) division supplied with couriers, and to obey his orders and nobody else's. It is needless to say that the lesson was laid to heart and closely followed thereafter.

The army bivouacked in Brown's Gap that night, and the next day the usual rain storm which follows a battle poured down upon them, as they still waited to see and do whatever "Old Stonewall" might decide upon as best for them; and two days after, the great commander put his people in camp at Mount Meridian, where, for several very beautiful June days, the troops passed away the time, fishing and bathing in the blue Shenandoah, and visiting the wonderful Weyer's Cave, while each day a regular detail was made to go to Port Republic and "make believe" build a bridge as if Jackson intended to try another campaign down the valley. When, in reality, he was preparing to march his army to the relief of the Confederate Capital, which was now closely environed by the magnificent army of McClellan, and was anxiously waiting the critical moment when the last spadeful of dirt should be thrown, and the "Young Napoleon" would replace his sappers and miners with the splendid battalions who were to immortalise the name of McClellan by taking, under his plans and direction, the now world-renowned City of Richmond.

White's company was in splendid condition, the ranks full, the horses thriving and the men all armed equal to any cavalry in the army, and all they wanted was for their captain to come up and take command again. While at Mount Meridian Gen. Jackson had divine service regularly, and appointed times for praise and thanksgiving to the God of battles who had crowned his arms with victory; while from all around our borders came news of Confederate successes, and rumours that foreign nations had recognised the independence of the Southern Confederacy. So that the future was brilliant with hope and no man in the army would have willingly exchanged his Confederate dollars for an equal amount of greenbacks.

5: Marching With, 'Old Stonewall'

About the 20th of June the army crossed the Blue Ridge, and moved quietly towards the beleaguered capital; but the men did not know any more about their destination than the enemy, who never knew, until his artillery boomed upon McClellan's flank at Richmond, that Jackson had left the Valley.

On arriving at Charlottesville, Capt. White, now entirely recovered from the effects of his wound, rejoined his company, and it now appeared that the little band of scouts and couriers was to be the foundation upon which a larger command was to be built up. For here the news was received that Capt. George W. Chiswell, of Maryland, was on the march from that State with a full company to join White's Cavalry, and all the boys began to look forward to the time when the irksome duty of waiting upon the generals and playing telegraph for an army, was to be exchanged for the more congenial and pleasant one of once more scouting on the frontier. Encamped at Charlottesville they had seen a battalion of men commanded by Major John Scott, of Fauquier Co., Va., and organised by that officer to act as Partisan rangers.

It seemed that mainly through the influence of Major Scott, a bill had been introduced into the Confederate Congress, and which afterwards became a law, authorising the formation of such bands, and offering premiums in captured property for an independent border warfare upon the outposts and communications of the enemy's army, and this idea struck the minds of White's men very forcibly as containing the very principle upon which their company had been formed, and the one they most desired to have applied to their own particular case, and they believed that in strict justice, Capt. White could get the authority under the law to become a Partisan, as soon as his command was large enough to justify it, and all hailed with joyful acclamation the report that Maryland men were coming to join them; in fact the advance guard of the company met them at Charlottesville in the persons of Ed. J. Chiswell, Sam. White, Frank. Williams and Elijah Viers.

Some anecdotes of Gen. Jackson, and the manner in which he was regarded by his men, and the enemy too, were current in the army during this campaign, and were true in idea if not in detail. Before leaving camp at Mount Meridian, an order was issued instructing the men not to tell what or whose troops they were, and to answer all questions on the subject with Gen. Ewell's abomination, "don't know," as a precaution against the enemy getting a knowledge of Jackson's movement from the valley. One day the general saw a soldier crossing a field towards some cherry trees, and as the great abundance of cherries along the route had caused any amount of straggling, he resolved to make an example of this man. So, riding up to him he inquired, "What division do you belong to?"

"Don't know," said the soldier.

"What brigade?" asked the general; and again, the soldier replied, "don't know."

"Well," asked Jackson, "what regiment do you belong to?" thinking he had now found an answerable question; but again, the man replied, "don't know," and with some asperity of tone the general exclaimed, "What do you know, sir?" when the cute "gray jacket" answered— "I know that old Stonewall ordered me not to know anything, and damned if I ain't going to stick to it."

The general turned and rode away without a word, smiling at the extremely literal construction of orders which had saved the soldier from the punishment he had meditated for him.

Gen. Jackson got aboard the cars at Louisa C. H., to go to Richmond, and took a seat in the same car in which a Yankee major, who had been captured among some of the raiding parties on the Rail Road, was being carried also to Richmond.

The major entered into conversation with the quiet officer, not knowing, of course, who he was talking to, and began explaining to him the absolute certainty of McClellan's capture of the Confederate capital. After listening for some time to the manner in which each division of Lee's army was tied up by a stronger force from the other side, "Stonewall" ventured the remark, "But suppose Jackson's army should move from the valley and strike McClellan in flank and rear while he is engaging Lee in front."

"Oh," said the major, "there's no danger of that, Jackson has been badly crippled in his engagements in the valley, and is now hemmed in closely by Fremont's army, so that he can't move."

"But," persisted the Confederate, "suppose he should getaway and come to Richmond."

"No, I say it's no use to talk about that," said the major, "for he can't get away, it is impossible."

"Yes," said the other, "and I say it is possible, for he has already whipped Fremont, and his army will be in front of Richmond in less than twenty-four hours."

The Yankee looked at him a moment, and with an anxious expression asked, "Who are you, sir?"

"I am Gen. Jackson," replied the hero; upon which the major smacked his hands together exclaiming, "Whipped again, by God!" and at once subsided into silence.

When the army of Jackson reached its position and it was plain to everybody that the time had come for the great battle, the men who had followed "Stonewall" all over the Valley, and had seen his banner wave in triumph on every field, were rendered still more proud of their great leader by seeing, about noon on the day of "Cold Harbour," the men whose names were already encircled with a halo of glorious deeds performed during the war, ride up and report to Gen. Jackson for instruction.

Longstreet, A. P. Hill, Magruder, and Stuart, all acknowledged the solemn soldier as their superior, and took his orders for the day's work.

That day's work too was a sad and bloody one, and when night ended the conflict, many were the corpses strewn over the carnage-stained ground, and terrible arose the groans and shrieks of mangled men; but the enemy still held the front and all thought the morning sun must look down on a repetition of the same unchristian work.

Gen. Ewell was found about midnight by the men who were sent to him to relieve the couriers who had passed with him through "Cold Harbour's" baleful death-fires, lying along his lines, which were drawn close up to the enemy, waiting for some sign to commence anew the work of slaughter; but when daylight broke over the battle lines the men in blue had disappeared, and soon after, Gen. Lee found one of White's boys and sent him to find Gen. Stuart and take him to the commander-in-chief.

This conference ended in Stuart posting off to see what had become of the enemy, and it wasn't long until that enterprising cavalier had found out all about him.

In the operations which followed, Gen. Ewell moved with his division to Despatch Station, on the York River Rail Road; and as a matter of course White's cavalry went with him. On their way to that place they passed Yankee camps where the fires were still burning, the camp-kettles of old ham and vegetables, and the coffee, still boiling; while at many of them there were wagon loads, in some instances houses full, of supplies of all kinds on fire; but what created the greatest excitement of all, was a report that the Yankees had poisoned the wells all around their camps by throwing into them the supplies of medicines which their surgeons could not carry away in their hasty retreat.

These rumours grew out of the fact that large quantities of powder and cartridges had been tumbled into some of the wells, and those who drank the water readily imagined it to be poisoned, not only from the taste, but also that several of them were made sick by it; and all threatened summary vengeance on the prisoners, but the true state of the case was soon discovered and the excitement quelled.

On arriving at the Station Gen. Ewell caused the railroad bridge over the Chickahominy to be destroyed and a part of the track torn up, and being now between McClellan and the White House, waited for whatever force might come down the road.

About 4 o'clock in the afternoon a sound as of an enormous train of cars was heard on the railroad, and every man was on the look-out for something interesting to occur, supposing that the Yankees did not know the road was cut and were attempting to run some trains through, and knowing that if this should be the case, they would certainly meet a bloody overthrow at the bridge. The 13th Virginia Infantry was lying on the railroad, and White's boys gathered on the bank of the river, when soon, in the distance, appeared the most singular looking affair any of them had ever seen on a railroad track. It was a train of cars certainly, but high up over the locomotive was built an affair that looked very much like a barn, being made of plank and very long.

The general impression of the men at first sight was that it was a contrivance from which the Yankees could fire at any rebels they might discover, and thus keep the track clear; but there was very little time to think much about it, for the iron-horse, under a full head of steam, was carrying it at a rapid rate towards them, and pretty soon the infernal machine leaped from the track into the Chickahominy, and at the same moment a blaze of fire went up from it that seemed to meet and melt into the blue of the sky, while an explosion, so terrible that men lying on the ground a hundred yards distant were lifted bodily, and in some cases had the blood forced from ears and nostrils, broke out on the evening air.

Just as soon as they got their senses together White's boys walked quietly off to their horses, which had been feeding in an oat field a quarter of a mile distant, and concluded they didn't want to be around when McClellan run his trains to the White House. This curiously contrived affair must have contained three or four tons of powder and artillery ammunition, for shells were exploding constantly from the time the machine blew up until dark, but fortunately did no damage.

The next day Col. Bradley T. Johnson, of the 1st Maryland, (afterward Brigadier General of the Maryland Line,) and Capt. White were prospecting along the river for the enemy, the colonel having with him a rifle cannon with which he occasionally "felt the woods" on the opposite side, and in the evening elicited a reply from several batteries, whose smoke rolled lazily up through the trees in white, foggy-looking masses, and showed that the "Young Napoleon" still had a line of battle there. During the firing Gen. Ewell, accompanied by White's company, rode out to Col. Johnson, who showed him the Yankee positions, remarking, at the same time, "and by the way, general, I think I heard the long roll."

By this time the colonel's one iron gun was attracting considerable attention from the Yankee artillery, and their shells were flying very plentifully around him, when Gen. Ewell turned his horse, and remarking to his escort "we'll go back now, boys," rode over the hill towards Despatch Station, and in so doing passed in full view of the enemy's line, who now opened warmly upon him, and just before reaching the woods a heavy shot passed between the general's head and his horse's neck, causing the old fellow to make a very sudden backward motion. But he instantly righted up, and noticing that the shot had struck a large pine tree about twenty feet from the ground, and cut it off so clear and sudden that the upper part of it came down perpendicularly and stuck in the ground beside the stump, he exclaimed "wasn't that beautiful; wasn't that well done!" but some of the boys remarked afterwards that they didn't know exactly whether he had reference to his dodge or to the cutting of the tree, and they were afraid to ask him.

On the 30th of June Gen. Jackson's corps crossed the Chickahominy at Grapevine bridge, and pushing on after the retreating Yankees came up with them at White Oak Swamp, where he had to fight them several hours with his artillery before his army could get over. During the arrangement for this fight Capt. White marched his company along the battle-line with "Old Stonewall," and after the latter had gotten his seventy guns in position, we halted to watch the result. The enemy was firing constantly, but Gen. Jackson made no reply until he had everything arranged to his notion, when he gave the signal to commence firing, and it was soon evident that he was more than a match for the Yankees.

While the roar of the guns was waking the echoes of swamp and forest, Gen. Jackson rode along the line, where the shells from the enemy's batteries were flying the thickest, and, greatly to our wonder, held one hand up as high as his shoulder nearly all the time, but wonder turned to reverence when found that our hero was praying to the God of battles to spare the lives of his men and crown their arms with victory.

Before long the bridge over the swamp was uncovered, and Jackson's infantry went across, capturing several of the enemy's guns and many prisoners. Here White's men got into a snap with some of the Pennsylvania Bucktail riflemen, but the captain led them in a charge, in which they captured a whole set of German-silver wind instruments for a band, and several prisoners, killing and wounding some of the "Bucktails." They also got a splendid suit of armour belonging to a colonel, over which they had a great deal of amusement, but in their experiments with the breastplate they learned that it was bullet-proof against Colt's army revolvers and all the guns they could find, with one exception, and that was the Maynard rifle, which tore a hole in it large enough for a hen's egg to pass through.

On the 1st of July we went to Malvern Hill, and the company was busy enough during all of that long and bloody afternoon, carrying dispatches for the several generals operating in connection with Ewell, and acting as provost guard to stop the soldiers from straggling.

At the close of the battle, which continued until dark, Capt. White took a detail of his men to Gen. Ewell, who had sent for him, and found that officer, in company with Gen. Whiting, lying on the ground to the left of the road, and with the advanced vedettes of the army, conversing in whispers, the enemy being so close that they could not talk in an ordinary tone without being heard by them; and when White and his boys had crawled up to the general, finding him with great difficulty, he sent them back, saying he was going to advance his infantry line pretty soon, and had no scouting to do, as he had found the enemy and they were in his front—so close that he could throw a stone over their line.

White and his men crept back in the same noiseless manner to their horses, where they waited anxiously for the opening fire of the intended advance; but it was not made, or, if made, the Yankees had gone, and the ever-memorable campaign of seven days' battle around Richmond was at an end; while with it ended the Northern policy of conducting the war according to the established rules of humanity recognised by civilized nations, for now McClellan, who had treated the citizens inside of his military lines humanely, and had respected their rights and protected their property, as far as possible, from the usual pillaging that attends the movements of every large army, was to give place to another who had nothing but his brutality to recommend him to the favour of the "greatest and best government the world ever saw," which was now represented in Washington City by a crew of foul birds of the devil's own hatching, whose names will make the cheeks of Americans crimson with shame as long as American history is read.

And Gen. Pope, from his "headquarters in the saddle," announced that henceforth the business of his army should be to investigate the colour of the coat tails of the rebels, and that the time had arrived when a new era in military tactics should dawn upon the astonished world through the transcendent genius of "John the Pope," and that under him the battles of Abolitiondom should be fought with fire and sword, according to the most approved rules laid down by the aborigines of North America, with all the improvements which the Spanish greasers of Mexico had been enabled to add from the familiarity of their fathers with the horrible scenes of the infernal inquisition; all of which had been revised and corrected within the sound of Mr. Seward's little tinkling bell for special use in the Grand Army of "John the Pope."

And the world was assured that the war had commenced in earnest; while those whose attention had heretofore been called, by accident, to the career of Mr. Pope, and had formed their opinion therefrom, predicted that women and children would suffer now, for the chosen *sachem* of the little-souled Yankee Nation was on the war-path, and the influence of the Northern people in whose hearts the God-given principle of chivalric forbearance towards the weak and helpless had an abiding place, was literally smothered to death in the smoky vengeance which the nigger crusaders had manufactured for crushing the rebellion—*vide* Brownlow, Stevens & Co.

6: The Meeting House Fight

For several days after the close of the seven days' campaign the army lay quiet, and White's people had a delightful camp at Meadow Bridge, about 7 miles from Richmond, on the Rail Road, from which they could send to the city daily for such luxuries as the markets afforded; and during this time there was not much to do in the way of carrying dispatches, so that there was little to do except rest. Here the company held an election for Orderly Sergeant, which resulted in the choice of C. M. C. Whaley, for that important position, and the list of non-commissioned officers was now full, *viz*: Edward S. Wright, 2nd Sergt.; Benjamin F. Conrad, 3rd Sergt.; John Dove, 4th Sergt.; and J. Mortimore Kilgour, 5th Sergeant and Quartermaster; John T. Tribbey, 1st Corporal; Daniel C. Pettingall, 2nd Corporal; William Snoots, 3rd

Corporal; and Peter J. Kabrich, 4th Corporal.

About the 10th of July, Gen. Ewell marched his division to his old camp near Liberty Mills, on the Rapidan, where for some weeks he remained watching "Mr. Headquarters-in-the-saddle," who was prospecting towards Gordonsville, in the new "On to Richmond" movement of his own and father Abraham's invention, and ravaging all the country inside of his lines in the barbarous manner which had been predicted of him from the beginning of his reign, which was as literally a "reign of terror," to the defenceless people under his dominion, as ever was the bloody revolution to the citizens of Paris during the days when flame and murder held high carnival at command of the devils incarnate who ruled in France.

White's company had now increased to nearly one hundred men, and the captain spent much time in scouting in Madison County, which was just on the border of the "grand army," and very much infested with its cavalry raiding parties.

On one occasion, with about thirty men, he drove a strong force of infantry and cavalry from Madison C. H., making the citizens imagine that they were once more free from the terrible dominion of Pope. And again, from the mountain top near Wolfton, he discovered a company of cavalry engaged in plundering a farm-house, and as rapidly as possible came down on them; but owing to the fact that some of his men had been seen by the enemy as they descended the mountain, he was only able to catch about half a dozen, chasing, however, the remainder *out* of their hats, and *into* their camp.

About the last of July, Capt. White left camp at dark, and marching all night, with twenty men, reached a farm-house five miles from Stanardsville about daylight, and halting his command, he sent Lieut. Myers, with the citizen pilot who had volunteered to guide him, to look up the Yankees. On reaching the Conway River, about sunrise, they discovered seven Yankees on foot, going from a camp over the river to a citizen's house for breakfast, and sending the guide with all haste to inform the captain, the lieutenant took a position at the gate, about one hundred yards from the house, to watch the "boys in blue" until the command could come up and get them.

After about an hour's watching and waiting, which, to the lonely picket appeared like four hours, the captain came up with a part of his squad, and before the Yankees knew it, the rebels were in the yard; when, hastily leaving the table, they each "took a tree," and with their carbines attempted to fight it out; but it was too late, and with what grace they could command, the foragers had to "on to Richmond."

The next expedition White made was for the purpose of bush-whacking a patrol of cavalry, which daily passed over the road from Robertson River to Madison C. H., and reaching the road in the evening, he dismounted his men and placed them in the woods along-side of it, sending Lieut. Myers, with Ferro and Spicer, up the road as a decoy, expecting the Yankees to chase these men past the ambuscade, when the others would open on them with their double-barrels and buckshot; but the—

Best laid schemes o' mice and men,
Gang aft agley,

—and the patrol failed to pass that evening.

In the morning the captain moved his people by the Poorhouse to another point on the road; but, after waiting about two hours, found the enemy advancing in strong force of infantry and cavalry to occupy the Court House, and on exchanging a few shots found a full brigade developed against him, when he retired.

On the way to camp in the afternoon the Confederate pickets at Jack's Shop, without any warning at all, fired upon the little company, fortunately without doing any damage, when the captain galloped forward alone and succeeded in rallying the retreating pickets and convincing them that they were running from their own men.

When White's men came up they found their captain talking very sharply to the pickets about firing on him before they halted him, and high words were passing, when one of the firing party said "if you wasn't a captain you shouldn't talk that way;" but the captain exclaimed "no I ain't; I'm no captain; I'm Lige White, and can whip you any way! Come on! I dare you!" But nobody took up the gaunt-let; and with a pleasant little malediction on cowards everywhere, but especially on picket, the ranger chief marched on to camp.

About the 6th of August Gen. Jackson commenced to show some uneasiness, and ordered Gen. Ewell down the road towards Louisa, but came back the next evening, and instead of halting at the old camp, kept right on towards Culpeper, and commenced picketing beyond Robertson River. The boys begun to have ideas that the man with the movable headquarters had better commence moving; but when they found that Jackson's quartermaster-general (Banks) was in front, they said they "just knew 'Old Stonewall' was getting scarce of supplies and only came up after some."

On the morning of the 9th, as White's boys were lazily lying around the shady yard of the house where General Ewell's headquarters were, talking about the prospects, in imagination, of ever seeing Loudoun again, and listening to the general's baby-talk to some little children he had coaxed to come to him on the porch, Gen. Jackson rode up, and very soon the two were studying intently some maps and papers which they spread out on the floor.

Gen. Ewell's ideas appeared to be in accord with "Stonewall's," and they soon laid themselves out for a rest; but after dinner everybody got busy all at once, and it wasn't very long until we found ourselves face to face with a Yankee line of cavalry deployed as vedettes, and apparently bent on investigating the rebel operations and ascertaining why they came so near to Gen. Banks' wagon trains at Culpeper C. H.

Their cavalry was commanded by Gen. Prince, who had been a classmate of Stuart at West Point, and was a fine officer, and a gentleman. His troops were splendidly drilled, and the first that White's men had seen who performed their evolutions on the field at the sound of the bugle. About 3 o'clock Capt. White and Lieut. Myers rode out on the lines, to gratify their curiosity, to see what was going on, and before they were aware of it almost, were witnessing the movements of a regiment of cavalry, that deployed most beautifully as the bugle notes floated musically on the air, and in a short time had advanced to a fence not a hundred yards from the curiosity hunters, who quietly rode off as a shell from one of Jackson's guns exploded in a group of Yankee cavalry.

While riding up the line a Yankee approached them from the woods, but scampered away again as Capt. White called to him "come here to me, you rascal." About an hour after this Gen. Ewell called for his cavalry to go with him, and riding at a gallop, soon reached the foot of Slaughter Mountain, where White's boys, by order of the general, dismounted, and dragged Lattimer's Battery of artillery to the top of the mountain, where the "Napoleon of the Valley," as General Jackson called Capt. Lattimer, commenced firing as soon as his first piece was in position, and until his own men came up with the remainder of the battery, White's men acted as gunners for him. By this time the blue and the gray were getting into a very warm fight down on the plain at the foot of the mountain, and Lattimer's first shot was a fine one, exploding exactly *at* a Yankee battery, but the blue jackets instantly replied with one gun, which sent a shell within two feet of the muzzle of Capt. L.'s piece, striking the trail of the gun-carriage.

The shells and solid shot now hailed thick around the Confederate position on the mountain, and the Louisiana brigade, which had taken post there, enjoyed it hugely, some of the men being on the open ground in front, instead of in rear of the battery, where they belonged, would run to the places where the Yankee shot tore up the earth and coolly sit down, saying they were safe now, "as lightning never struck twice in the same place," but some of them lost their heads by the operation in spite of the proverb.

The battle raged with great violence until dark, and even when her sable wing had spread over the wild scene of blood and death, the artillery continued to fire, and if there is anything in war that can be called splendidly beautiful, it is a night cannonade, when high overhead, in the very middle, apparently, of the black field, the hissing shells fly in curving lines of beauty, leaving behind them a track of sparkling flame, until the explosion blazes a lurid glare all around the sky, which can he likened to nothing better than to the fitful flashings of Aurora in her most gorgeous masquerades.

When the firing ceased White's men had left the mountain and advanced to a house near where the Yankee battery which had been the recipient of Lattimer's first compliment had stood, the enemy having been driven back a considerable distance, and here they laid down and slept soundly till daylight, when their first notion was to look around for Yankees and plunder, in which interesting occupation they passed the time until noon, having secured a number of prisoners and quite a large quantity of arms and other trophies of the battlefield.

About 1 o'clock the company retired to a large spring, near the house before spoken of, and unbitting their horses, turned them out to graze, while the men lay in the shade of the trees around the spring reading the Yankee papers they had gathered up. The captain was very busily engaged in conversation with Mr. Henry Ball, who had just come from Loudoun, and brought to the captain the delightful intelligence that his wife was near the old camp at Somerset, having accompanied Mr. Ball through the Yankee lines without difficulty.

A small detail of the company was assisting Major Christie, ordnance officer of the division, to remove a quantity of ammunition from a broken-down wagon, about a quarter of a mile above, when the officer in command of the infantry skirmish line passed along and informed the captain that the pickets were all withdrawn from his front and he must look out for Yankees. "All right," responded White, and straightway forgot all about it in the interest of his talk with Mr. Ball.

Soon after this a commotion was heard in the direction of the ordnance detail, and before the men had time to get up, a squadron of Yankee cavalry charged down upon them, firing, yelling, and making everything look very blue. There was of course great consternation among White's people, but all scrambled to their horses—the captain mounting his own before putting the bit in its mouth—and as soon as they found themselves in their "headquarters," the confusion manifestly subsided, so that when Capt. White called on them to follow him in a charge upon the enemy, they responded gallantly, and chased the Yankee squadron in most splendid style over the same track they had come, at the same time rescuing Major Christie and his detail from the hands of the Yankees.

Two of the men who were with the major had already effected their escape, *viz*: Jas. H. Mock, by splendid riding, and Thomas Spates by literally outrunning his horse, a thing until then entirely unheard of. The old major was doing his best to get away on foot, but the enemy had him surrounded and were striking him over the head and back with their sabres, but they instantly left him when the pistols of White's boys begun cracking among them, and the old man mounted behind Lieut. Marlow, who carried him out of danger; and always thereafter there was no difficulty in Capt. White's men getting all the ammunition they wanted from the ordnance department of Ewell's Division.

The horses of Lieut. Myers and Sergt. Conrad carried them some distance in pursuit of the enemy after the balance of the company had retired, and were not stopped until the two men found themselves exposed to the fire of a line of infantry, which wounded Conrad's horse, when they too fell back, but not until the sergeant had cursed heartily the Yankees who shot his steed. From his position on the top of Slaughter Mountain Gen. Ewell had witnessed the whole of the gallant affair, and he complimented the captain very highly, calling it "a beautiful thing."

This advance of the Yankees, and skirmish of White, brought on a fight among the cavalry of both armies, which resulted in the discomfiture of the enemy and capture of Gen. Prince.

The next morning Capt. White obtained permission to visit his wife, and the command of the company devolved upon Lieut. Myers, who was called upon to go, with a few men, to see that the Yankees did not raid upon the wagon train, and on reaching them found everything in great confusion owing to a report that the enemy's cavalry was about to attack the train; but the lieutenant and his party soon rallied, and formed into line, about two hundred infantry stragglers who were about the wagons, and thus restored order among quartermasters and teamsters.

After dark, when the company had rejoined the general, the division withdrew from the mountain, and White's men were left to keep up the fires and make the Yankees believe the whole force was still there; and once, when Sam White and John Marlow piled hay on a fire, making a blaze that lighted up the side of the mountain, the general threatened to "throw a pistol ball among them if they did so any more," but they quietly promised to return all the pistol balls he threw them; however, they put no more hay on the fires. About midnight the general ordered Lieut. Myers to take his company and march rapidly to the bridge at Liberty Mills, with instructions to hold it and prevent the Yankees from destroying it before the infantry could get up.

About daylight they reached the bridge, and in half an hour an order came to send ten men, as couriers, to report to the general on a road north of the Rapidan, but after considerable difficulty in finding that number of men whose horses could stand the trip, the detail was sent on the wrong road and missing the general, excited his ire against Lieut. M., and when he reached camp and met the lieutenant he abused him considerably for not obeying his order, winding up with asking why he had not sent the detail; and as the lieutenant commenced to explain he unfortunately used the expression, "I supposed, general," when the general broke out, "You supposed; you supposed, you say; what right had you to suppose anything about it, sir; do as *I tell you*, sir; do as *I tell you*." That was the end of it, and during all the whole tirade of words the subordinate had only had an opportunity to use three.

The whole force was again in the camp at Somerset, and now the captain and his people began to talk about a raid to Loudoun for the purpose of chastising a band of renegades and Yankees which, under Sam. Means, was reported to be harassing the people of that county very severely; but, like foreign recognition and rumours of peace, it appeared to be more talk than anything else, and the men, as a general thing, hardly thought it possible to reach the "promised land," although it was the heartfelt aspiration of each to once more behold it and enjoy the pleasure of sweet companionship with homes and loved ones again.

On the 16th, one week after the battle of Cedar Run, General Jackson marched across the Rapidan towards Culpeper C. H., and

59

now hope burned brightly in Southern hearts, for all the men believed that Gen. Lee could march into the North Country and conquer a willing peace treaty from the government at Washington.

Pope made a stand on the Rappahannock, and while waiting for the Southern army to drive him back again Capt. White perfected his plans for the Loudoun expedition, and at Warrenton White Sulphur Springs got Gen. Ewell's sanction to it. When, on the 25th of August, "Stonewall" left the main army and started on his flank movement to Manassas, White marched with him, crossing the river opposite Orleans, after which he made as fast time as possible in order to gain the front of Jackson's corps, which he succeeded in doing at Salem. Just as his company passed the last regiment the men, who had halted to rest, called out, "you wouldn't have caught up with us if the colonel's horse hadn't given out."

At sunset the raiding party, having cleared all the troops, marched to the Bull Run Mountain, which point they reached about daylight, and where they proposed to lie over until night of the 26th. During the day the true-hearted citizens of the neighbourhood brought in plenty to eat, and some of them spent a great part of the day in the camp, among them Mr. Ball, Mr. Simpson, Mr. Wynkoop and others.

When the dark came down over the mountain the captain formed his men, consisting of about twenty of his own company, with Lieuts. Myers and Marlow, about twenty of Capt. Randolph's company, with Capt. R. and Lieuts. Redmond and Mount, and half a dozen of Gen. Jackson's scouts under that splendid soldier Dr. Gallaher. After the line was formed White made a short speech, telling his command that his object in the expedition was to *whip* Means' men, and that no matter how much force they had he intended to do it; that he knew where they were, and if the expedition failed it would be the fault of his own men; closing by saying with King Henry, if any man among them had no stomach for the fight upon such terms he was now at liberty to return.

The little force, augmented by the addition of Messrs. Henry Ball and J. Simpson, now took up the line of march for Waterford, passing along the mountain all the way, and arriving at Franklin's Mill an hour before daylight, when a halt was ordered and scouts sent out to ascertain if any changes had been made in the disposition of Means' command.

While lying here a party of eight was heard passing the road from Leesburg, who, from their conversation, were rightly judged to have been scouting all night to learn if there was any movements of the Southern army to the northward, and their words proved that they were perfectly satisfied and felt entirely secure, for among other things their leader was heard to declare, as they watered their horses within ten feet of one of White's scouts, that "there wasn't a rebel soldier north of the Rappahannock."

As soon as this party passed beyond hearing, White moved his people to Mr. Hollingsworth's barn-yard, where about twenty of them were dismounted, under command of Capt. Randolph, and ordered to march to the enemy's quarters, which were in the Baptist meeting-house, about one hundred yards distant, with instructions not to fire until they entered the house, or, in case the enemy was outside, to get into the yard with them before firing, and then to rush upon them and go with them into the house. The captain held the remainder of his men mounted, and rode to the brow of the hill in the road by Hollingsworth's gate to wait for the movement of Randolph to drive the Yankee boys from their quarters, when the cavalry would dash down and capture them.

Dawn was just beginning to turn the black of night to the grey of early morn when the movement commenced, and on Capt. Randolph's party getting near enough to see, they discovered Means' whole force standing in the yard listening to the report of their scouting party, which had just come in, and though they looked wonderingly at the infantry advance of White's army, not one of them said a word; but in spite of his orders, which could have been executed with perfect safety, Randolph ordered his men to fire as soon as they reached the corner of the palings around the yard.

This caused the Yankees to break and rush into the house in great confusion, having their commander, Lieut. Slater, badly wounded; and now, instead of following them, as his orders required, Randolph retired to Virts' house, just opposite; but the gallant Gallaher, with Jack Dove and a few others, tried to execute the order, and while Gallaher, springing into one window, fired his revolver bullets among the demoralised "boys in blue," the others poured their buckshot in at the other windows.

As soon as the firing commenced White brought his cavalry down the road at a gallop, and halting long enough to fire a round or two at the side windows of the meeting-house, discovered quite a number of Means' men leaping from the windows and making the fastest kind of time across the lots below the house, so calling on his boys to follow the captain made a dash down into town, but only succeeded in capturing two of the fugitives. From here some of the men galloped down to Means' house in the hope of getting that gentleman, but he was by that time "over the hills and far away," according to his custom when rebel bullets were on the wing.

Returning to the meeting-house, in broad daylight, White found his infantry laying close siege to it, and standing in the vestibule was the daring Webster, who had assumed command of the Yankees, and who, seeing White's mounted men riding up, supposed them to be a reinforcement for himself, and began firing upon Randolph's men at Virt's house, calling, as he did so, for his own men to come out and fight. A few pistol balls near him showed him his mistake, when he deliberately turned on the cavalry and emptied his revolver at them, after which he stepped back into the house and commenced to barricade the doors.

White's whole force now dismounted and opened a brisk fire at the windows, which was returned by Webster, Cox, and a few others, whom Webster succeeded in bringing from under the benches long enough to take a shot; but pretty soon it was discovered that ammunition was running short in White's ranks, and knowing the impossibility of taking the place by assault now, the captain prepared to withdraw his people, but on reaching the horses of the dismounted men he resolved upon shooting the horses of the Yankees, which had been tied in the yard during the fight, and presented to the gaze of the now baffled Confederates a prize well worth fighting for, composed as they were of the very best horses of Loudoun, a land always noted for fine ones, and equipped in the most superb style of the U. S. A.

Previous to this, however, an attempt had been made to negotiate a surrender by sending Mrs. Virts, under a truce, to make the proposition, but on her second mission the enemy informed her that if she came again they would shoot her; and now nothing remained but to get away in safety, which could only be done by depriving the Yankees of the means of following; and collecting the remaining cartridges a detail was sent to kill the horses; but while this party was getting in position around Virts' house it appears that the enemy were so badly frightened they were trying to force their commander to make terms, and a few shots from Ben. Conrad and Ross Douglass at some Yankees they saw by a window, precipitated matters and brought Webster out with a flag of truce.

He demanded the usual terms in such cases, *viz*: his men to be released on parole, their private property respected, and officers to retain their side arms; which White immediately granted, and the affair was concluded as soon as possible, the victors getting fifty-six horses, saddles and bridles, about one hundred fine revolvers and as many carbines, with a vast quantity of plunder which they were unable to carry off; and paroling twenty-eight prisoners, which, with the two previously captured, made thirty in all.

White lost Brook Hays, killed, and Corporal Peter J. Kabrich, mortally wounded; both gallant soldiers as ever drew a sabre. A few others were slightly injured. The enemy lost about seven or eight in killed and wounded.

The scene at the surrender, when Means' men, after being formed in line, laid down their arms, was a curious one. Many of them were old friends, and had been schoolboys with some of White's men; and in one instance, brothers met: one, Wm. Snoots, being a sergeant in White's company, and the other, Charles, a member of Means' command. Rebel and Yankee had swallowed up the feeling of brotherhood, or rather, that feeling had intensified the bitterness and hatred with which enemies in the hour of conflict regard each other; and the rebel would have certainly shot his Yankee brother, even after the surrender, but for the interference of one of the officers.

As soon as possible, after getting everything in movable shape, and arranging for the care of Kabrich, who was too badly hurt to be moved, and for the burial of Hays, the raiders turned their faces towards the South again, expecting to rejoin Gen. Jackson that night. At the point where the line of march diverged from the Leesburg road, Capt. White left Lieut. Myers in charge of the column, and taking with him a small detail, galloped into Leesburg, where he created quite a commotion, causing a few Yankee soldiers there to depart in the shortest time imaginable, and making the Southern people of that extremely Southern town almost wild with joy.

They had been under the galling rule of Yankeedom, as administered by such as Geary, until simple endurance had almost culminated in despair, and the advent of White, so unexpectedly, among them, was hailed as an omen that their day was beginning to dawn; and consequently, in their freshly blooming hope, they petted and lionized to their heart's content the little band of boys in gray who came to assure them that soon they would be free from the rule of their hated tyrants.

The two parties united about sunset, at Aldie, where all partook of an excellent supper at Mr. Henry Ball's, and where the captain again met his wife, but not for long could he remain in this earthly Eden, for while here the Rev. John Pickett notified the command that he had found a brigade of Yankee cavalry at the Plains, on the Manassas Gap Rail Road, and immediately the overloaded little band prepared for a night march to Manassas, making the third night of sleepless travel.

But all kept up, and about 9 o'clock on the morning of the 28th August, Capt. White reported to Gen. Ewell, and when evening came the boys carried their general from the battlefield to the house of Mr. Buckner, he having been badly wounded in the leg. And it now appeared that what they had considered as irksome duty, that of acting as couriers for Gen. Ewell and his brigadiers, was to the company the easiest and most pleasant they had ever or would ever perform; and they felt bitterly the loss of the best friend, of influence, they had in the army, in the person of Gen. Ewell. After this the company took but little part in the battle, but lay quietly in the yard around the house where their general was, until the close of the battle, when the country was cleared of the enemy to such an extent that people from the border could get out to the army, and here many young men came and enrolled themselves in White's company.

Citizens, also, who had heard of the capture of Means' horses at Waterford, came to look at the stock, and as that command had been mounted on horses taken from the people of Loudoun, and Capt. White invariably returned their property, it was not long until all the captured horses, so far as White's men were concerned, were among the things that had been.

Pope's army, too, as an army, was in the same situation, and the quarters for "Stonewall Jackson and 16,000 prisoners," which the mighty bummer had ordered to be prepared at Washington, were not occupied—for John had to "skedaddle," and just in his rear "old Stonewall" with that identical little party of 16,000 "foot cavalry" pushed bravely on, and with him went White and all his mounted men fit for duty, while Myers was sent to Loudoun in charge of dismounted men, and such as had broken down horses, for the double purpose of recruiting in both men and horses.

7: Snicker's Gap

Never were the veteran hearts of the men whom Lee and Stonewall led to victory, so thrilled with triumphant pride as on that morning in September, when the wild refrain of "Maryland, my Maryland," echoed from a thousand throats, rolled on the morning breezes over the border, and the ragged men in gray marched through the waters of the old Potomac which some of them had made to run red with the life-blood of the invading hosts of Yankeeland, who made their boasting advance, at almost the same point the year before, and added the name of Ball's Bluff to the list of Southern victories.

But none other than those born on the soil of Maryland could fully enter into the feelings that filled the heart of our captain when he saw the army that had tramped over the heaps of dead men, strewn from the blue and billowy James to the dashing surges of the Potomac, actually marching through the boundary that had, up to this time, been considered the *de facto* line of separation between the two Confederacies, and felt that of a truth the hour had come when another star would blaze in the Southern Cross, and *that* star the sign that Maryland, by aid of the iron legions of the Southland, had broken the rod of the Blackamoor's god, and joined, at last, her sisters in their crusade for freedom.

It will avail nothing, however, to revert here to the bitter disappointment which quenched these proud feelings in the hearts of the brave sons of the State of Maryland, who had been battling for the cause of Southern rights, when they found no responsive greeting from the now pitifully cowed spirit of poor, conquered Maryland, and felt that in spite of the hero-blood that had baptised the wreath of glory woven for her queenly brow by such hands as Carroll, Howard, May, and a thousand others, who, in the days of yore, had made her name so famous, she was now a subjugated thing, too much afraid of the power that had bound the slavish chain upon her very soul, to lift the folded hands from which the tyrant's fetters had just been so bravely torn, even though upon her own soil the conquering battle-flag of Dixie waved high above the bloody Northern standard.

Through treachery at the council board, she had been betrayed into the power of her enemies, and had not enough spirit left to do more than gaze with sad-eyed wonder upon the war-worn soldiers whose mission to their State was to give her people an opportunity to draw their swords in an equal fight for their desecrated altars.

Maryland was dumb before her shearers, and lamb-like she submitted, while the Southern Army looked vainly for the lion to awake to glory again.

At Frederick City, Capt. White fell under the displeasure of General Stuart, and was ordered by that commander to return with his company to Loudoun County, Va., but the captain protested, saying that he was a Marylander by birth and had fought as hard as any man for the privilege of fighting once upon the soil of his native State.

The general seemed only to want an excuse to become offended with him, and exclaimed, "Do you say you have done as much as any man, for the South?"

"No, sir," said Capt. White, "I did not say that; but I have done my duty to the South as a soldier, so far as my ability extends, as fully as anybody."

Again, the general broke out with, "You did say you had done as much as any man." And the captain replied, "I did not say so."

Thus, the quarrel went on, and finally Stuart ordered White to go back to Loudoun and watch for a flanking force of the enemy expected by way of Dranesville, or Fairfax C. H., from Washington. But White refused to go, saying he would go see Gen. Lee.

"Come on," said Stuart, "I'll go with you." And the two proceeded at once to Army Headquarters. Arrived there, Gen. S. passed in, and White saw that Gen. Jackson was also there.

Gen. Lee met White at the door and asked him his business, when the captain replied, "I want to see you, sir." "Very well," said the general, "just wait a little while and I'll see you."

Pretty soon General Jackson came out and approached White, who was walking in front of Headquarters, and actually so much excited over what he considered the injustice of Gen. Stuart, that he was crying.

"Stonewall" asked him his difficulty, and was told that Stuart wanted to send him back to Loudoun, and he didn't want to go. The general appeared surprised, and remarked, "Why, I just heard Gen. Stuart tell Gen. Lee that you *desired to be sent back*, and recommended that it be done."

At this the captain tried to tell Gen. Jackson that it was not so, but before he could explain, his feelings so overcame him that he completely choked down and could not say anything.

Presently, Gen. Jackson said, "Capt. White, I think I can understand your feelings, for I was once situated just as you are now. During the Mexican war I was ordered to the rear just as a battle was about to take place, and I knew of no reason why I should be so unjustly treated; but I obeyed, and it so happened that by doing so I had an opportunity to acquire distinction that I never could have had in front, and captain, my advice to you is to obey orders, no matter how unjust they may be. We are poor, short-sighted creatures at best, and in the very thing that *seems* hardest for us to bear, Providence may have hidden a rich blessing for us. Go, captain, and obey orders."

White says he knew Gen. Jackson was too good a man for him to talk to, and consequently he made no reply. But Gen. Stuart now came out and calling him to his side said, "Capt. White, did you say you was a Marylander?"

"Yes, sir," said White. "Ah!" said the general, "I didn't know that. Gen. Lee wants you. Go in and see him."

As may be supposed, the captain lost no time in appearing in the presence of the commanding general, and his orders were to scout towards Harper's Ferry and report to Gen. Lee. This meant that for the present he was free from the spite of Stuart, and he at once commenced his scout, learning of the condition of affairs about Harper's Ferry, and gathering much valuable information; without, however, being required to engage the enemy.

"He had now been joined by the long-expected company of Capt. Chiswell, and on Saturday night, September 12th, the two companies crossed the river into Loudoun County, and on Sunday evening marched down to Waterford, where they bivouacked in the same meeting-house which Webster had tried so hard to hold against White's men a few weeks before. Here they were joined by Lieut. Myers, whose detachment had grown into a very respectable company; and the next morning White moved with his squadron towards the river, intending to make an examination of the enemy's force which was following Lee's army up through Maryland.

On the top of Catocton mountain, they had a partial view of the cannonading at Harper's Ferry, where Gen. Jackson had penned up Gen. Miles in the "nose of the tunnel," just as Jo. Johnston had declared, in 1861, that he (Johnston) would not be caught.

About noon Capt. White reached his own farm on the river, and in the bottom, near the ford, discovered a party of Yankee infantry and cavalry, which he immediately charged, capturing all the infantry, in number thirty-five, with the lieutenant in command, but the cavalry made their escape over the river. From here the command went to Leesburg, from which place a detail from the two companies was made to guard the prisoners, and Lieut. Myers placed in charge, with orders to deliver the Yankees to the provost marshal at Winchester, while the captain moved his command back to Waterford, where he spent the next day; but on the 17th he received a notice that a force of the enemy was advancing on Leesburg from towards Washington, which caused him to hastily return to Leesburg.

On arriving there he found the troops preparing to leave the town, but he prevailed on them to remain for a short time at least. The force there consisted of Co. A, 6th Va. Cavalry, under Capt. Gibson, and about forty Mississippi infantry commanded by Capt. Young, who was the provost marshal of the town. Captain White, owing to the rapidity of his march from Waterford, did not have more than thirty of his men with him. The force of the enemy was about four hundred cavalry, with four pieces of artillery, under command of Gen. Kilpatrick, who had come up to see if there was any Confederate force in Loudoun County.

Capt. Young, with his infantry, halted on the turnpike above town, and Capt. Gibson did the same, while Capt. White moved his command below Leesburg, and found the enemy still advancing, but rather slowly. Here he exchanged a few shots with them, and seeing them placing a battery in position he retired through the town and halted near Capt. Young.

Kilpatrick now, in perfect wantonness, and without any warning, opened fire from his artillery upon the town, and the women and children of Leesburg only knew that they were to be bombarded when the shrieking shells came crashing through walls and roofs in the centre of their town.

After a while a party of cavalry advanced, and the firing having stopped they marched through and came out on the road near where the little force of Confederates were standing, upon which Capt. White ordered his men to charge, but just as he was riding forward the infantry fired a volley at the Yankees, one ball from which struck him just under the shoulder blade, and lodged under the skin in front of his throat. This unfortunate affair stopped the charge which, had the captain not been wounded, would undoubtedly have routed Kilpatrick's whole force, as citizens on the road reported him and his men to have been very much excited and in great confusion when the party which the infantry had fired on returned at a run from their advance through Leesburg.

Capt. Gibson's men and the infantry of Young now retired, and White's men, bearing their wounded Captain, followed them slowly up the turnpike as far as Rice's house, where they left him in charge of Boyd Barrett, and went on to Hamilton, where Lieut. Myers and his party from Winchester met them. Myers at once took command of the squadron, and as it was now dark halted for the night in the village, and when morning came marched back to Leesburg; shortly after which the captain was moved to Colonel Vandevanter's, where he remained for a few days; but the Battle of Sharpsburg having now been fought and the Southern Army forced back across the Potomac, and the border country, in consequence, being overrun with parties of the enemy's cavalry, it was thought best to move him nearer the mountain, which was done, and for some time he sojourned at Mr. Humphrey's, near Snickersville, care being taken not to let his whereabouts be known, as the Yankees desired nothing better than to get possession of Capt. White, the guerrilla, as they called him.

In fact, a party of them had come very near capturing him while he was at Colonel Vandevanter's, only missing him by having been wrongly informed as to his location, they having gone to Mr. Washington Vandevanter's instead of the colonel's. After this Lieut. Myers established his camp in Snicker's Gap, from where he scouted the border to Fairfax C. H., under the orders of Gen. Jackson, and reporting directly to that commander, whose headquarters were in Winchester.

Some time passed in this manner, the two companies operating actively in Loudoun and Fairfax, occasionally picking up a few Yankees, and to a great extent stopping their incursions in the country, except in large bodies, one of which came near gobbling up the little command. Maj. Foster, of the Quartermaster's Department, had been instructed by Gen. Stuart to call on Lieut. Myers for assistance in bringing out a lot of cattle from the Lovettsville country, and had fixed upon the 16th of October to meet at Wheatland for that purpose; but Myers, knowing that Gen. Kenley, with a strong force of infantry, cavalry and artillery, was somewhere near Leesburg, thought it best to let the cattle alone for that day. He, however, sent scouts to find where the Yankees were, and with about thirty men went to Wheatland, according to instructions, where he halted, and threw out pickets.

Pretty soon the picket on the Waterford road, who happened to be a young soldier (E. H. Tavenner) on his first tour of duty, came in and reported the enemy advancing, saying they had come within fifty yards of him and refused to stop when he told them to do so; and being asked why he didn't fire on them, he replied that he "did try, but his carbine kept snapping, and that was why they got so close to him before he left his post." The lieutenant concluded that as green a man as that didn't know a Yankee when he saw him, and sending "for the other pickets to come in, trotted off to see for himself, and before getting to the post his picket had occupied, he saw, and heard too, for the advance guard of Kenly's brigade opened fire on him from a turn of the road, and charging upon him at the same time, nearly captured him with Dick and Sam. Grubb and Ben. Conrad, who came to his assistance; but they were in luck and escaped without injury, or losing any of the command.

That night, John DeButts, with Tom. Spates and one or two others, captured Kenly's pickets near Hillsboro', and the general marched to Harper's Ferry before day.

Previous to this, a company commanded by Lieut. James Anderson, one under Capt. John H. Grabill, and one under Lieut. Wood, had reported to Lieut. Myers, and these with the two companies of White and Chiswell, and about fifty men raised by R. B. Grubb, formed a battalion which Myers did not feel disposed to command. The companies of Chiswell and Grubb, not being yet organised, and were moreover attached to the old company as a part of it, he could manage very well, but Capt. Grabill refused to command the whole force and the delicacy Myers felt in assuming the command of officers higher in rank than himself, made the matter a very awkward one in the new battalion, but all the officers insisted upon his occupying the position, and he finally did so, and commanded until the 19th of October, when Capt. James F. Trayhern, whose company, under Anderson, was already in camp, came in and assumed the command.

Capt. Trayhern immediately resolved on an extended scout to find the enemy, and for this purpose ordered all the available force of the battalion then in camp to mount and form for the expedition. The whole force thus called out was about one hundred and thirty, in two squadrons; the first, commanded by Lieut. Myers, was composed of portions of the old company and of Chiswell's and Grubb's men, the Marylanders led by Sergt. Henry Sellman, and Grubb's boys by Sam. Grubb. The second squadron was commanded by Capt. Grabill, and composed of his own company, that of Trayhern under Lieut. Anderson, and part of the Albemarle company.

Capt. Dick Grubb acted as Adjutant; and thus organised, the battalion marched out of the mountain, assured by its commander that "he intended to go wherever he heard of Yankees across the Potomac." On the 20th, the command halted on the river hills opposite Berlin, and looked at the long line of bluejackets on drill on the Maryland side of the line, but none had yet been discovered or heard of south of it. About sunset Capt. Trayhern retired to the old Rehoboth Church and disbanded his command, in order that the men could get something to eat in the neighbourhood for themselves and horses, but gave instructions for all to report at the church by nine o'clock, which they did, and the pickets were duly posted by Lieut. Myers, who was detailed as officer of the guard for the night; and all, except the guards, unsaddled and went into the church to sleep.

About an hour before daylight, Myers started out for his last visit to the outposts that night, and on reaching the post at Bolington was surprised to find all the pickets missing; and a further examination convinced him that the Yankees had certainly been down and carried off the whole business—guards, reserve and all. Returning to the command, he informed Trayhern of the affair, and rode on to the other pickets, whom he found all right, not having heard or seen anything more alarming than cattle during the night.

Taking his pickets with him, the lieutenant went back to the battalion, and after a consultation, it was resolved by Trayhern to follow the enemy, who, according to the testimony of some persons at Bolington, had not been gone long, and endeavour to recapture the prisoners; and sending Sam. Grubb with a squad in advance, the command pushed forward rapidly; but soon met Sam. coming back with the information, that Lovettsville was full of Yankees, and that an infantry force was posted in a piece of woods on the grade, a short distance from town.

And here Capt. Trayhern committed the fatal error of attempting to drive this force from their position, which was all the enemy wished, hoping to keep him occupied until the flanking party from Harper's Ferry could gain the rear of the Confederates. After a short skirmish, Trayhern decided to go back, and on his way, halted for a short time at Morrisonville, and then moved on towards Hillsborough.

Pretty soon he met some of the men from the latter place, who informed him that Hillsborough also was occupied by a strong force; and counter-marching, the little battalion took the road to Wheatland; but on arriving at Smith's, about a mile from that place, firing was heard in front, and soon the advance returned at a gallop, closely pursued by a body of Yankee cavalry.

Capt. Grubb now gave the order "by fours right about," and the Confederates retreated rapidly to Maj. Geo. L. Moore's gate, where Grubb turned the column into the field. All this time the Yankees were firing rapidly, and the halt made here in passing the gate enabled them to come up with the battalion, and here a party, with Lieut. Marlow and Sam. Grubb, left the command and struck for the mountain.

Reaching the barn-yard gate at Moore's the Yankees were in thirty yards, and Lieut. Myers, who in the "right about" on the grade had been thrown in rear of the command, found it a difficult matter to get the gate shut and chained again after the command had passed, for the "blue jackets" fired fast at him, but he finally succeeded, and on the hill in the field joined Capt. Trayhern, who, with Captains Grabill and Grubb assisting him bravely, was endeavouring to rally the men and make a stand until an opening for escape could he made in the post and rail fence, but only twenty men could be got in line.

In a few minutes the Yankees came through the gate, and about two hundred of them charged the little force on the hill, but received a volley which checked and caused them for a moment to retire; but now, notwithstanding the efforts of Capt. Trayhern, who displayed great gallantry, and of other officers, the men broke and crowded down into the corner of the field, and the Yankees coming on again captured twenty-two of them and about thirty horses. They could just as easily have gotten the whole party, but on charging with drawn sabres to about ten yards of the crowd in the corner, and receiving a fire from a few men with pistols, they halted and commenced firing in return.

The fence was now broken open, and the Confederates began leaping their horses over. Here one man was killed and one wounded, but by good horsemanship the others all got clear. The pursuit was continued as far as the mill of Mr. Caldwell, on the Waterford road, and during it a Yankee lieutenant, in the attempt to capture Lieut. Myers, who was poorly mounted, was mortally wounded.

On arriving at camp and counting up the losses, it was found that twenty-three were captured; Lycurgus W. Bussard, a gallant soldier of the old company, was killed, and Jacob H. Robertson, also of the old company, badly wounded. The squad that with Marlow and Sam. Grubb escaped to the mountain, came down in the Yankee rear at Hillsboro, capturing six prisoners, whom they brought out; which with the eight killed and wounded in the chase, made the enemy's loss fourteen.

Their whole force consisted of two regiments of cavalry, three of infantry, and a battery of artillery, in all about four thousand; while Trayhern's command, when he met the Yankees, did not number more than seventy-five.

Gen. Geary, who commanded the Yankees, felt himself the hero of a most wonderful exploit, and on his return to Harper's Ferry arrested and carried with him the Rev. S. S. Rozzle, but the parson so cut the general's feathers in his conversation with him, that he was glad to permit him to go home, not even requiring his parole, although if he had asked it Mr. Rozzle was not the man to give it to such a bombastic bag of gas as Geary, who could not look him in the face after talking with him half an hour.

Captains Trayhern and Grabill both lost their horses, and only saved themselves by taking refuge in the top of a cabin which stood near the field, and where they lay until dark undiscovered by the Yankees, although many of them were in and around the house for some time.

When Capt. Trayhern returned to camp, he found his company highly exasperated against him for having, as they said, gotten them into such a trap; and under the excitement of the moment, that high-spirited officer resigned his commission, and left the battalion, never to meet it again until the morning after Gen. Lee surrendered the Army of Northern Virginia.

The command again fell upon Lieut. Myers, and under instructions from Capt. White, he went diligently to work preparing the battalion for organisation.

The captain had moved his quarters from Mr. Humphrey's to the home of Mr. Park. Shepherd, in Clarke County, where his devoted and heroic little wife joined him, and under her care he was soon convalescent.

On the 28th of October, Col. Bradley T. Johnson, (afterwards Brigadier-General of the Maryland Line,) then A. and I. G. on Stuart's staff, came over, and after superintending the organisation, mustered White's Battalion regularly into the service.

Capt. White was unanimously elected Major, and Lieut. Myers became Captain of Company A, with Barrett, Marlow and Ben. F. Conrad, for his lieutenants.

Company B, organised by electing George W. Chiswell, Captain; Joshua R. Crown, 1st Lieutenant; Nich. W. Dorsey, 2nd Lieutenant; and Ed. J. Chiswell, 2nd Lieutenant, Jr.

Company C, elected Richard B. Grubb, Captain; W. Flavius Dowdell, 1st Lieutenant; and Sam. E, Grubb, 2nd Lieutenant.

Company D, was already organised, being Trayhern's old company, and now officered by Lieuts. Anderson, Spangler, and Sam. Baker.

Company E, had Capt. Grabill, Lieut. Grubbs, and —— ——, for officers.

There was some difficulty in the case of the other company, which had been organised in Albemarle County, under Capt. Geo. N. Ferneyhough, for service in Scott's Battalion—and although it was present, under command of Lieut. Woods, was not mustered in until some months later.

Capt. Grubb and Lieut. Anderson were both prisoners, having been captured a week before, in the battle of Glenmore.

Major White now appointed Lieut. Crown, Adjutant, and Capt. J. Mort. Kilgour, Quartermaster. After which, he rode back to Mr. Shepherd's again, leaving Capt. Myers in command, with instructions to look out for the advance of the Yankee army, which, under Burnside, was about to "on to Richmond" again.

Besides White's Battalion, there was now stationed in Snicker's Gap, a company of the 2nd Va. Cavalry, under Capt. Tebbs, and a detail from Capt. Chew's battery with one 12-pounder howitzer, making a total force of about three hundred men.

About the 1st of November, a heavy body of the enemy's cavalry, under Gen. Pleasanton, advanced on the gap, creating no small excitement among the garrison; but as soon as possible, preparations were made to dispute possession, and while Capt. Tebbs held his company, mounted, near the toll-gate, Myers dismounted two companies of the battalion under Capt. Grabill, who was an old infantry officer of the "Stonewall brigade," to operate as sharpshooters on the side of the road, and with the remainder in the saddle, took post near the artillery, which was advanced to within five hundred yards of Snickersville.

About this time the Yankees dashed into town, and gave a few of White's men there a lively chase up the road, in which John Stephenson was severely wounded. In a few minutes the enemy's column appeared in the road just above the town, and on the instant, the little howitzer blazed forth its "thus far and no farther," in the shape of a three-second shell, which exploded precisely in the right place, killing and wounding several men and horses, and causing the remainder to retire in great confusion, which was increased by the fire of Grabill's infantry.

Before the gun could be reloaded the Yankees were out of range, and the fight over, for Gen. Pleasanton took up his line of march for the Potomac at once. This affair took place on Thursday, and on the Sunday following, just at sunrise, the Yankees were again discovered making for the gap; but this time it appeared that the whole land was covered with infantry, long blue lines of which moved up the mountain; and Major White having reached the scene of action, ordered the battalion, which, with the howitzer, had taken the same position

74

occupied on Thursday, to fall back, and the whole force retired to the river hill.

Very soon the Yankees were on the mountain in heavy force, and hardly noticing the shells from White's little howitzer, they placed a battery in the gap from which they threw shells clear over his position, and killed men in A. P. Hill's division, a mile beyond the river. White's men thought it was time to be leaving, but the major held on until dark, when, leaving Lieut. Dowdell, with Company C, to watch the enemy, he crossed the river and encamped for the night.

About noon the next day, Dowdell sent a courier over to the major, saying that the Yankees had flanked his pickets off their posts on the river hill, and he thought they were coming down the mountain in force. The major called for volunteers to cross the river with him, when about thirty of his men mounted their horses and followed him. Reaching the foot of the mountain they met Dowdell, with his company, who gave the particulars of the night-watch, and told how the Yankee infantry crawled through the bushes around his men, very nearly capturing his party.

The major at once started up the mountain with about ten men, to see for himself the position of the enemy, and when nearly on the top of the river hill, Sergeant-Major L. B. Stephenson and Capt. Myers, who were in the advance, each at the same moment discovered the Yankees in the woods on both sides of the road, and not twenty yards distant. They immediately wheeled their horses to retreat, but before they could tell the major what they had seen, the infantry sprang out of the woods and opened a heavy fire which sent the whole party in a hurry down the road, and when about half way met the reserve coming to their assistance.

The enemy was advancing rapidly, and telling his men to cross the river quick, the major formed a rear guard to fight the Yankees until the main body could get over; but very soon the heavy masses of blue jackets pouring out of the mountain in front, and on the right, forced him to cross also; and now the most exciting scene of all transpired. Most of the men were over, and Major White, last of all, was not more than one-third the way across, when a heavy bank of Yankee infantry lined the river shore and poured their fire upon that solitary man; but calmly he rode amid the storm, the bullets raining around him and making the water appear as if it was boiling, while his horror-stricken men looked on, expecting each moment to see him fall; but on he came, apparently as cool as if there was not a Yankee in five miles, and finally rode out of the river, unscathed.

Dense masses of the foe were still rapidly marching down the mountain, and just as White got through, the batteries of Gen. Hill opened from the Clarke hills a most horribly destructive fire upon them, as they stood, wedged closely in the small space between the river and the mountain, and from which there was no way of escape, the road being full of troops, batteries and ambulances, all hurrying towards Castleman's Ferry. For some time, the slaughter was terrible, and all the while not a shot was returned from the Yankees; but bye-and-bye an officer appeared with a flag of truce, asking for a cessation of the firing, until they could remove their wounded, and to the surprise of all, Gen. Hill granted it, although he must have known that ten minutes more of such firing would have forced the enemy to surrender.

Shortly after the firing ceased Maj. White, with a party of his men, crossed the river again, and found the mountain road literally running with blood, while the dead lay thick along it, and the busy ambulances, as they carried their mangled freight to the rear, left a trail of blood on the ground. The fight was over, for while moving the wounded and dead, the Yankees continued to take their sound and live ones back too.

Shortly afterwards the following note was received from Gen. Stuart:

Headquarters, Cavalry Division,
November 9th, 1862.

Major—I am directed by the major-general commanding, to say that he has heard with much pleasure of the successful operations of your command in the actions with the enemy at Snicker's Gap, and hopes that it may be a forerunner of still further deeds of daring, skill, and success by your command; and to assure you of his high appreciation of its conduct, and the gallantry and skill of its commander.

I have the honour to be, Major, your obedient servant,

Norman R. Fitzhugh,
Major and A. A. Gen'l.

To Major E. V. White,
Commanding White's Battalion Cavalry.

For a few days after this affair the battalion lay quietly in camp about a mile from Castleman's Ferry, with nothing to do but look at the Yankees on the mountain. But one evening it was noticed that a great fire was burning in Snicker's Gap and spreading along the ridge on either side, which induced the major to believe that the enemy was leaving; so hastily calling out his command, he crossed the river and advanced into the gap, without meeting any of the blue-coated boys who had been there so recently.

From here he pushed forward to Snickersville and learned that the rear guard of Burnside's army had passed there three hours before, and finding a number of sutler wagons following the Yankee line of march, White's boys very quietly took possession of them, and now the battalion divided into several detachments and ranged the country nearly all night, arriving in camp shortly before daylight with about twenty wagons loaded with all manner of supplies, and upwards of two hundred prisoners.

The next day the raiding on the enemy's rear was resumed, and several wagons and prisoners brought in; and about dark the major learned that a Yankee train had deposited a quantity of tents and baggage in an old house at Neersville. So, putting his people in line again, he started for them, and about midnight took quiet possession of exactly the supplies needed by the command for winter quarters, all of which were safely brought away. The same day was marked also by a gallant exploit of four members of Company A, which was highly complimented by the major.

The half wild Henry Simpson, in company with Mort. Palmer, Dave Lee and Bob Ritacor, were at Philomont when the 91st Pennsylvania infantry passed that place. The wagon train followed close in rear of the regiment and just behind the wagons the commander, Col. W. P. Wainwright, with some members of his staff, rode leisurely along, when these daring fellows made a dash at the train, cutting out and bringing safely to camp the colonel's headquarter wagon; the colonel himself narrowly escaping capture by flight.

The last expedition in Burnside's rear was a raid on a camp of sixty infantry at Mount Gillead, who had been left to guard a quantity of stores at that place, and who surrendered after a sharp fight, and these stores composed the richest capture yet made.

The total number of prisoners made in the whole series of operations was about one thousand, and fully two hundred wagons were destroyed and brought out together, besides an immense amount of stores and arms destroyed by the Yankees themselves, to keep them from falling into the hands of White's men.

A considerable number of the men had been taken prisoners during the fall, and although most of them were promptly exchanged under the Dix-Hill cartel, yet some few were detained and treated by the enemy with great rigor, under a charge of being guerrillas, and the major had done all in his power, through appeals to the Confederate authorities, to procure their release by retaliation, and took occasion, on sending the beautiful sword of Col. Wainwright as a present to Gen. Jackson, to call that officer's attention to the matter, which elicited the following reply from "Stonewall:"

Headquarters, V. Dist., Nov. 15th, 1862.
Major—The beautiful sword with which you have so kindly presented me, and also the other much prized presents, have been received from Lt. Marlow of your distinguished command. Please accept my thanks for them.
I have watched with great interest your brilliant exploits. Your men may well feel proud of having such a leader. Press on in your successful career.
Let your men know that their comrades who are maltreated at Fort McHenry are not forgotten. I deem it a solemn duty to protect, as far as God enables me, every patriotic soldier of my command. I regret being driven to retaliation, but the enemy, from time to time, have been warned against their inhumanity. I have directed three Federal prisoners, of the rank of captain, to be detained at Staunton. I intend to have this outrage of which you complain thoroughly investigated, and not only see that the two men of your company, but also the one belonging to Capt. Ball's, are exchanged, and also that indemnification is made for any wrongs which they may have suffered.
With high esteem, I am, Major, very truly your friend,
T. J. Jackson, Lt.-General.
To Major E. V. White.

As an evidence that "Stonewall" Jackson took no half way measures, and also that he kept his promises, the prisoners referred to were released in about ten days.

8: In Maryland

The battalion now encamped on the turnpike, about three miles from the river, and near Berryville, and under orders from Gen. W. E. Jones. The major posted his companies at the fords on the Shenandoah, from Front Royal to Key's Ferry, to picket. The camp was lumbered up with a great quantity of captured property, having wagons and tents sufficient for three times the number of men; in fact, no regiment in either army was better supplied with camp equipage than White's battalion.

On the night of the 28th November, a dispatch was received from Company B, at Berry's Ferry, saying that the enemy was crossing at that point, and Mr. William Dove, or as he was familiarly known in the command, "Uncle Billy," the active and efficient wagon-master, went to work loading the wagons, preparatory to a move; but by the time everything was ready, another courier came from Company B, saying the alarm was false. At this time the only force in camp was Company Q, composed, as every old soldier knows, of men who are disabled or on detail.

Company A, which was to play the most conspicuous part in what was about to transpire, was on duty at Castleman's Ferry, commanded by Lieut. Barrett.

For several days a party of about one hundred Federal cavalry had made regular trips up the Aldie turnpike to Snickersville, thence through the Gap to the river bank, and returning at once as quietly as they came. They never disturbed citizens, and no one knew their object, but all supposed it was nothing farther than to notice the disposition of the Confederates in the Valley, and it is singular that they were permitted to operate in this manner with so much regularity and not be molested; certain it is that no such thing was ever permitted by White afterwards.

On the 29th, this party made its appearance at the river as usual, and Barrett's men, on their first appearance, were not prepared to receive such company; some of them being engaged in fishing, some were boating, and nearly all had their horses unsaddled, so incautious had familiarity with the motions of this particular party of Yankees rendered them; but the visitors seemed to linger on the river bank for a longer time today than usual, and Barrett ordered his men to saddle up, at the same time sending a courier to camp to inform Capt. Myers, who was in command there, that the Yankees were at the river, and he thought they intended to cross.

He hailed the enemy, and when they replied, asked them "what they wanted," and invited them to "come over," to which they answered by telling him "not to be uneasy," that they "would be over presently," which the lieutenant began to think was highly probable, as their number was increasing every moment in a most alarming manner. As soon as possible he had the company mounted, and sending a man down the river to order the guards below him to fall back, he prepared to do the best he could, under the circumstances, to delay the enemy as long as possible, in order to give the men in camp time to get the baggage away, for their intention to accept his invitation to "come over" was rapidly becoming apparent and certain.

It is now time to go to the camp and see what arrangements have been made there for the visitation that will soon be made on the west bank of the Shenandoah.

Thanks to the alarm from Company B, the night before, the wagons were all loaded and ready to move. All the tents had been struck, with the exception of Capt. Grubb's, who having been sick for some days, and unable to move, resolved to stay in his tent. About twenty-five men were in camp, either entirely dismounted or with broken-down horses. Some were sick, and besides these the number on detail in the quartermaster's department would make a total of about sixty in all when Lieut. Barrett's courier arrived.

This man came up very leisurely, and did not report to Capt. Myers at all, but who accidentally saw him, and knowing him to be one of Barrett's men, asked him the news at the river, when the fellow responded that there were "some Yankees on the other side."

Myers asked if Barrett thought it was only the usual scout, or if they looked like crossing, and he replied that he "didn't know." This was all of Lieutenant Barrett's dispatch that reached the commander, and I have always entertained the opinion that the courier ought to have been court-martialled and shot.

After a few minutes' reflection and study about the matter, Myers gave the order for the wagons to move out on the road, but was induced to do so more because "Uncle" Billy Dove was anxious to move now that everything was ready, than from any apprehension that Yankees would come.

Capt. Kilgour and "Uncle Billy" at once set all the machinery of the quartermaster's department in motion, and very soon the train begun to move.

We will now go back to the river where we left Barrett and his boys watching the enemy; but their watch was of short duration, for suddenly the whole force of Yankees moved off briskly, and unmindful of the pistol shots fired at them, dashed into the river and came over. The Confederates soon gave way, and the affair turned into a horse-race for camp.

One of the men ran in at Mr. Shepherd's to notify Major White, and found him lying down, but he soon got out and mounted his horse, reaching the pike just as the Yankees came up. They were now about a mile from camp and all together, pursuers and pursued, rode like "Tam O'Shanter," and all together reached the camp, but here the Yankees made a halt until their reserve came up, before charging in upon the scattered crowd of demoralised men in the camp.

The major had been wounded in the thigh, and Lieut. Barrett, with about twenty of his men, taken prisoners, and now the question was, "How are the wagons to be saved?"

Major White, notwithstanding his wound, rallied such of his men as were mounted and armed, and from every hill-top in the fields fired upon and checked the enemy, while all the men except the dozen with him, did their best running.

An old citizen of Clarke County, Col. Morgan, whose residence was near, saw the flying fugitives racing across the field; he came out and attempted to rally them, but seeing that they only ran the faster, the old gentleman, with the spirit of his famous ancestor, "the wag-oner general of the revolution," swore he would fight them alone; but when the carbine balls began to clip the blue grass around him, he thought better of it and went home.

The Yankees pressed White and his party very closely as far as Ber-ryville, and captured one wagon, but not the team, the driver having cut his horses loose and made his escape. Capt. Kilgour stuck to his train bravely, and with "Uncle Billy," directed its movements until the Yankee bullets commenced singing around him, when he gave it up, and made "Toney" show his speed and bottom too.

At Berryville, the 12th Virginia Cavalry, under Lt.-Col. Burke, made its appearance and charged gallantly into the Yankee column, but were soon compelled to retire, when they came on again after White and his boys, one of whom, Mag. Thompson, was badly wounded and taken prisoner, but the enemy was generous enough to parole him and leave him in the care of some ladies at a house near the road.

At the 7th mile post from the river the pursuit ceased, and the Yankees went back to Berryville, just in time to miss the capture of the baggage wagon of Company A, from which the driver had cut the lead horses, only about two hundred yards from where they halted.

The major now went on to Winchester, whither most of his men had preceded him, while Capt. Myers, with a small party, waited by their wagon until the horses were brought back, which was about dark, when they too rode on up the pike, and met General Jones and staff at the Opekon, who made them turn back and go to Berryville to learn if the enemy was still there; but on arriving at that place they found the Yankee rear guard retiring towards the river. The miserable affair was over, but it left its influence upon the command, and their pride in the battalion was clashed by the shame of the surprise.

The surgeon, Dr. Wootten of Maryland, who had never seen the battalion, but was just on his way to join it, was met by the Yankees and carried off with the others.

As before stated, Capt. Grubb was in his tent sick, when Gen. Stahl's people (for that Dutchman was in command) came up, and many of them crowded around, asking questions, among which they wanted to know what was the matter with him. "I don't know," said Dick, "but they tell me I have the smallpox."

After that he wasn't disturbed at all for some time, but finally an adjutant who was *seasoned* to it came to see him, treating him very kindly, however, and assisted him to move to some negro quarters nearby, where he took his parole and left him, while the officer returned and set fire to his tent.

The enemy was about twelve hundred strong and all superbly mounted, especially the advance column, so that all the men in Company A who were on indifferent horses were easily picked up in the three-mile chase from Castleman's, where the only error of their commander was committed, in keeping his men at the river until the Yankees were nearly over.

Lieut. Conrad related, that on their run up the pike, he having staid in the rear as long as it was possible to do without letting himself be taken, he passed Lieut. Barrett, who was mounted on a large racking horse that had the name of "John," (and "John" had no motion faster than his rack, either,) and was doing what Conrad called his "level best." Just as Conrad rode by, he called out, "You must go faster than that, lieutenant, or they'll get you." But Barrett, casting an eye over his shoulder, and giving at the same time an extra dig with his spurs, coolly remarked, "No they won't; they'll never catch me while old John racks this way." Lieut. Conrad says that in three minutes they were all around him, and soon after he made an unconditional surrender of "old John" and all.

Lieut. Barrett wore a pair of U. S. A. lieutenant's shoulder straps, and on the way down the pike some of the Yankees cut them off for him, saying no rebel had any right to wear their officers' rigging.

The next morning, Major White got his command together and made a scout over into Loudoun, but the enemy had all disappeared, and for many a day Gen. Stahl considered this exploit of whipping "dat dam Bob White," as he called him, the chiefest plume in his cap; and some of his men, who were afterwards captured, say that he insisted on being made General-in-Chief of the U. S. Cavalry for it.

Two days after Stahl's expedition, Gen. Jones ordered his brigade to assemble at Winchester, and when dark came down with night, he marched it to Strasburg, where he halted for a little time.

It was here that the old general tried to teach White's men how to bivouac in winter nights with no comforts but fires and their blankets. Said he, "Lie down by the fire on the opposite side from where the wind blows, and the fire keeps the wind from you while the smoke blows over you and keeps off frost or dew."

"Oh, but," said one of the men, "the smoke is a little too bitter for me."

"Yes," replied the general, "you get some of the bitter, but you get a damned sight of the sweet, too." There is good philosophy in this, apart from the profanity—and all who are compelled to camp out would do well to practice it.

General Jones did not move any further up the Valley, but marched back towards Winchester and encamped near Kernstown.

Here it was that the same Capt. Webster, who had been with Means' men in Loudoun, and whom White had paroled at Waterford, in August, came out to the camp of the battalion, in company with Charley Cooper, who rode with him from Upperville without taking from him his arms. Webster gave himself up to Myers, who happened to be in command of the camp at that time, and to whom he told his plans and purposes, and explained the feasibility of capturing Means and all his party, so very clearly, that Myers fell very much in love with the scheme, and was sure that Major White would embrace the apparently certain opportunity to break up the Loudoun Rangers for the war.

Webster's proposition commenced with explaining that Means had driven him from his company, and also had caused him to be arrested and confined in the Old Capitol prison in Washington, from which he had escaped and now only lived to revenge his wrongs by being instrumental in putting Means in the power of White's men, who he was sure would not permit him to live.

He proposed to be tied on a horse, placed in charge of as strong a

guard as Maj. White should deem necessary, the guards to be instructed to kill him if he made one step that did not please them; and for
White to take his battalion, and with Webster thus bound and guarded
for a guide, go to Means' camp and capture it. Or, if not willing to go
with him, to leave him at Gen. Jones' headquarters and then move the
battalion by his directions, with the absolute certainty that he would
be hung or shot if the expedition failed, under his instructions, to get
Means and all his men.

Capt. Myers thought Webster's life was sufficient pledge of his sin-
cerity in the matter, and in imagination already saw the pet scheme
of the whole battalion fully executed, being certain that White would
gladly avail himself of the opportunity thus opened for it. But, alas
for human calculations! when the major arrived in camp, he not only
refused to speak to Webster at all, but instantly ordered him to be securely tied with ropes, hand and foot, and placed under strong guard,
at the same time bitterly censuring his subordinate for holding conversation with him instead of tying him as soon as he came in camp,
and declared his belief that Webster had only come there for the purpose of killing him. At the same time, he ordered Cooper to be confined in the general guard house, where he remained in confinement
until February, when he was acquitted by a brigade court-martial.

About dark, some of the officers visited Webster and found him
suffering severely from the manner in which he was tied, the ropes
having cut into his flesh, and they applied to the major, asking to have
him relieved, but were refused. They then made the following request
in writing:

Camp 35th Va Cavalry, Dec. —, 1862.
Major—We have seen the prisoner, Capt. Webster, tied in such
a manner that his hands are blackened from it, and we respectfully propose, that if you will permit, we will untie him and
guard him ourselves.
We are perfectly willing to hang or shoot him, if you say so, but
desire to see him treated with humanity while a prisoner.

F. M. Myers, Capt. Co. A
Wm. F. Dowdell, 1st Lieut. Co. C.
B. F. Conrad, 2nd Lieut., Jr., Co. A.
W. Dorsey, 2nd Lieut. Co. B.
S. E. Grubb, 2nd Lieut. Co. C.
R. C. Marlow, 2nd Lieut. Co. A.

The major returned the paper endorsed as follows:

Headquarters, White's Battalion
Dec. —, 1862.

Capt. Myers—You can have Webster untied if you choose, but I shall hold the officers signing this paper personally responsible for his safe keeping.

E. V. White, Major Comd'g.

Webster was at once freed from his bonds, and his self-constituted guardsmen sat with him all night, listening to the story of his life, which, supposing all he said to be true, was as full of romantic adventure as any ever depicted by old Sir Walter; and I doubt if in the annals of rascality, a more finished character than Webster ever had a place, for certainly, by his own confession, no sin in the decalogue had been untouched by him. When morning came, he was sent, in charge of Lieut. Sam. Grubb, to Richmond, where we will leave him for the present, to the tender mercies of Gen. Winder.

About this time, White received permission from Gen. Jones to scout into Loudoun, and arrived there just while Slocum's corps was passing through to the aid of Burnside, then fighting the battle of Fredericksburg, and the battalion immediately beheld visions of captured trains and prisoners. The major's first bivouac was in the Baptist meeting-house at Ketocton, from which point he sent Lieut. Dowdell with a party to Hillsboro' to find, under the friendly shadows of night, the situation of affairs in the rear of Slocum's march.

Dowdell pushed on and found no enemy until he reached Wheatland, where he learned that a considerable number of infantry stragglers were asleep in the mill, and the lieutenant immediately went in, taking quiet possession of the arms of the sleeping soldiers, and demanding a surrender, which, under the circumstances, they deemed it prudent to comply with.

When morning broke, Major White marched his command towards Wheatland and met Dowdell, who informed him that the enemy's rear guard had camped the night before at Bowie's, on the turnpike. Moving quietly along the road the battalion picked up about one hundred prisoners, whom they sent back to Gen. Jones, and learning that a wagon train was lost somewhere in the neighbourhood of Hamilton, the major sent a party to bring it in, but it could not be found. He then marched to Leesburg, and there was informed that some wagons, with a small guard of cavalry, had passed through the town on the Ball's Mill road, about two hours before, and he at once resolved to capture them; so ordering Lieut. Crown, of Company B, to take the advance with a party of his men, and to keep all the blue-coats in front to deceive the enemy, he pushed on as rapidly as possible after his prize.

In a short time, Crown sent him a report that the enemy had halted a few miles ahead to feed their horses, and thinking there could be no escape for the wagons now, he ordered Crown to go ahead and make the attack; and very soon the ringing pistol shots in front proclaimed that the advance guard was among the enemy.

The gallant Lieut. Crown had, in fact, pushed ahead so rapidly that he struck the escort of the train, which was vastly superior to his force in point of numbers, too far in front of the battalion to receive timely support, and his men had been hard pressed before the major could get up; but they had fought as Company B always did it, and with their sabres were clearing the ground when their comrades reached them. But the enemy had held out long enough for the wagons to get started and for a regiment of infantry to return to their rescue; which latter circumstance *induced* the major to wheel his men off the road to avoid the fire, which was very hot, and to *permit* the train to rejoin the army.

All that men could do had been done; the escort of the wagon train had been whipped fairly, in open fight, by Crown's boys, and nothing remained to be done but turn the wagons and go back, and but for the unforeseen accidental circumstance of the officer com-manding the rear guard of the army sending the infantry regiment to see what had become of the train, the raid would have been perfectly successful.

As it was, with as good a grace as might be, the baffled battalion re-turned, after considerable skirmishing, to Leesburg, and the major was there informed that a few wagons were wandering in the direction of Waterford, having, so report said, taken the wrong road at Wheatland, and thitherward the battalion marched, but on reaching the village of Waterford learned that no such train had been in that neighbourhood, and there was no longer a doubt but that the reported straggling wag-ons were the same which the timely arrival of infantry had saved from capture beyond Leesburg.

The major then turned his attention to Means' gang, and to make sure of them, if they were over the river at all, went down into town after dark, but the "rangers" were not around, and after frightening the intensely tory citizens of Waterford half out of their wits, the battalion marched to Beans' mill and encamped for the night.

The next morning, very unexpectedly, but greatly to the discomfort of the people there, the major moved his column back to Waterford, and very much to his own surprise, as himself and Dr. Wootten were riding a considerable distance ahead of the command, met Means' people in full force advancing to meet the battalion, not intending to find it of course, but they did so nevertheless, and the result was a horse race, in which the rangers, on their fresh, fast nags, made such extra time that only two of them were captured.

From this point the battalion crossed the Potomac, and struck out for Poolsville, Md., reaching that town about 8 o'clock, p. m., and finding the Federals there entirely oblivious to danger, knowing, as they did, of Slocum's march through Loudoun, and besides, they felt perfectly safe anyhow, because the old Potomac rolled its watery barrier between themselves and the fighting boys of Dixie, and they felt so easy, that no guards were posted at all, and many of them were at church (it was Sunday night) listening to a sermon from the Rev. Mr. ——— ———.

As may well be imagined, there was great commotion in the congregation at the sudden apparition of the Confederates, but from the pulpit the preacher proclaimed to the people that they had gentlemen to deal with, and urged them to be quiet, which assurance and advice served to quell, in a great measure, the fears that, with the rebels, would come destruction and death to town and inhabitants. The portion of the reverend gentleman's audience who wore the uniform of Uncle Sam, took no encouragement from that portion of his discourse, but as rapidly as they could, passed out and endeavoured to reach their quarters in the town hall.

One of them, the orderly sergeant, was killed in the street, and the others surrendered. Those who were at their quarters in the hall made a sharp fight, but were also soon compelled to give up to the victorious raiders. Only one man on the Confederate side was injured, and he was killed, but by a singular circumstance the battalion lost nothing by his death, he being an independent and had volunteered to take his brother's place, who was unwell when the command marched from camp. His name was Jenkins.

After spending some time very delightfully in the village, where nearly all of Company B was perfectly at home, the battalion crossed the river with a large amount of captured property, including about sixty horses, and marched to White Post, in Clarke County, where the major had stored a quantity of the supplies drawn from the commissary department of Gen. Burnside's army, in November, and here they halted for some days, learning that Gen. Jones had moved his headquarters to New Market.

The major made another scout in Loudoun, soon after, but nothing could be accomplished, and his time of his absence having expired, he returned to the brigade, arriving at camp on Christmas Day.

General Lee noticed the Poolsville raid in the following note to Gen. Jones:

Headquarters, Army N.V.,
January 31st, 1863.

Brig.-Gen. Wm. E. Jones,
Commanding Valley District:
General—I have received Major E.V. White's report, dated Dec. 24th, 1862, of his scout to Poolsville, Maryland, and have forwarded it to the Adjutant and Inspector-General at Richmond, calling the attention of the War Department to the gallant conduct of Major White and his command.

I am much gratified at the manner in which Major White conducted his scout, and the substantial results accomplished, with such slight loss on his part.

I have the honour to be, General, very respectfully,
Your obedient servant.

R. E. Lee, General.

General Jones was on the eve of marching to Western Virginia at the time White reached him, and leaving the major in command of the Valley District, with his battalion and such portions of other regiments as could not move with him, that enterprising officer went on his raid. Here the battalion learned for the first time that its independence was gone and it was a portion of Gen. Jones' brigade permanently, and that the men were regular troops.

Insubordination, and almost open mutiny, was the result, especially in the two Companies A and B. The members of the old company claimed that theirs was an independent command, organised to serve on the border, and that they joined it under the assurance that they never would be attached to any regiment or brigade, but be always on the border, and report to the nearest commanding general, and according to the terms of their enlistment they were never to forfeit, without their consent, the independent character of their command.

This was the second time the same issue had arisen in its history, the first being the time when the company was thrown under command of Lieut.-Col. Munford, in March, 1862, and the men watched jealously any movement which threw them, for ever so short a time, with any other command.

Company B claimed, that as Marylanders, they owed no allegiance to the Confederacy. They had come over voluntarily, because their sympathies were with the South, but being foreigners, they had the right to select for themselves the manner in which they would serve her, and in accordance with their privilege had united with the command of Major White, under the assurance and belief that his was an independent organisation, and that now, the contract having been broken on the part of the government, they were no longer bound to remain in the battalion.

There can be no doubt as to the justice of the claims advanced by both companies, but soldiers *must* submit to the powers that be, and as soldiers they had no right to question the validity of the orders which removed from one branch of service and assigned them to another. A Napoleon or a Jackson would have had somebody shot for such conduct, and in so doing would have totally destroyed the efficiency of the battalion, for after the first military execution, double their number could not have kept three companies in service a day longer. Their homes were in the enemy's lines, and among the mountains, and wild as they were, they would have remained untamed for the war, under such discipline as this.

The other companies were all quiet, but Company C was resolved to share the fortunes of the old company, and only waited for its action to be defined to come out and join her. The dissatisfaction was intense, and the major absolutely alone and unaided in his efforts to stem the tide of sedition and mutiny in his camp, but his firmness and coolness made him master of the fiery spirits with whom he had to deal, and simply by appealing to their better nature won them from their desperate resolves, and very soon peace reigned in White's battalion. But never for a day did the men forget their first love, or turn away their longing hearts from sighing after their lost independence.

Gen. Jones soon returned from his raid to Petersburg and Moorfield, and from now until February nothing occurred to mar the monotony of camp life, save the interminable drilling and sabre grinding which the general imposed upon his men.

Early in February, Major White was promoted to Lieutenant-

Colonel, by the President, and an election was held to fill the vacancy occasioned thereby, which resulted in the choice of Capt. F. M. Myers, of Company A, to be Major of the battalion.

About this time Gen. Lee, through Gen. Jones, ordered White to report to Gen. Jackson, and the following letter from Jackson explains the duty upon which he was to engage while under the orders of "Stonewall:"

> Headquarters, 2nd Corps, A. N. V.,
> February 5th, 1863.

Major—The courier who bears this has an order from Gen. R. E. Lee, through Brig.-Gen. W. E. Jones, directing you with the whole, or part of your battalion, as may be necessary, to report to me for orders.

The object to be accomplished is explained by the accompanying papers from Gen. Cooper.

I wish you to take such of your battalion, or the whole of it, if necessary, and arrest the witnesses and send them to Gen. Cooper in Richmond.

Charge those who may have the securing of them to treat them kindly, unless it should be necessary to do otherwise. Say to the witnesses, it has been thought, that by *arresting* them, they would not be so likely to be annoyed by the enemy, as if they had only been summoned and gone to Richmond.

I hope that you will take special pains to see that all of them are safely delivered to Gen. Cooper.

I think that you had better arrest them all during the same night; but I leave you to decide upon this, and I have such confidence in you that I leave the whole process of securing them to your discretion.

I have written to Gen. Jones to let you take your entire battalion, if you think it necessary, and in the event, you only require part of it to let you make the selection.

Keep your instructions, and also your destination, confidential, until your plans require you to make them known.

I hope sometime to have the pleasure of being with you again.

I am, Major, your obedient servant.

T. J. Jackson, Lieut.-Gen'l.

Major E. V. White,
Commanding Cavalry Battalion.

It is important that you move at once. Please write to me on your return, respecting your success.

T. J. J.

The accompanying papers contained the names of Isaac Vandevanter, John Ross, Gen. R. L. Wright and Henry S. Williams, as witnesses against Capt. Webster, whom White had sent to Richmond in December, and against whom two charges had been preferred, one of which was that he had murdered two citizens of Loudoun county, *viz*: Richard Simpson, formerly a captain in that gallant command, the 8th Va. Infantry, but at the time of his murder not in any manner connected with the service; and John Jones, of Hillsborough, whom Webster wantonly shot in his own door. The second charge was, that he had broken his parole, given at Waterford, in August, 1862, when he surrendered to White at the Baptist meeting-house.

In following up this subject, we may as well dispose of Webster finally, by remarking that he was found guilty of both charges, and on the second was condemned to be hung, which sentence was shortly afterwards executed in Richmond. Just before his execution, Webster confessed that the charges were correct, and also that he had been married seven times, five of his wives being alive.

Many persons, especially among the ladies, expressed the opinion that he richly merited his doom on the last count, even if neither of the others had been sustained; and many others thought that if the remedy for this case had been applied in all, the Abolition army would have been very nearly broken up, for in the eyes of the civilized world, and by the laws of nations, they were all murderers or worse.

White moved promptly, and without any incident worthy of note, executed General Jackson's order to the letter.

9: The Battalion in Camp

The battalion returned to camp, near New Market, about the 20th of February, and for two months there was nothing to mar the monotony of camp life, save the interminable drilling and sabre grinding ordered by Gen. Jones, which was really the most monotonous part of it as well as the most vexatious, for White's men didn't like to drill, and they had a small opinion of the sabre as a weapon to fight Yankees with, no matter how sharp it might be, and the regular Saturday grindings were looked upon as perfect nuisances.

Discipline in the command was at a low ebb, in fact it was hard to keep it up to any degree of perfection at all, for several reasons; first of which was, that Col. White himself was naturally much better qualified for the stirring and active life of a partisan, whose parade ground is the enemy's picket line and wagon camp, than to command the choicest body of troops behind the army lines; and experience gives as a rule, that as the colonel is, so is the regiment, and it is one that holds good under all the circumstances of the camp, the march and the battlefield.

The carelessness of the colonel very soon showed itself to a far greater degree in the battalion, and really, as of necessity it must, impaired the efficiency of it, for there is a vast difference between the dashing tactics of the raider, in which numbers are little considered, and all depends upon the suddenness of the attack and surprise of the enemy, and the operations in the face of a prepared enemy, where the success of an army depends upon its different parts performing the proper evolutions at the right moment and best manner, amid the din and roar of battle, where the "flying shot and reeking steel" are performing their bloody work.

Early in 1863, the colonel had most fortunately secured the services of an excellent Adjutant, in the person of Lieut. R. T. Watts, formerly of the 2nd Va. Cavalry, and a native of Bedford County, Va., who had been recommended to him by Col. Munford, of that regiment, and many persons thought that the very existence of the battalion was due to the precision and care with which Lieut. Watts performed his duties, for the company officers, with few exceptions, were as careless as the colonel.

Lieut. Crown, Co. B, Lieuts. Dowdell and Tom White, Co. C, and Capt. Grabill, Co. E, were disciplinarians, and did their best to make soldiers of their men; but Capt. Myers and Lieut. Conrad, who formed the character of Co. A, Lieut. Sam. Grubb, Co. C, Lieuts. Dorsey and Chiswell, Co. B, and Lieut. Strickler, Co. E, all officers of great influence with their companies, cared as little for drill and discipline as possible. Company F had, for some time, been rendered rather inefficient through the carelessness and indifference of its officers, but it was finally raised to the position of being one of the best in the service, by having two first-rate officers given it in Capt. French and Lieut. James; but previous to that, Capt. Ferneyhough was seldom with it, and Lieut. McVeigh was like the majority, willing to let matters take their course. Lieut. Barrett was unfortunate in being for a long time a prisoner, and Lieut. Marlow was so frequently on detached service in the quartermaster's department, and elsewhere, that his services were to a great extent lost to his company.

The quartermaster's department exhibited the same lack of system observable in other places, and it was soon discovered that high attainments in law and literature, and brilliant talents as an orator, did not fit Capt. Kilgour to perform the duties of this important position, and he resigned in favour of John J. White, who had been his sergeant, and who was vastly better calculated for the office in question than the distinguished gentleman who had preceded him. The business was now managed by Capt. White, aided as he was by active and energetic assistants, such as Wm. H. Luckett, Quartermaster-Sergeant; Thomas Brown and Jack Simpson, Frank Saffer, and last, but by no means least, "Uncle Billy Dove," as forage and wagon-masters; in a systematic and highly satisfactory manner.

The medical department, under the management of Dr. Ed. Wootten, was almost a farce, from the fact that medicines of all kinds were scarce in the Confederacy, and worth almost their weight in gold, so that the office of Surgeon, except on battle days, when wounded men were to be cared for, was almost a sinecure; but in the absence of medicine, the doctor, by all the little arts known only to the profession, would work upon the imagination of his patients and bring them out, generally, all right, except in cases of camp itch, which active disease prevailed widely, and positively refused to succumb to the imaginary efficacy of bread pills.

While in winter quarters, the first court-martial in the battalion was convened; composed of Captains Myers, Chiswell and Anderson, and Lieutenants Watts (Co. F,) and Strickler, (Co. E,) and proceeded to the trial of a number of cases of absence without leave, and similar offenses.

After the court got through with its business, the report of their proceedings, showing that they had awarded only such light penalties as extra duty, walking a beat, &c., was handed to the colonel for his approval, as military law required, when, after examining the report, he came out in a general order at dress parade, denouncing the action of the court as folly, fit only for schoolboy nonsense, winding up by setting aside all its judgments and discharging the delinquents unconditionally, which ended the court-martial business for a year.

Gen. Rosser used to tell a story which illustrated Col. White's attention to the *minutiæ* of the business of the battalion, and which will not be out of place here.

On one occasion Gen. Lee wrote to Rosser, saying that no reports had been received for a long time of the ordnance department of White's Battalion, and asking him to look into the matter, to which Rosser replied that he had never been able to get an ordnance report from that command, and if Gen. Lee could do so he would be glad to see it. This brought a staff officer from army headquarters at once, to get a report; and Gen. R. tells the story as he received it from the officer, who, after calling at Rosser's quarters, rode over to the battalion, and introducing himself to Colonel White, explained his business.

"Very well, sir," said the colonel, "go ahead."

And by aid of Adjt. Watts, the report was made out pretty well, until the officer, reading from a paper which he held in his hand, said, "I see, colonel, that 340 guns have been issued to your command; what report do you make of them?" (White's men *never* would carry guns.)

The colonel turned to the adjutant and asked how many guns were on hand, to which he replied, "eighty, sir."

"Well," said the officer, "how do you account for the 260?"

At which, White seemed somewhat perplexed; but Gen. R. says that while he was studying the matter over, one of the young "Comanches," in a corner of the tent, said: "Why, colonel, ain't them the guns that busted in Western Virginia?"

"I golly, yaas;" said the colonel, "they did bust; you sent us a lot of them drotted Richmond carbines, and they like to have killed all the men."

The staff officer put down on his report: "260 guns bursted in Western Virginia," and took his departure, everything being now accounted for.

10: The West Virginia Expedition

On the 21st of April, 1863, Gen. Jones marched his brigade from their camp, now near Harrisonburg, for the memorable expedition through West Virginia, intending to damage the Baltimore and Ohio Rail Road, and to threaten the enemy in that country, so as to not only prevent troops from going to the Rappahannock where "fighting Joe" Hooker was confronting the Army of Northern Virginia, but to draw forces from his army to protect the Rail Road and keep Western communication with the capital unbroken; a scheme which originated in the far-reaching mind of General Lee, and one that exerted a telling influence upon Hooker's operations at Chancellorsville.

Gen. Jones' brigade was a noble one, consisting of the 6th, 7th, 11th and 12th Regiments of Virginia Cavalry, 1st Maryland Battalion of Cavalry, 35th Battalion of Va. Cavalry, 41st Battalion of Va. Cavalry, (Witcher's mounted rifles,) Col. Herbert's Battalion of Maryland Infantry, Captain Chew's Battery of Horse Artillery, and the Baltimore Battery of Light Artillery; in all, four regiments, commanded by Cols. Flournoy, Dulaney, Lomax and Harman, and four battalions, under Lieut.-Cols. Brown, White, Witcher and Herbert; with two batteries, of four guns each; making a total of about four thousand men.

The brigade marched through Brock's Gap, in the North Mountain, and passing Howard's Lick, soon had a view, full and complete, of the famous Moorfield Valley; and great was the gratification and delight of all the men as they looked down from the mountain top upon the lovely scene, lying as it did like a picture of beauty at their feet, girt with its dark mountain frame, and fringed with its evergreen bordering of hemlock and cedar; white snow-caps all around, but everything fresh as springtime in the valley, where the South Branch was foaming and dashing over its rocky bed, sometimes winding along the base of one mountain, then crossing to the other, and sometimes rolling gloriously through the carpet of living green in the centre of the valley.

The brigade encamped at Moorfield, until the morning of the 24th, when the general marched it to Petersburg, nine miles above, where the men forded the river.

The ford at that place is covered with rocks of almost every size and shape, making it a difficult passage at any time, but now the mountain stream was full to overflowing, and the waters foamed over the rocks as from some enormous mill-flume, increasing infinitely the difficulty and danger of crossing, so that some of the men, in viewing the angry flood, turned and fled in greater dismay than if an army of Yankees had faced them; but by aid of some noble-souled citizens, who rode through the water and guided the horses of the men, the crossing was effected, and the cavalry found themselves fairly started into the mountains, but the infantry and artillery, being unable to cross, were sent back to the Shenandoah Valley.

On the 25th, the command approached Greenland Gap, in the eastern front ridge of the Alleghany mountain, Col. Dulaney, with his regiment (the 7th) being in front; and when, about sunset, the enemy's pickets were discovered, the 7th charged, driving them in and finding a force of infantry strongly posted in an old log meetinghouse and some other buildings nearby. Col. Dulaney himself was

Private Philip Carper, 35th Battalion, Virginia Cavalry

badly wounded, and his regiment cut in two, as the enemy fired so heavily upon it, after the leading squadrons had passed their position, that the remaining ones were unable to follow, and halted in front of the meetinghouse.

Gen. Jones soon came up, and at once began his arrangements to take the place. He had brought several kegs of powder with him to blow up the Cheat River trestle work with, and he now determined to try the effect of some of it just here in his first encounter with the enemy. His pioneer corps, made up by details from each regiment and battalion, was provided with axes and bundles of straw, the first to be used to break open the windows of the fort, while the latter was to be set on fire and thrown into it, and at the same time Lieut. Williamson (his engineer) was to get the powder under the building.

He dismounted his three battalions and placed White's men in front; Brown's Marylander's in the rear, and Witcher's mounted riflemen at the end of the house, and it being now dark, the general rode down near it, and politely informed the Yankees that "he had them surrounded, and a barrel of gunpowder under the house," and that, unless they surrendered, he would "blow them all to hell in five minutes;" to which they, with equal politeness responded, by requesting him to "go there himself."

The general's information as to the surrounding was correct, but Williamson's gunpowder plot was a failure, owing to his inability to approach the fort without getting shot, and they knew that if he had powder under them he wasn't likely to tell them, for they were fully persuaded he would greatly prefer blowing them up, if possible, to having them surrender on any terms; and Gen. Jones, thinking they had received sufficient warning, ordered his storming parties to advance, telling the men to "go right up to the building and punch out the chinking of the logs;" "that the pioneers would throw blazing straw into the house, and then all were to fire their guns and pistols through the cracks, by the light of the straw inside;" and assuring the men that "a signal would be given for them to retire before the powder was touched off."

The battalions advanced promptly to the positions assigned them; White's men being compelled to wade a stream that ran through the gap, nearly waist deep, three times; and all the while exposed to a withering fire, for the Yankees opened fire from the house the moment the troops began to move, and kept it up incessantly.

The Marylanders, led by Col. Brown, moved quickly to the rear of the house as White's battalion marched up in front, and here was a great blunder, on the part of General Jones, in placing these two commands in such a position, for their fire was far more fatal to each other than to the enemy, as they both commenced firing at short range, with the old house exactly between them.

As for Witcher's men, they were mountaineers, and fired from behind the rocks at a safe distance, scattering their bullets promiscuously all about the house, but really doing quite as much good as the other two commands which charged immediately up to the walls.

The Yankees fired coolly and rapidly, and almost before the pioneer corps could light the first bundle of straw and throw it into the house, every man of the corps was down, either killed or wounded, but they acted nobly while they were allowed to act at all.

The affair lasted about fifteen minutes, during which the firing was very heavy and constant, and at one time the powder business very nearly caused a stampede among the Confederates, as one of them suddenly called out to his comrades to "look out for the powder," and they all took it to be the promised signal of Gen. Jones.

The panic was soon over and the assault renewed with unabated vigour, but no impression was made upon the intrepid garrison, who all stood to their work bravely, until Thos. E. Tippett, a gallant soldier of Co. A, White battalion, climbed up the stick chimney and placed some burning straw upon the roof of the house, which very soon brought out a flag of truce, and finally an unconditional surrender of the Yankees, but a party of them in a house near by kept up a scattered firing a few minutes longer.

There were only seven of the enemy killed and wounded, and their whole force was less than eighty, but they were all Virginians, from among the mountains, and were fighting in the gate that if opened would let the Confederates right among their homes, and they left no stain upon the honour of Old Virginia in their defence of the pass, for they held out until their fort was wrapped in flames.

The loss of the two battalions was nearly one hundred; but much of it was due to the miserable position they occupied, by which they were constantly firing upon each other.

Just as soon as everything was arranged, and the wounded who were able to move, together with the prisoners, had been sent back, the brigade continued its march without further halt, until daylight, when the almost worn-out people were allowed to stop awhile, to rest and refresh themselves and horses. But soon the march was resumed, and followed without any special incident, until it led to Evansville, in Taylor County, where a halt for half a day was made; and here the bushwhackers were discovered in considerable numbers for the first time.

It is true, that in passing what is known as the "Shades of Death"—a dark and gloomy gorge in the Shenandoah Mountain, which is shadowed to twilight gloom even at noonday, by the rocky wall which on either side is covered with the hemlock, the cypress and the towering white pine—the advance guard had skirmished with and captured a few of the "Swamp Dragons," as they termed themselves, but at Evansville bands of armed men, in hunting shirts, could be seen on all the mountain crags, viewing from a safe distance the army of rebels, lying quietly in their country; but they seldom approached near enough to the main body to get a shot or be shot at.

While here, some of the men, who had been engaged in plundering a store on the route, came up, and Gen. Jones finding two of them, one of whom had a hoop skirt and the other an umbrella, compelled the hoop skirt man to wear his plunder around his neck, and the other to hold the umbrella over him during all the afternoon, in full view of the whole command. That night the brigade crossed the R. R., at Independence Station, and pushed rapidly forward to Morgantown, at which place the "home guard" was found drawn up in battle order on the hills; but they fell back as Jones advanced, not firing a gun, and finally disappeared, when the town authorities sent an old citizen out to meet the raiders, and negotiate a surrender of the town.

This gentleman approached in great trepidation, making all the Masonic signs he was master of, and on being brought to Gen. Jones, was informed that no damage was intended the town, provided the town people did not attempt to damage the troops, which greatly pleased him, and he returned from his mission highly pleased with Jones and his men.

Here again the general exercised all his authority to prevent plundering, and was so very strict that he compelled Adjt. Watts to leave some calico he had bought and paid for in U. S. money, swearing that his men should not carry any such rubbish; but a few of them managed to smuggle some calico, by folding it in their saddle blankets. His protection, however, did not extend to stock suitable for the army, but on the contrary, it was his policy to drive with him as many such horses and cattle as he could find.

The brigade lay at Morgantown from about 10 a. m. until dark, when the march was resumed, and the whole force pushed forward to Fairmount, where it arrived about the 1st of May, and found about nine hundred "home guards" and militia concentrated for the defence of the town. The raiders reached the vicinity of the place about sunrise, but the morning was dismal and foggy, and as Jones formed his line in front and flank of Fairmount, the enemy formed theirs on the hills above, and appeared resolved to do battle valiantly for their town and the R. R. bridges. They had three pieces of artillery, one an old iron twelve-pounder and the others brass guns, brought upon a platform car from Wheeling, with about twenty soldiers to work them.

The general dismounted his men, and taking charge himself of the 7th and 12th regiments and the Maryland battalion, moved to the right, while Col. Lomax, of the 11th, with his own regiment and the 6th, together with White's battalion, commanded the left, and leaving Capt. Myers with his company, and a number of men from the other regiments, mounted and stationed on the road that leads directly to the wire suspension bridge. Witcher's riflemen had dismounted long before, and were approaching the place by a march up the railroad to the left.

Col. White, with his battalion and part of the 11th, was ordered by Lomax to advance upon the right of the enemy's line, which he did, driving them like sheep, and at the same time the mounted men charged into town, and took possession of the bridge, which compelled the Yankees to ford the river above the town, followed closely by White and his men, who, immediately after crossing, turned to the right, and forced the enemy to take refuge in the R. R. bridge, where most of their force was now concentrated, and from which they opened fire with their artillery, but Gen. Jones was moving quietly to their rear, which being discovered, caused the men in charge of the two brass pieces to beat a hasty retreat, a thing very easily done considering the fact that they were still mounted on the car to which a locomotive, under steam, was attached.

A dash was now made upon them, in which the iron gun was captured, and very soon after the whole force, to the number of seven hundred, surrendered, the others having made their escape into the mountains.

The affair was a decided success, not a man being hurt on either side, and now after destroying the Rail Road bridges, and damaging the track and rolling stock of the road very seriously, the raiders passed on towards Clarksburg, in Harrison county, on the N. W. Rail Road, at which point they found a heavy force of infantry in fortifications, and after some skirmishing, Gen. Jones deemed it advisable to let it alone, especially as he learned that the gallant Irishman, Col. Mulligan, of Missouri fame, was in command; consequently he flanked Clarksburg to the left, and marched to Philippi.

The Maryland battalion was badly cut up in a fight with infantry at Bridgeport, caused by charging among the post and rail fences on the Rail Road, in which Col. Brown was wounded.

The attack on the Cheat River works was a failure, owing to the 6th Regiment being driven back by a heavy infantry force, which defended the ugly mountain gorges leading to the rail road, and which fought from barricades inaccessible to cavalry, even with no enemy to hold them.

Reaching Philippi, the general sent back to the Valley all the prisoners and stock, and marched his command to Buckhannon, in Upshur County, where he halted for a short time to watch a party of the enemy that came down from Clarksburg, intending to guard the party conveying the stock and prisoners from an attack by these fellows; and after all danger from this source was over he passed on by Weston, Lewis county, to West Union in Doddridge County, near which place he again operated on the Rail Road at Cairo Station, where there were quite a number of short tunnels.

These tunnels had been blasted and bored through almost solid rock, and inside of them a frame work was built wide enough for the track, and the space between the frame and side of the tunnel was filled with cord wood, an immense quantity of which was used for the purpose. There was a large force of home guards and militia at the station, and by the way, all the troops of this kind were invariably in U. S. uniform, and armed with U. S. muskets, while the "bushwhackers," or "Swamp Dragons," carried only their old sporting rifles, and dressed in homespun.

The Yankees only made a show of fight, and a cavalry charge soon brought them to terms without losing a man; some of them, of course, escaped, but about three hundred were made prisoners.

The Rail Road buildings were burned, and White's men were detailed to work on the tunnels, which they did most effectually by pouring coal oil on the cord-wood and setting it on fire, which caused the rock to burst and fall in, so that the destruction was complete.

From Cairo the march was continued through the counties of Pleasants, Ritchie, and Wirt, to the Little Kanawha River, and at every turn the bushwhackers enlivened the route by popping away with their old rifles, but they would not venture in range of the Sharpe's carbines and Colt's revolvers carried by the brigade, and consequently did no damage, but on the contrary did much good, in acting as provost guard, to keep up the stragglers; and their sprightly style of warfare kept Jones' men in a good humour all the time, in fact the most pleasant part of the whole raid was through the bushwhackers' special territory, for without anything to vary the monotony of the march, this continual roaming through that apparently interminable sea of mountains was a very tiresome business.

The command reached the oil works about noon, and a detail was sent forward to Elizabeth City, while the main body halted at Oiltown. There were a large number of wells in operation, worked by steam engines, and up to the last moment the oil men kept busily engaged, but after a while they learned the character of their visitors, and surmising their object, the workmen turned away from the wells, and shutting off steam, remarked, with doleful faces, "I guess oiling is played out now," and of a surety their guess was correct, for destruction was the watchword of Jones' brigade at Oiltown, and nowhere, except in a powder mill, could it be more speedily and generally accomplished. The oil was all around, some of it in barrels piled up, and some in flatboats in the river, the boats being built water-tight and filled with the oil, some of them holding a thousand barrels each, which was run into them by pipes directly from the wells.

These boats, after being set on fire, were cut loose from the shore and allowed to float away, and as they burst, letting the blazing oil spread over the water from shore to shore, the truly wonderful spectacle of a river on fire was presented, while to heighten the grandeur of the scene, explosion after explosion boomed out upon the night air, and columns of dense black smoke twined with the red flame from the wrecks of the boats, loomed skyward a hundred feet from the blazing sea; and on shore the oil barrels were burning and bursting, their contents flowing in streams of liquid flame all over the ground, and from the wells themselves great fiery pillars rose up, and added to this, the many buildings contributed their quota of flame to the great conflagration; in fact no better illustration, on a small scale, could be presented of the popular idea of the burning brimstone lake, where—

The devil sits in his easy chair,
Sipping his sulphur tea,
And gazing out, with a pensive air,

On the broad bitumen sea,

—for from pump to river all was flame.

The amount of oil destroyed was estimated at one hundred and fifty thousand barrels, and this has been fully confirmed by reports of owners published since the war; and taking into consideration the destruction of boats, machinery, buildings, &c., the damage was immense.

As soon as the destruction was complete, the raiders went out into the night, leaving a bitter remembrance of their visit in the hearts of the people who dwelt on the desolated shore of the Little Kanawha, and many an oilman was heard to wish, in substance, as the brigade marched away, that "he might never be any nearer hell than he had been that night."

These things occurred about the 10th of May, and now the little army of Jones passed on through the counties of Calhoun, Gilmer, Braxton, Nicholas and Fayette, to Lewisburg in Greenbrier, during part of which march the command was divided for the better securing of rations of forage, and Col. Lomax with his regiment and White's battalion took a new route through the mountains. Arrived at Lewisburg, the command halted from Saturday noon until Monday morning, and visited the celebrated Greenbrier White Sulphur Springs, where many of the men, by Gen. Jones' permission, spent Sunday, the 17th of May, 1863.

On Monday morning, the brigade marched on by the noted Hot, Warm, and Alum Springs of Bath County, through Augusta to the camp near Mount Crawford in Rockingham, where it arrived on the evening of May 21st, having been absent thirty-two days.

Owing to the loss of papers and diaries, by the circumstances of war, it has been utterly impossible for the author to give more than the most meagre outline of the Western Virginia expedition of General Jones' brigade, which took rank among the army campaigns as a very important one, it having aided, to no small degree, in securing to the Confederates the great victory at Chancellorsville, by accomplishing the objects for which it was intended, as explained in the beginning of this chapter.

The visible fruits of the expedition, besides the damage to the rail roads and oil works, were about nine hundred and fifty of the enemy killed, wounded and captured, about one thousand small arms and one cannon destroyed, twelve hundred horses and one thousand cattle brought safely through to the Valley.

About twenty bridges and tunnels on the Baltimore and Ohio and North Western Rail Roads had been destroyed, and the Southern sympathizers, of that country for a time relieved from the domineering rule which invariably characterized the home-made Yankee, wherever he had the power to annoy his Southern neighbour, and finding by this raid that it was not as impossible as they had thought, for the Confederate troops to come among them, these Tories took the lesson to heart and acted more like men towards the people who differed with them in opinion and feeling, than before.

The turning point in the fortunes of the young Confederacy had been passed, during the absence of the Ashby brigade, and with the fall of "Stonewall" Jackson her star began to wane.

The news of his death had reached the brigade while in the wildest part of its mountain campaign, and it clouded the spirits of the whole command; many of the men having such implicit faith in him that his death was to them the dreary sign which told that all their hopes were dead, like their hero, and buried in his grave; and from that time their march took the character of a funeral procession.

The following touching poem was written by Capt. J. Mort. Kilgour, a day or two before the return to camp:

THE DEATH OF GEN. THOMAS J. JACKSON.

Give me the death of those,
Who for their country die,
And oh! be mine, like their repose,
When cold and low they lie.
Their loveliest mother earth,
Enshrines the fallen brave,
In her sweet lap, who gave them birth,
They find their tranquil grave.
                    Montgomery.

Come, comrades, come, with lowly hearts come,
And grief's cypress wreaths let us borrow,
Whilst the trumpet's long wail, and the muffled drum,
Will bespeak our tear-burdened sorrow.
Come, comrades, come, a chieftain has gone,
A beacon with victory beaming,
Which through the dark battle-cloud brilliantly shone,
Where our war-tattered banners were streaming.

With slow, solemn steps let us gather around,
The spot where his ashes lie sleeping,
And we'll feel in our souls that 'tis hallowed ground,
Whilst in anguish unspoken we're weeping.

The hero has gone, but there's still left behind,
The beauteous light of the story,
Which history will tell, as the passing years bind,
'Round his name, fresher garlands of glory.
No more will he cheer the brave columns he led,
Where the lightnings of battle were flashing,
And over the heaps of the dying and dead,
Its volleying thunders were crashing;
But his clarion voice from his grave we will hear,
Through the conflict in melody flowing,
And the fire of his eye will beam radiant and clear,
In the pictures of memory glowing.

Oh, come maidens, come, and together we'll strew,
O'er his resting place, Spring's sweetest flowers,
And the stars will shed on them their tear-drops of dew,
As they watch through the night's stilly hours.
We will strew them in silence for our souls are opprest,
With an anguish too deep to be spoken,
Which can only be told by a sob in the breast,
That speaks of a heart nearly broken.
Farewell, matchless chieftain!—kind Heaven will forgive
The rebellious spirit of sorrow,
As it whispers—'though dead, his example will live,
Growing brighter each coming tomorrow.'

Yes! his name will be written, in letters of gold,
On the crest of each sky-kissing mountain;
In music's sweet measures his fame will be told,
By the murmur of streamlet and fountain;
It will haunt each green spot with its magical spell,
It will live in the song of each river,
In the bowers and aisles of each forest 'twill dwell,
Like a spirit of beauty, forever!
But come, comrades, come, let us back to the field,
'Tis there our duty still calls us,
With a tear and a sigh for our leader and shield,

And a heart for whatever befalls us.

J. Mortimer Kilgour."

White's Battalion, May 17th, 1863.

After the return to camp, and until the 1st of June, the company officers were busy with muster and pay-rolls, and other business which a month's neglect had left upon their hands, and on the 28th May the State election was held, in which poll-books were opened in the various regiments, so that all the soldiers who were entitled to do so could vote.

The weather was beautiful, rations and forage plentiful and good, and the political horizon, apart from the gloomy shadow left by the death of General Jackson, was brighter than for many months. True, the army of Hooker still lay on the North bank of the Rappahannock, but the bloody defeat at Chancellorsville had wrecked the hopes of its general and its men to compete successfully in a battle with Lee's army, and all they did, or could do, was to watch the Southern Army, and keep close to their entrenchments until their ranks were again filled; but Gen. Lee did not propose to be so very quiet while his adversary was recruiting, and on the last day of May an order was issued for tents and baggage to be stored and the Ashby brigade prepared to join the army East of the mountain.

Capt. George N. Ferneyhough, of Co. F, by virtue of being the senior captain in the battalion, had, during the absence of the command in West Virginia, succeeded in getting the election held some time before, for major, set aside, and himself appointed to the position.

11: Brandy Station

On the morning of June 1st, 1863, the brigade marched from the Valley for Gen. Stuart's camp in Culpeper County, the battalion having the following officers: Lieut.-Col. White, Major Ferneyhough, Adjt. Watts, Dr. Wootten, Quartermaster White, and Sergeant-Major Stephenson, in field and staff; Co. A, Lieuts. Barrett and Conrad; Co. B, had her full corps of officers; Co. C, Capt. Grubb and Lieut. Grubb; Co. D, had all her officers present; Co. E, Capt. Grabill and Lieut. Grubbs; Co. F, Lieut. Watts. Capt. Myers and Lieut. Marlow, Co. A, were left sick in the Valley; Lieut. Dowdell, Co. C, was on detail there to settle up the quartermaster's business, incident to the change just made in that department; one lieutenant of Co. E, and one of Co. F, had been removed for misconduct on the raid to West Virginia.

Soon after the brigade reached the army, the grand review of all the troops begun, that of the cavalry being held on the 8th of June, in which General Stuart brought a division of full fifteen thousand troopers, in fine condition for service, but all the generals confessed that Jones' was the peer of the best brigade in the line.

The morning of June 9th, while the men, worried out by the military foppery and display (which was Stuart's greatest weakness) of the previous day's review, were yet under their blankets, the enemy sounded for them the *reveille* from the smoking muzzles of carbines and revolvers, as they drove the 6th Regiment vedettes from their position on the river, and it was very soon discovered that a heavy force had crossed at Kelly's and Beverly's fords for the purpose of continuing the review, but in a different style, and but for the prompt action of Gen. Jones, would have had all of Stuart's artillery almost before that officer waked up.

The regiments moved rapidly to the front, as soon as the men could obey the boot and saddle bugle call, and with the first that came, which were the 6th and 7th Regiments, Gen. Jones met and checked the enemy, and arrangements for the battle, which was now inevitable, were made as quickly as possible. Col. White was ordered with his battalion, to support the 12th Regiment, which was ordered forward to make a charge; and he at once began to form his men in line of battle, but before it could be completed, Gen. Jones called to him to charge, which he immediately did, riding at a gallop towards the point where the firing showed that the 12th was into it heavy,.

But after going about two hundred yards, was met by that regiment in full retreat, and whose disordered ranks threw the right wing of the battalion in confusion, and checked for a time the advance of the "Comanches," but order was quickly restored, and again dashing forward they threw themselves upon the enemy, whose column, flushed with their successful charge on the 12th, was rapidly advancing, but after a sharp fight of a few minutes were compelled to retire before the irresistible onset of White's men. The colonel says, in his official report, that not a man faltered, but with yells that a "Comanche" might envy, they pressed forward, each man striving to gain the foremost rank and ride with his commander.

The Yankees were driven over the field and about a hundred yards into the woods, where they met fresh troops coming up, and White's people were in turn compelled to retire, but rallying at the edge of the woods, they again charged upon the overwhelming forces of the

Battle of Brandy Station

enemy, and not only checked their advance, which was all the colonel hoped to do, but completely routed them and drove their demoralised line for half a mile through the pines.

In this charge they captured about forty prisoners, and killing General Davis, who was vainly endeavouring to rally his flying troopers, and also a brave major, who, after a fierce sabre fight with Wm. Shehan, of Co. B, in which both were severely handled, was compelled to surrender to the gallant Confederate.

While the battalion was thus occupied in front, a regiment of the enemy came in their rear and attempted to charge, but wheeling his left squadron, the colonel met and drove them back in splendid style, the men all fighting with the greatest enthusiasm, but Lieut. Crown, Co. B, especially distinguishing himself.

About this time, Gen. Jones became aware that a strong party of the enemy had succeeded in flanking Stuart's position, and were approaching from the direction of Culpeper Court-House, and he at once sent the information to General Stuart, who said to the courier, "Tell Gen. Jones to attend to the Yankees in his front, and I'll watch the flanks."

When this reply was communicated to Jones, he remarked: "So he thinks they ain't coming, does he? Well, let him alone; he'll damned soon see for himself." And he *did* see, for about one o'clock the flanking force appeared exactly in rear of, and very near Stuart's headquarters; and again Col. White was ordered to follow and support the 12th Regiment in case of need; but on arriving near the house, Gen. Stuart ordered White to form his battalion on the right of the road leading to the Court-House and charge the squadrons of the enemy on the high ground around the general's headquarters.

And here again, just as Col. White commenced to move, a squadron of the 12th, which had met the enemy and been defeated, broke the line of the battalion, badly deranging its right wing, and causing the loss of valuable time, but the colonel ordered Major Ferneyhough to charge with the first squadron (Companies A and D) which had not been broken, upon those squadrons of the enemy in front of the house, while with two squadrons (Companies B, C, E and F) he charged a regiment in rear and to the left of the building.

Both charges were successful, the enemy being driven down the road towards the Rail Road, but while the colonel with his party was pressing them, a regiment passed between him and the hill, cutting off the first squadron and again occupying the ground from which they had just been driven.

As soon as the colonel discovered this situation of affairs, he withdrew all but twenty men from the pursuit, and renewed the contest for the possession of the hill, which, after a spirited fight, he succeeded in gaining, driving off the regiment and killing its colonel.

In this fight around Stuart's headquarters, Lieut. Barret was wounded and captured, and Captains Grabill and Anderson made prisoners.

The battalion was now reinforced by a company of the 6th Va. Cavalry, and ordered by Gen. Stuart to charge a battery which had been playing on White's men during all the fighting on the hill. Without a moment's hesitation the charge was made, and the wreath of glory which White's battalion had been weaving and twining around its name, during all that long summer day, was completed.

The gallant fellows at the battery hurled a perfect storm of grape upon the "Comanches," while from the supporting cavalry a rain of bullets fell in their ranks, but with never a halt or a falter the battalion dashed on, scattering the supports and capturing the battery after a desperate fight, in which the artillerymen fought like heroes, with small arms, long after their guns were silenced. There was no demand for a surrender, nor any offer to do so, until nearly all the men at the battery, with many of their horses, were killed and wounded.

While most of the men pursued the flying cavalry that had supported the battery, Col. White with a few others attempted to turn the guns, and work them on the Yankees who were rapidly closing in upon him in heavy force both on the right and left, not doubting for a moment that General Stuart would support him, but nothing seemed further from the general's intention, and feeling that he was being wantonly sacrificed, Col. White rallied his men, and charging with desperation upon the enveloping ranks of the foe, cut through to safety again, but the deliverance cost half the number of the battalion.

In the Battle of Brandy Station, the battalion had captured and brought out two regimental standards, (besides two others taken, but lost in the escape from the battery,) and upwards of one hundred prisoners, with a great quantity of arms and equipments and many horses, but many of its gallant men had been lost.

Capt. Geo. W. Chiswell was badly wounded, so badly that he was never again fit for service, and the brave Lieut. Watts, of Co. F, was mortally wounded, both of them in the charge upon the battery.

The whole loss was ninety men killed, wounded and missing, and but few of the latter ever returned to the command, some having died of wounds in U. S. hospitals, some in prison, and some escaping from the battle after being wounded died at the houses of citizens in the neighbourhood; as it was, only four of the dead were found and buried by the battalion.

The following general order issued by Stuart, shows the conduct of the battle and the desperate valour of the men who fought and fell at Brandy Station, a name rendered famous forever as the scene of one of the greatest cavalry battles of modern times:

Hdqrs., Cav. Div., Army N.Va.,
June 15th, 1863.
General Orders, No. 24.

The Major-General commanding congratulates the Cavalry of the Army of Northern Virginia, upon the victory of "Fleetwood," achieved under Providence, by the prowess of their arms, on the 9th instant.

Comrades, two divisions of the enemy's cavalry and artillery, *escorted* by a strong force of infantry, "*tested your metal*" and found it "proof steel."

Your sabre blows, inflicted on that glorious day, have taught them again the weight of Southern vengeance.

You confronted with cavalry and horse artillery alone, this force, held the infantry in check, routed the cavalry and artillery, capturing three pieces of the latter, without losing a gun, and added six flags to the trophies of the nation, besides inflicting a loss in killed, wounded and missing, at least double our own, causing the entire force to retire beyond the Rappahannock.

Nothing but the enemy's infantry strongly posted in the woods saved his cavalry from capture or annihilation. An act of rashness on his part was severely punished by rout and the loss of his artillery.

With an abiding faith in the God of battles and a firm reliance on the sabre, your success will continue.

Let the example and heroism of our lamented fallen comrades prompt us to renewed vigilance and inspire us with devotion to duty.

J. E. B. Stuart,
Major-General Commanding.

The orderly sergeants of the several companies of the battalion made the following reports of the losses of the companies:

Co. A—wounded 9, missing 7—total 16.

Co. B—killed 1, wounded 7, missing 12—total 20.

Co. C—wounded 5, missing 12—total 17.

Co. D—wounded 3, missing 5—total 8.

Co. E—killed 2, wounded 2, missing 8—total 12.

Co. F—killed 1, wounded 1, missing 15—total 17.

After the Battle of Brandy Station, Col. White's command was detached from the Cavalry Division, and ordered by Gen. Lee to report to Lieut.-Gen. Ewell, who had again taken the field and been assigned to the command of the old 2nd Corps A. N.V., the men whom General Jackson had so often led to victory, and who believed that the mantle of military inspiration of their now sainted chieftain had fallen upon the person of the lion-hearted Gen. R. S. Ewell, and soon after his disabling wound at Manassas, which now caused him to appear with an artificial leg, Gen. Ewell had told White that if he ever again took the field he wanted White and his boys to be with him, an assurance never forgotten by either of them.

At the time Gen. Ewell crossed the mountain and made his attack upon the enemy at Winchester, adding another to the invariable whippings the bombastic coward and cow-stealer, Milroy, received every time he stood long enough for the rebels to reach him, Col. White asked and obtained permission to make a raid on the Point of Rocks, in the hope of striking again his old enemy, Means.

Crossing the Potomac below Berlin, the colonel divided his force, sending Lieut. Crown, with sixty-two men of Co. B, to pass along the Frederick road and come up in rear of the point, while he marched with the remainder, about one hundred, directly down the tow-path of the Chesapeake and Ohio Canal, intending to attack the enemy in front, while Crown should intercept the retreat of any who attempted to escape by the road to Frederick.

After a quick march of about two miles, Lieut. Crown observed the rear of a body of cavalry about a mile in advance, and wishing to ascertain what force and command it was, he sent Lieut. Dorsey forward with six men to capture a straggler, which was soon done, and the prisoner reported that the force in front was two hundred men of Cole's battalion, commanded by Captains Vernon and Summers. Not disposed to take one Yankee's evidence without having it corroborated, Crown again sent Dorsey forward, instructing him as before, to capture a Yankee but to avoid the use of fire-arms, if possible; but this time "Nich." rode up on two of them, one of whom he captured but was obliged to shoot the other, and as soon as Crown heard the firing he moved his command rapidly to the front, only halting long enough to assure himself that the story of the last prisoner tallied exactly with the first.

The enemy halted after crossing Catocton creek, and forming their line of battle, waited for the Confederates to come up, which they very soon did, and Crown discovered that as the advantage in position, numbers and arms, was all greatly against him, he must trust to charging and close quarters; and he at once gave the order to charge, which Company B executed in her usually gallant style, but now with more of fiery valour than ever, for they were that day upon the soil of their native State, and to add to their enthusiasm, knew that the blue jackets in their front covered the forms of Maryland men.

The Yankees poured a heavy fire upon them from their carbines, but Company B was moving at a gallop and on the lowest ground, so that most of the bullets flew over the heads of the men, while those that were low enough only tore their clothes or wounded their horses, and the fact that Cole's men had not been drilled to fight at sabre's length was soon evident, for the moment that Crown's boys gained their side of the creek the Yankees broke, and notwithstanding the efforts of one of their officers fled like sheep from hungry wolves.

A running fight for about four miles was kept up, when finding his men overloaded with horses and prisoners, and fearing too that Col. White might need him at the Point, Lieut. Crown recalled his men and turned towards that place, taking with him thirty-seven men and horses of Cole's battalion, many more having been captured, but in the darkness and confusion made their escape.

When Company B joined Col. White at the Point of Rocks, they found that he had already taken the place, having routed Means' command and captured about twenty prisoners and horses, and was then engaged in setting fire to two railroad trains that had just come down, one of which he destroyed where it stood, but after getting the other in a good way to burn some of the men let steam on the locomotive and started the blazing train at full speed for Baltimore.

After getting all the men together, and taking plenty of time to secure the plunder they wished to take away, the colonel marched his battalion to Loudoun, and encamped near the Blue Ridge, above Hillsborough, where his people enjoyed themselves finely until the order came calling them to join their general, who was now leading the advance of Lee's army through Maryland and opening the way for the brilliant but fruitless campaign in Pennsylvania.

12: Gettysburg

The battalion crossed the Potomac at Shepherdstown, and passing on by Sharpsburg and Hagerstown, reached the head of Ewell's column at Greencastle, from which point it took the advance, and under orders from Gen. Ewell marched directly to Gettysburg, where a heavy body of Pennsylvania militia was assembled to keep the rebels out of town. Company E, commanded by Lieut. H. M. Strickler, a gentleman, a gallant soldier and good officer, but above all an earnest Christian, and who is now (1870) a devoted minister of the M. E. Church South, led the advance, and charged bravely upon the enemy, who were drawn up on the left and in front, as the battalion moved forward, to the number of thirteen hundred infantry and about one hundred cavalry.

The battalion did not have over two hundred and fifty men in ranks, but they came with barbarian yells and smoking pistols, in such a desperate dash, that the blue-coated troopers wheeled their horses and departed towards Harrisburg without firing a shot, while the infantry who could do so followed their example, and those who could not threw down their bright, new muskets, and begged frantically for quarter. Of course, "nobody was hurt," if we except one fat militia captain, who, in his exertion to be first to surrender, managed to get himself run over by one of Company E's horses, and bruised somewhat.

Most of White's men pushed on after the cavalry, who were finely mounted, but they had been on the run while the others were losing time in the camps, and were, of course, too far gone to overtake, and the battalion rallied in the town, where the citizens gave them all they wanted, and more, so that in a little while all who ever did indulge in the ardent were in a half-horse, half wild-cat condition, and each man imagined himself to be the greatest hero of the war; in fact, some were heard recounting to the horrified citizens of Gettysburg the immense execution they had done with the sabre in a hundred battles.

But about five o'clock, after the "Comanches" had been in town two hours, Gen. Early came in and ordered the battalion to go on up the railroad and catch some Yankees, but after a long chase they returned without any "boys in blue," and bivouacked that night with the citizens—about a mile from town.

Next day was passed in scouting and in gathering up horses, supposed from their fat, sleek appearance, to be fit for service, but no greater mistake was ever committed, for a Southern cavalry horse, after being entirely broken down, could travel farther and better than the fine-looking steeds just from a Pennsylvania stable, and many a man bitterly repented him of exchanging his poor old horse for a new one, even if he got a watch to boot.

The battalion marched to Hanover Junction, where there had been about eight hundred Yankee infantry, but who retired to their fortifications, about two miles off, as the "Comanches" advanced, nor did the latter deem it prudent to attack them; so after skirmishing with them a short time they passed by and encamped for the night, moving out the next morning, in front of Gen. Early's division, to Little York, where they arrived about noon; and as soon as the general came up he ordered Colonel White to scout the country and destroy as much railroad as possible.

Here the colonel divided his command, sending Captain Myers with his company off to the left of the town, several miles, to picket and scout, while with the remainder he moved forward to the Susquehanna, where he destroyed the bridge, and on his return from Wrightsville to York burned twenty-two railroad bridges.

When Gen. Early was ready to march to Gettysburg again he called in his cavalry, and sent them in advance, with orders to watch carefully the left flank; and in the afternoon of the same day a strong force of the enemy appeared, and in a dash upon Company A captured one man (Thos. Spates) who was *picketing* in a cherry tree. This opened the eyes of the men to the fact that they now had something more than militia to deal with, but no one imagined that it was anything but the army of Hooker, which had been beaten on the Rappahannock, and no people were ever in finer spirits than those who had followed the stars and bars to Pennsylvania.

The weather was extremely hot, but the marching was easy, and they were in a land where abundance of everything could be obtained for men and horses, while all the floating news and rumours that reached the soldiers' ears were of the "good time coming," and had never a tinge of gloom to mar the brightness which flooded the future as the *seeming* hand of destiny lifted the veil which divided that shadowy land from the now, giving a glimpse of the glory and peace beyond; and looking back to the "auld lang syne" they said, in the language of holy writ, "the thing which hath been, it is that which shall be, and that which is done is that which shall be done; and there is no new thing under the sun;" for had not America been the land of rest to the oppressed of the Old World; and had not Liberty always ground the tyrant's power to dust beneath the tread of Freedom's legions in this—her chosen home? and now the finger of events was tracing the same old story before the eyes of the wondering nations.

One current story was that Gen. Lee had said that he would "winter his army on the Hudson," and another, that France had recognised the Confederate States and was sending a fleet to open the blockade; and just then an old soldier would break out with "Confound French recognition and all the rest of them, the English and French wouldn't recognise us when we wanted them to, now we don't thank them for it, because we will make the Yankees themselves acknowledge our independence in a month;" when, as if to confirm the opinion and make it prophecy, a newspaper would proclaim in big letters, "Hurrah! the war is over! Commissioners from Washington and Richmond have met at Fortress Monroe to arrange terms for separation and peace!"

This was the atmosphere in which the soldiers breathed while campaigning in Pennsylvania, and many of them expressed *fears* that they would not be permitted to fight the Yankees "just once more" before the war ended, but as they approached Gettysburg on Wednesday evening, July 1st, all such *fears* were dispelled, for there stood the Army of the North in battle order, and before the Southern troops were within two miles of the place their foes came out to meet them. White's battalion, then the only body of cavalry with the A. N.V., was sent by General Ewell to the left of his corps, and as they gained the high hills in that direction, they had a full view of the battle between Ewell's Corps and the 11th Corps of Meade's army, particularly that part of it fought by Heth's Division.

The enemy was posted at a fence and ditch which ran together across an open, level meadow, and Heth's men came out of a woods about four hundred yards in front, their thin line marching beautifully over the smooth meadow towards the enemy's position, and although under a fire from the moment of their appearance, that increased rapidly as they advanced, the line moved without any more falter or waver than if they had been on dress parade, paying no attention to the men who occasionally fell out of ranks smitten by the fire, but on reaching a point about one hundred yards from the Yankee position an officer on horseback gave an order.

116

And with a shout Heth's men sprang forward in a charge, and now the line which had before been keeping step and moving so regularly began to spread out as the fastest men would leave the slow ones in the race of death, and the fire of the enemy was now a perfect blaze and roar of musketry, but in a few minutes the Confederate bayonets drove them from the fence, and in utter route the Yankees fled across the open ground to the railroad, their men falling thick beneath the withering rifle shots of the Confederates, who had now no danger to affect their aim, and the rout and pursuit disappeared from view through the streets of Gettysburg.

Soon after this one of Ewell's brigades marched to the left of the town and into a large wheat field where lay a line of men in blue, who raised up when the gray jackets were in about fifty yards, and throwing down their guns, surrendered in a body—in all over one thousand.

The battalion passed on, and soon met some of the Yankee skirmishers from a division of infantry on Rocky Creek, whom they captured and sent back, and in a short time Gen. Gordon marched his brigade to the support of the cavalry.

About this time a battery, from the Cemetery Hill, was fiercely shelling White's men, and as Gordon's skirmishers appeared on the field a storm of shot and shell ploughed the ground along the line, causing part of it to falter; but the major who commanded was a splendid officer, and brought his people up to it handsomely; once, indeed, he displayed almost more than human coolness and daring—in reforming a part of his line that had broken under the fire,.

Just as the major reached it a heavy shell exploded exactly under his horse, causing both it and the rider to roll over on the ground in a cloud of dirt and smoke, all who saw it thinking that they were surely both killed, but amid the cloud the beautiful bay sprang up, with the gallant major still in the saddle exclaiming, "Steady men, steady; no use to break; keep the line steady;" and the men were steady after that.

At dark the troops encamped, and in the morning the battalion was broken up into scouting parties for the generals of the left wing, the colonel sending Captains Myers and Grubb with six men each to find the right flank of the Yankee Army. They crossed the creek, and separating, scouted through a rough, broken country, for probably two hours, when they united exactly in rear of the enemy's right wing, and sent a courier to inform the colonel that they had found it; Myers having gone around the right flank, while Grubb passed through an opening in their line without knowing it until he found himself in the rear.

Here they saw a long train of wagons, and determined to capture some of them, but on arriving in about two hundred yards of the train found that a cavalry force had passed along in their rear, while a line of infantry was marching directly towards them, and from this interesting situation they agreed to retire, without wagons, if they could.

It was a very particular business, but by passing off for Yankee scouts, which Captain Grubb could do to perfection, they got clear, taking five prisoners with them.

During the remainder of the day the battalion did little but watch the flank and listen to fighting along the lines to their right, and when night came, they bivouacked near a deserted farmhouse on the bank of Rocky Creek.

The morning of July 3rd opened very clear and very hot, and the stillness along the lines of battle was at times almost oppressive, but the occasional shell from Round Top and the Cemetery kept the boys from going crazy with their anxiety to interpret the long intervals of silence, and when one of the Yankee bombs set fire to their farm-house they became perfectly satisfied, certain now, they said, "that the Yankee Army was still there."

About noon, while the men were idly lying along the fields in the full blaze of the July sun, with no motion of the air to mitigate the oppressive heat, they noticed that the artillerymen were posting their cannon in a long curving line along the hills, and to all appearances meant business, although no firing was heard anywhere, but about 1 o'clock one single gun, (a long black Whitworth,) pealed out its sharp, ringing battle-note, and in an instant, from two hundred and ten guns, boomed forth a raging tempest of lightning and thunder that fairly shook the solid ground and made every man leap to his feet in bewildered excitement; but soon came the reply from the lines of Gen. Meade, where the white powder smoke, tinged with the lurid flashings, puffed from the blazing muzzles of two hundred and seventy cannon, and the great Battle of Gettysburg was fairly joined.

This firing continued until the veterans of Lee had gone through the valleys and reached the fire-crowned heights where lay the Northern army, when the Southern guns ceased their bellowing; but of the general battle the great historians have written, and we have only to tell of what White's people did.

About 2 o'clock the colonel marched his battalion up the turnpike towards York, and no sooner did he get clear of the infantry lines than

118

he became aware that the enemy's cavalry was on the ground.

Gen. Stuart had not yet appeared, and all that was heard from him was that he was actively operating in Meade's rear, destroying trains, and had even gone so far as to make a demonstration on the fortifications around Washington City.

White's people found the Yankee pickets on the pike and drove them to their reserves, which were drawn up in a body of timber running parallel with the road and separated from it by an open line of level grass fields, about three hundred yards in width, and as soon as the colonel found that a heavy force of cavalry was here, he reported it to Gen. Lee, who sent Gen. "Extra Billy" Smith with his infantry brigade to support the battalion in guarding the flank.

There had always been a feeling of dislike between the infantry and cavalry, the former regarding the latter as the most favoured branch—in not being compelled to walk—but nothing so thrilled them with dread as a cavalry charge, while the cavalry feared even more to attack the infantry of the enemy; and Napoleon, at the Pyramids, proved that cool courage and scientific handling made infantry invincible against the finest cavalry in the world, for such the Mamelukes certainly were; but for all that the infantry preferred to have their foes on foot.

White's battalion moved up the turnpike, with Gen. Smith's brigade in support, but very soon the general found that he was becoming separated from the army, while on the flank and front the enemy's cavalry was threatening him, and fearing to be cut off if he advanced further he decided to retire, which he did, halting at a cross-road a mile back, and White and his boys had a great deal more than their hands full, but what they could do they did, and in constant dashes, first up the road in front and then out on the right, they drove back the enemy's parties as often as they advanced.

The situation was full of excitement, to which the roar of the great battle, raging at its hottest in their rear, added force; but by-and-bye long lines of cavalry were discovered marching quietly from the woods on the left, and now it did appear that the enemy was all around, for no one doubted the new force being Yankees.

Making one last charge up the turnpike, in which a regiment of the enemy was driven wildly back, Col. White turned his command and retired slowly toward the position of Gen. Smith, but pretty soon, in a cloud of dust, Gen. Stuart and staff galloped up the road, inquiring eagerly for news; and just then, as the colonel called his attention to the new forces on the left, the wind unfurled their banners and

TRAIN DERAILED BY CONFEDERATE CAVALRY

displayed the battle-flag of Dixie, while Stuart remarked, "that is Gen. Fitz Lee's Division;" and a perfect storm of cheers and glad shouts of welcome went up from White's excited battalion.

As soon as General Stuart could get his division up he opened the battle by sending a regiment across the fields before spoken of to the woods, but when half way to the timber a regiment of the enemy came out, and in a few minutes was driven back, but being reinforced by another the Confederate regiment retired, when Stuart sent a second regiment to aid his first, and thus the battle spread, growing fiercer as the numbers engaged increased, while the artillery played upon all points where it could be managed without injury to its own troops.

A story was told in '62 to the effect that Gen. Lee had said he would give ten dollars for every cavalryman killed or wounded in battle with the sabre, and if he had been held to the contract now, he would have been ruined, for the men appeared to use their sabres that evening from choice, and numbers on both sides fell under the bloody blades.

After watching the conflict for some time, Col. White noticed a Yankee regiment wheeling on the right of Stuart's line, and ordering his men forward met it fairly, driving it back to the woods in gallant style, for which he received General Stuart's thanks.

"When night had stilled the battle's hum" the troops bivouacked on the ground over which they had fought; but the news from the lines was discouraging, saying that General Lee had failed to take the heights; and when, an hour before day, the orders came to mount and fall back silently, for fear the enemy's batteries would open fire again, the soldiers knew that the battle was lost, but they still trusted to the genius and generalship of their great leader to turn the defeat to their advantage in some way.

The 4th of July, a dismal day of rain and gloom was passed in gathering the stragglers and wagons together, and in burying the dead, but when evening came the battalion was divided; Colonel White, with Companies B, C and E, acting as rear guard for Ewell's Corps, which brought up the rear in the retreat, as it had led the van of the army in the advance; and Maj. Ferneyhough, with Companies A, D and F, was sent to A. P. Hill, to be advance guard for his Corps, as it held the front of the army.

The whole march was full of harassing attacks by the enemy, but White fought those who followed, from every hill-top, only being compelled once to call upon the general for aid, when Gen. Gordon, the fiery Georgian, marched his brigade back and administered a reproof that made the Yankees chary of pressing Ewell's rear guard too closely again.

Major F.'s command pressed forward under A. P. Hill's orders, driving the enemy's pickets as they went, and whipping a force of cavalry from the town of Waynesboro', but when the army reached Hagerstown the battalion united again, and remained with Gen. Ewell.

Nothing of special interest, other than what was done by other commands, was performed by White's battalion in the further progress of the retreat, and the history of it has been told by other pens so fully that were mine capable of the task there is nothing new to write, and when the army of General Lee, baffled, it is true, in its Northern campaign, but still in fighting trim and ready for battle, reached the South bank of the Potomac at Williamsport, the men felt that they were at home once more, and believed that the only result of the Gettysburg disaster would be to prolong the war a few more years, and indeed all hope of a speedy termination had died in the hearts of the battle-scarred soldiers of the Army of Northern Virginia, when, in connection with their own defeat, they counted the bloody siege and final surrender of Vicksburg, the news of which saluted their ears almost as soon as their own battle was over.

Almost as soon as he crossed the river, Colonel White reported to Gen. Stuart, and asked permission to take his battalion to Loudoun County, which that officer readily granted, and the "Comanches" marched rapidly to Castleman's Ferry, but found the Shenandoah so high, from the heavy rains which had followed the battle, that it was impassable, and the colonel encamped his men a short distance from the river to wait for it to fall.

13: Poole's Farm

The battalion remained on the bank of the Shenandoah for a day, but seeing no decrease in the flood, impatience got the better of prudence, and the colonel, giving way to the wishes of his men, (which in this case coincided so fully with his own,) marched them to the river, and such as were not afraid to "take water," swam the horses across, while the others went over in a skiff. When about fifty men had got over, and the shades of an early twilight commenced to gather from the low-hanging clouds, a courier from Lieut. Moon, of the 6th Va. Cavalry, who had charge of the pickets in the gap, came down the mountain and informed Col. White that the Yankees were moving into the gap.

The boys hastily dressed, and mounting their horses marched up to see if the report was true, but before going far they met Lieut. Moon retiring, while behind him came a large force of Yankee infantry; and with many a curse on the delay in crossing the river, the detachment turned back and passed up between mountain and river to the Shepherd's mill road, which brought them out at the Trap. The next day they learned that Meade's army was in Loudoun, following the track of Burnside, and as nearly all the men who had been scattered through the county, at their homes, returned to the command, the colonel retired to Ashby's Gap, where he resolved to make a fight, if anything like his number advanced upon him.

On Sunday morning, July 19th, the long lines of the Yankee Army were seen marching along to Southward, and when the sun was an hour high, a few cavalry scouts rode up towards the mountain position where White and his men were standing, but showed no disposition either to be captured themselves or to attempt to drive the rebels from the gap. After waiting and watching a long while for such an advance as they had made at Snicker's Gap, the colonel ordered Capt. Myers to "send some men down there to stir up those fellows," and a party of half a dozen was instructed to ride down and drive away the pickets below Paris.

This party went down, and making a dash drove the picket out of sight over the hill, but in an instant was seen coming back at full speed, while along the hills, a blue line of infantry, deployed as skirmishers, sprang up as if by magic and advanced at a quick march towards the gap, and in the pike beyond, at least a brigade was seen marching in the same direction.

Capt. M. now turned to the colonel, and asked if he would "have those fellows stirred up any more?" to which he replied that he "thought *that* would do just now," and sending Captains Grubb and Myers to the village to check the advance, he prepared to leave the last corner-stone of Loudoun. When the men with Grubb and Myers reached their position at Paris, they dismounted, and as the Federal advance on the turnpike, which was a party of cavalry, came up, they commenced a fire which drove them back; one man, Harper, of Co. A, bringing down the Yankee major in command, and his horse, at one discharge of buckshot from his musket. The battalion now took the mountain road to Manassa Gap, and on reaching that place saw and captured a Signal Corps, which was operating on the side of the mountain, near Linden.

The Yankees marched through towards Front Royal, but were met and driven back by A. P. Hill's people.

Col. White now crossed the river again, to wait until the remainder of his battalion could come up, but gave permission to Captains Myers and Grubb to take a party of their men on foot and make a scout along the mountains to capture wagons, if possible.

With eighteen men, they went down among the enemy's camps near Piedmont, at dark, but found nothing but infantry, and the next day went to Ashby's Gap, where they discovered a heavy force holding that position, which forced them to cross the river at Berry's Ferry, and passing down to Shepherd's mill they again went over, climbing the Blue Ridge near Snicker's Gap, only to find that pass strongly guarded by both infantry and cavalry, while all the wagons passed along with the army, keeping entirely clear of the mountain, it being pretty evident that Gen. Meade had learned a valuable lesson from the mistakes of Burnside the year before.

Everything was now at a stand-still, and thus they remained for several days, when the colonel came over with the battalion, and moving down into the lower country begun to trouble the enemy's scouting parties, and succeeded in capturing a number of horses and prisoners. On the morning of August 7th, he went to Woodgrove, where he learned that a regiment of Michigan Cavalry had come out from Harper's Ferry to Hillsborough, and moving cautiously to the latter place, found that they had passed on towards Waterford.

The colonel had about one hundred and twenty men with him and determined to attack them, so passing down the road he halted at a favourable position near Mr. Vandevanter's, and made his arrangements for an ambuscade, thinking the enemy would return to Harper's Ferry in the evening, but in this he was mistaken, for after waiting some time, he learned, about sundown, that they were preparing to encamp at Waterford for the night. He now moved his command into the woods on Catocton Creek, near Mr. J. E. Walker's, and waited until about 9 o'clock, when, leaving their horses, he marched his people over toward the camp, as he had discovered it, on a high hill south of the town.

He instructed his men to march quietly up to the enemy's position without firing, and when he gave the signal, to rush upon them and secure as many horses and prisoners as possible; and to prevent mistakes in the confusion of the attack gave as challenge and reply the words "Bob" and "Joe."

On getting into the field, the men found a great number of hay-cocks, which caused them to become somewhat scattered in their march, and as the colonel advanced in front, holding his pistol ready to fire, he accidentally fell over one of the cocks, in which his pistol was discharged.

This caused a panic, and while some of the men, imagining that they were beset by the enemy, commenced to retreat, the others looked upon it as the signal for attack and rushed forward firing their pistols, although nearly two hundred yards from the enemy. The flying ones were speedily rallied and brought back, but the Yankees were all mounted and ready to retreat, which they did with all haste, after firing one volley at the Confederates, killing a very gallant young soldier of Co. C,—John C. Grubb.

Three or four of the enemy fell, and a few horses were captured, but the most of them made their escape. A part of the command, under Captain Grubb, were standing in the road when two or three pickets, who had been stationed on the Hamilton road, alarmed at the firing, came up, and were halted with a demand for a surrender. Some of Grubb's men drew up their pistols to fire upon them, but the captain prevented it, saying, "don't shoot them, they will surrender," when one of the Yankees discharged his carbine almost in Captain Grubb's face, and at the same time exclaimed, "I surrender," and the whole party gave themselves up as prisoners.

Capt. Grubb fell, mortally wounded, and with mournful hearts his men carried him back to his father's house near Hillsborough, where he died in about two hours, and the battalion met with a loss that was well-nigh irreparable, for he was one of the best, if not the very best officer in it. He had been in the service from the commencement of the war, first as a member of Capt. N. R. Heaton's Company, (A,) 8th Regiment Va. Volunteers, and the gallant Heaton bears willing testimony to the noble daring of R. B. Grubb, while under his command, at the bloody battles of Manassas and Ball's Bluff, while Gen. Eppa Hunton pronounces him one of the best men he ever had in that regiment of heroes, whose name is crowned with the glory that beams brightly upon the fame of Virginia, won in a hundred battles.

In the Spring of 1862, "Dick" Grubb was discharged from the infantry service, and going to the Valley, attached himself to the 7th Va. Cavalry, where he distinguished himself as a scout for Colonel (afterwards Major-General) Wm. E. Jones.

In the fall of that year, he obtained permission to raise a company for White's battalion, in which he was entirely successful, as has been shown.

After this affair at Waterford, which had been fruitful only in disaster to his battalion, Colonel White established a camp on the Blue Ridge near Mr. Howell's, where he remained for several days, during which time the business of the command was, to some extent, brought into shape, as it was highly necessary to do, for it had begun to suffer for want of proper attention.

The old Company of Capt. Grubb was now officered by Capt. Dowdell and Lieut. Sam. Grubb, who were promoted, and by Lieut. T. W. White who was elected Second Lieutenant.

Marcellus French had been made Captain of Co. F, with Charles James as his First Lieutenant, and everything put in order, as far as possible, to make the battalion efficient.

One morning, about the middle of August, Triplett, of Co. F, reported to the colonel that a regiment of Yankee cavalry, encamped on the Rappahannock, near Orleans, in Fauquier County, was in the habit of sending a party every day, about 3 o'clock, to Barbour's Cross Roads, on a scout; and the colonel at once resolved to attempt their capture. So, starting with about one hundred men he reached, just before midnight, an admirable place of concealment in the thick pines near the Cross Roads, where the command halted to wait until the scouting party came along the next day. The time passed wearily enough in that hot, piney encampment, but every man knew that an absolute certainty of success depended on their lying hid until the enemy came.

Lieut. Chiswell, with seventeen men of Co. B, was stationed in the thick bushes close along the road, with instructions to fire when the Yankees came opposite them, and a picket was placed on the Orleans road half a mile below, to watch for the enemy, and now nothing remained but to wait for the game.

About 3 o'clock, the picket came quietly in and reported above one hundred approaching, when all the men got up from their lounging among the broom sedge and mounted their horses, and notice being sent to Lieut. Chiswell, everything was, as the man-o'-warsman would say, "cleared for action." After waiting anxiously, with ears strained to catch the sound, for about ten minutes, the carbines of Chiswell's men rung out, and with a shout, away dashed the mounted men to charge. On emerging from the pines into the road, the Yankees were seen in the field on the opposite side, in great confusion from the unexpected volley they had received, but as soon as they saw the battalion they dashed off towards a gap in the fence, to gain the road again; but now one of those unaccountable things, which so often occur without any reason at all, and just at the moment when their influence is most damaging, happened; and as Col. White, Adjt. Watts, and Capt. Myers, who were a little distance in front of the command, galloped up towards the gap to cut off the enemy's escape, and thinking they were followed by the men, the major, who was exactly at the head of the column, wheeled it down the road, leaving these three officers to meet the sixty Yankees alone.

In a few minutes the colonel and Capt. M. were dismounted, both of their horses being shot at the same moment, and the Adjutant was among the blue-jackets without any assistance at all, but pretty soon Lieut. Conrad managed to turn Company A back, and with part of Company B, under Lieut. Crown, who had not been in the column when Major F. started it away from the Yankees, dashed in and made the scene look something like a fight, for the Yankees were resolute fellows from the 6th Ohio Cavalry, and in spite of their surprise, fought bravely.

Conrad, with a few men, followed a part of them nearly to their camp, and on their return met another portion, who had made a circuit towards the Cross Roads at the first fire, and were now going full tilt towards camp with Crown and his boys right behind them.

Conrad and the few men with him were encumbered with prisoners and horses, but attempted to halt the Yankees, and fired into them as they came, but they only called to the Confederates to "clear the road," and passed on with their sabres flashing so dangerously that their foes gave them room.

The whole force now returned to the Cross Roads, having taken about twenty-five prisoners and thirty horses, besides killing and wounding about ten of the enemy, with no loss to themselves except the two horses before spoken of.

Strange as it may appear only one man was killed by the fire of Chiswell's men, although they had a rest and the distance was scarcely twelve yards, but that one man had seven bullets through him.

That was the usual result of ambuscades, for under the most favourable circumstances they seldom did much damage; and it would appear, (so miraculous did the escapes from them seem,) that Providence guarded in a special manner the unsuspecting party who became entangled in the murderous snare of a hidden enemy, no matter how cunningly devised the plan might be; and it must be confessed that such a mode of fighting is a poor school in which to learn lessons of chivalry and honour, the old adage that "all is fair in war," to the contrary notwithstanding.

After Barbour's Cross Roads, there were many attempts to strike the enemy's scouting parties, but they always came in such force it was impossible to do anything with the slightest show for success, and the colonel turned his attention to the camps of the foe in Fairfax and Maryland.

About the last of August, he learned that a force, entitled "Scott's 900," was stationed at Edwards' Ferry, and crossing the river some distance above the ferry about midnight, with one hundred and fifty men, the colonel hid his force along the bank to wait until the patrol which passed up and down the tow-path of the canal, every half hour, should go down, and at the same time he placed two men near the tow-path, with instructions to notice closely the patrol, and if they appeared hurried or excited, to stop them, for that would be evidence enough that they had learned something of his presence on the Maryland side, and they must not be permitted to reach the camp, but if they came along quietly, as usual, to let them pass, for they evidently would know nothing of his movement

It so happened that old "Uncle" Charley Butler was along, and moreover that he was about half drunk, and when the patrol of two men came riding very leisurely along, "Uncle Charley" sprang up and caught the bridle of the leading Yankee, who raised his gun to fire on Butler, and to save him the other boys had to shoot the Yankee, and of course the firing alarmed the camp.

Col. White now urged his people across the canal as rapidly as possible, and coming up in rear of the camp, (which he knew to be fortified in front,) halted long enough to form his line and ordered a charge, in which they received a volley from the enemy that badly wounded one man, and several slightly; and on reaching the camp found that it had a regular fortification all around it, but the men spurred their horses on, leaping the ditch and riding recklessly over the breastworks. Most of the enemy, thanks to Butler's drunken blunder at the canal, had escaped, and the daring and desperate assault only resulted in the capture of about a dozen, but their whole camp equipage fell into the hands of White's people.

The wounded man, Robert W. Jones, a splendid soldier of Company A, was so badly hurt that it was impossible to move him, and he was left at the house of a citizen nearby where he was kindly treated, even by the Yankees; and up to this time, (1870,) although more than seven weary years have passed, he is still unable to walk, the bullet having lodged near the spine.

This, and the affair at Barbour's Cross Roads, was acknowledged by Gen. Lee, in the following letter to Gen. Stuart:

Headquarters, Army N.V.,
Sept. 9th, 1863.

Major-Gen. J. E. B. Stuart,
Commanding Cavalry:

General—Your letter, enclosing reports of Lieut.-Colonel E.V. White, of the operations of his battalion at Poole's farm, on August 27th, and his previous attack on Kilpatrick's Cavalry, have been received, and forwarded to the department as an evidence of the great boldness and skill of that officer.

The activity and energy of his command, and the gallantry of his officers and men, especially in the attack on Poole's farm, reflect great credit upon the service. I hope his operations will always be attended with the same success.

I am, very respectfully, your obedient servant.

R. E. Lee, General.

Soon after this, an order was received through General Lee, from the Secretary of War, and the execution of which has caused great blame to be attached to Col. White, by those citizens of Loudoun county, who, denying the ground-work upon which the Federal Constitution was built, claimed that the rights of the States were not merely delegated but irrevocably transferred to the General Government, the testimony of common justice, common sense, and of the fathers and framers of the Constitution to the contrary notwithstanding, held their allegiance to the Northern government; and while the praise or blame of traitors to their State, in matters connected with the war, is of small importance, yet to show that the colonel was blameless in this case, I make the explanation.

Two citizens of Loudoun, who, among many others, had, at the tinkling of the "little bell," been dragged to a Federal prison, and although no crimes were charged against them, were held in durance on the ground that they refused to take an oath of allegiance to the

United States, a government to whom they owed none, and which was incapable of protecting them in it if they did. These were Henry Ball and Campbell Belt, and their friends, after appealing time and again to the United States authorities for their release, without success, and the health of both being so delicate as to excite grave fears that confinement would speedily end in death, sought by retaliation to effect their discharge from prison, and procured of the Secretary of War an order for the arrest and confinement of William Williams and Asa M. Bond—two prominent Union citizens—until Messrs. Ball and Belt should be released, and simply for the reason that Col. White was in a situation to execute the order it was sent to him.

Owing to the inefficiency of the men detailed to make the arrest, Mr. Bond escaped, and they substituted R. I. Hollingsworth in his stead, who, with Mr. Williams, was sent to Richmond, and now their friends used their influence with the United States authorities, which soon brought about the release of both parties.

About the middle of September, the colonel was informed by one of his scouts that there would be several carloads of horses sent down on the Baltimore and Ohio Rail Road on the 16th, concluded to attempt their capture, and having decided to take only Company B with him, sent Lieut. Crown, with his people, on the night of the 14th, to a point on the Catocton mountain near Mr. Gray's, above Leesburg, with instructions to remain there until he (the colonel) should have examined the fords and fixed upon a place to cross the Potomac, and as there is some difference of opinion as to who was to blame for the disaster that followed, I deem it proper to give all the particulars, and let the reader settle the point.

No one was admitted by the colonel into the secret, but Lieut. Crown, and as the colonel was about to leave the battalion in charge of Major Ferneyhough, he sent for Capt. Myers, and telling him that Cole's battalion and Means' men were in Waterford, gave him permission to go, if, he so desired, and try to capture their pickets.

Lieut. Crown says, that Col. White promised to send a force to attack the party at Waterford before he would consent to take his company into the mountain as White desired him, and that Col. White informed him he had given such orders, before he left the camp; but he certainly did not order Capt. Myers to make an attack, or tell him that anything depended on its being made, and he merely told him he could go down and capture their pickets if he desired.

Crown took his company to the appointed place, and Myers, with his people, went down near Waterford, but learning that the pickets were drawn in after dark to the town, and that the force there was composed of Cole's battalion, a regiment of Connecticut Cavalry, and Means' Company, all commanded by Col. Cole, he retired without making any attack, his orders being entirely discretionary.

The next morning Cole's command left Waterford and marched straight to the camp of Co. B, a spy having reported their position, and whether Lieut. Crown is blameless entirely, and all the fault lies with Col. White and Capt. Myers, or not, it does appear that Co. B. was surprised in the fullest sense of the word, for the first intimation they had of Cole's approach was the firing of his advance guard among them, and both Lieuts. Crown and Dorsey were at the house of Mr. Gray, waiting for breakfast and listening to the piano.

Both officers were captured before they could reach the company, and nine of their men were made prisoners at the same time, but the others, with great difficulty, made their escape. There is no doubt that if Lieut. Crown had had a picket out, and had notice of the enemy's approach, he would have whipped them, for he had about fifty of the best fighting men in the army, and Crown and Dorsey never counted odds in any kind of a fight. So, it is self-evident that situated as they were there, they would have whipped Cole's four hundred easily, for the latter had not the best troops in the world, in fact they were morally opposed to the usual dangers of the battlefield.

Col. Cole treated Lieut. Crown just as cowards always do those in their power, and even went so far as to threaten him with hanging for being a Confederate soldier so unfortunate as to be a prisoner to Cole.

Of course, this disaster wound up the projected horse capture in Maryland, and Col. White returned to camp with his spirits considerably below zero, but he was never heard to charge the damage to the misconduct of anyone, and only seemed to look upon it as one of the natural misfortunes of war.

★★★★★★★★★★★★★★★★★

Note.—Since writing the above, a letter from Lieut. Chiswell has been received, which makes some correction necessary.

Lieut. C. says, that at the time of the attack, himself and Lieut. Dorsey, with several of their men, were in Leesburg, and as soon as they heard of it, Lieut. Dorsey, with one man, (a member of the 8th Va. Infantry,) started to the scene of action at Gray's, but at a turn in the road they came suddenly upon the enemy's column and were captured, the man with Dorsey having his thigh broken, and the lieutenant himself being severely handled in the conflict.

Lieut. Chiswell and his party were hard pressed, and with the greatest difficulty effected their escape.

At one time Chiswell's horse fell with him, and rolling over lay prone upon his leg, but he managed to withdraw it, leaving his boot in the stirrup, and having gotten his horse up, the lieutenant took the boot in his hand, and though the Yankees were close upon him, he got clear. He says, "boots were boots" in those days, and he couldn't think of losing his.

★★★★★★★★★★★★★★★★

Col. White had frequently been called upon by General Lee to destroy the Rail Road bridges in rear of Meade's army, in order that their supplies might, to some extent, be cut off; but such enterprises were very difficult and hazardous, more especially as he had no men who knew the country well enough to pilot him at night to the scene of operations. On several occasions he attempted to accomplish something in this way, but to no purpose; however, having learned something of the bridge over Pope's Head creek, on the O. and A. Rail Road, he resolved to attempt its destruction, and with nineteen men of Companies A and C, he started in the evening from his camp in upper Loudoun, with John Davis of Fairfax, for his guide, and marching all night, camped about daylight on the Hatmark creek, below Fairfax C. H., where the company remained all day with nothing to eat but fox grapes; the enemy being so thick around that part of the country that the men would have been discovered if they had ventured out of the friendly shade of the pine woods.

When night came, the little party moved out, and passing Barnes' mill on the Accotink, arrested the miller and carried him along with them.

On arriving within half a mile of the bridge, the colonel, accompanied by Jack Dove, rode out to reconnoitre, finding a guard of four or five men on the bridge and a reserve of some twenty or more lying around a fire about a hundred yards from it. Returning to the command, the colonel moved it forward, intending to charge and drive off the guards, but on reaching the bridge found they had already retired, but whether they had become alarmed at something they had heard, or, as a patrol, had passed during the time he was gone for his people, the colonel could not determine, nor did he waste much time in speculations on the subject, but setting his men to work splitting and piling up rails on each end and in the middle of the bridge, they soon had a good lot of kindling ready to fire up, and after emptying a few canteens of coal oil on it, the fire was applied, and the boys withdrew a short distance and watched until the whole frame of the bridge was burning well, when they started on their return.

It was long past midnight when they left the bridge, and consequently could not go far before daylight compelled them again to hide themselves, and here another day was spent with nothing but grapes to eat. Some wagon trains, from Fairfax C. H., passed them, and could have been easily captured, but this would have almost insured the capture of the whole party, and consequently they were permitted to drive on.

When dark came the third night, the now half-famished band started again, this time for the nearest point where rations could be obtained, and very soon they were being well fed by the good people of upper Fairfax, who, no matter how hard pressed they were themselves, always had something to divide with the Dixie boys, and no people in the whole Confederacy would more gladly share their last morsel with the Southern soldier, than these very ones whose homes were constantly overrun by the blue-coated gentry who looked upon all they had as lawful spoil for Uncle Sam, and treated all of them as if they were rebels only wanting arms and an opportunity to show their hand.

When the colonel started on this expedition, he had left Major Ferneyhough in command of all the battalion except Capt. Myers and his company, and had instructed the latter to scout around the river country, mainly for the purpose of collecting a supply of long-range guns, in which his command was always very deficient, and for which he had special use in a contemplated attack on Cole's battalion. The major moved the rest of the command to the old camp at the Trap, and here Major Cole paid him a visit, causing the whole thing to move at a quick march into the mountain, while Cole encamped for the night at Bellfield, and strange to say he only lost one or two pickets by the operation, whom "Moll" Green, of Co. B, accidentally came in contact with.

As Cole was returning the next day, he came near breaking up the blacksmith department, by capturing Jo. Conner and Wm. Horseman, who were at work shoeing horses at the Woodgrove shop. Several other soldiers were at the shop, but they made their escape.

Myers in the meantime had been scouting around in the neighbourhoods of Hillsborough and Lovettsville, and the night Cole was at Bellfields, his party lay near Waterford, listening to the music of a party of infantry left at that place as a reserve for Cole in case he should need it.

What had been considered an impossibility the year before was now demonstrated to be perfectly feasible, and to the great discomfort of the border land both uniforms were daily seen by the citizens, and very frequently followed each other so rapidly that when not in actual chase, one party would scarcely be out of sight before the other would be demanding rations and horse-feed, and making awful threats against Rebels or Yankees as the case might be.

Not long after the bridge burning expedition the colonel sent Capt. Dowdell with his company and a part of Co. A, under Lieut. Conrad, to look after Yankee scouting parties "between the hills," as the country lying between the Blue Ridge and Short Hill from Hillsborough to the Potomac is called, while with seventeen of Co. A he started himself to arrest a notorious Yankee spy and guide, in Fairfax County, named Amey.

Capt. Dowdell, with fifty-five men, marched to St. Paul's church below Neersville, at night, and waited quietly in the woods for his game, but no blue-jackets put in an appearance until about noon the next day, when Dowdell's scout, who was none other than the famous John Mobberly, reported about one hundred Yankees coming from Harper's Ferry. Soon after this, the pickets on the Short Hill side came in at a gallop, saying the enemy was in their rear, which caused the captain to wheel about and march his command in that direction, and he soon came upon an interesting little fight between Lieuts. Sam. Grubb and Ben. Conrad, who, while reconnoitring, had run upon two of the enemy's scouts engaged in the same business, and had attempted their capture.

After this was over they started back to the grade, but the Yankees there had heard the firing and were retreating towards the Ferry, and owing to difficulties presented by the rough and broken country, considerable time was lost by Capt. D.'s command in reaching the road, but those of the men who were best mounted soon came up in the enemy's rear, and chased them under cover of the batteries on Maryland heights, wounding two and capturing five, together with eight horses of the enemy, who proved to be a scouting party of Means' command, numbering about seventy-five men, with three days' rations, on an intended scout, but owing to Capt. Dowdell's interference with their plans, they did not get more than two miles from their headquarters.

On their arrival at Harper's Ferry, a brigade of cavalry was sent out, which followed the Confederates to Hillsborough, but travelled too slow to overtake them.

Col. White with his party had, in the meantime, passed through Fairfax, by Hunter's Mill, Lewensville and Vienna, to Green's Store, where he succeeded in taking Amey; and on his return was told by "Jack" Dove, who got his information from Albert Gunnell, that a strong force of the enemy had passed up after Col. Mosby, who had been troubling them, as was the custom of that gallant and enterprising officer; and Col. White turned out by Thornton's Mill, but just before reaching that place, about midnight, the prisoner, who was riding behind one of the men, leaped from the horse and escaped into the woods.

Several shots were fired at him, but with what effect no one could tell, and the party moved forward again, and just before reaching the mill were fired upon by a party hid behind a fence. The colonel, supposing them to be citizens, wheeled about and rode up to the fence, but some of his men told him they were wounded, and the firing being kept up, he turned to his guide saying, "They shoot too well for citizens; show us the way out of here."

They now passed a barn, from behind which a party of about one hundred opened another fire upon them, at very short range, and Col. White ordered his men to cross the Rail Road, but in attempting it were met and fired upon by a third party of Yankees, when they turned to go up the Rail Road and in a few yards were again exposed to a galling fire from a fourth party. It now seemed that escape was impossible, but the colonel determined to make one more attempt, and his men following, he rode over the Rail Road bank and got clear of the trap into which they had so unwittingly wandered.

They lost two or three horses killed, but managed to get all the wounded men out, and making the best time possible, were five miles from Thornton's when daylight came.

It was afterwards ascertained that the force of Yankees engaged in this affair was over four hundred, and that the captured spy and guide knew of the ambuscade, which induced him to risk so much in his escape.

The next affair of importance was the raid to Lewensville, which occurred about the 10th of October. One of his scouts had reported to the colonel that a cavalry camp of about two hundred men and horses was located near that place, and taking with him about sixty of Companies A and B, he secured the services of George Tramell as pilot, and started on the hazardous expedition.

On arriving within five miles of the camp, about noon, the colonel halted his command to wait for night, and on cross-examining his scout, elicited the fact that he had never seen the camp and knew nothing except what citizens had told him, and not having anything at all reliable from this source, upon which to base a plan of attack, the colonel resolved to find out for himself the enemy's situation, and putting on a Yankee uniform, he, with his guide, started about sunset for the camp, leaving orders for the command to meet him about 9 o'clock, at a designated point near the camp.

He reached the place at dark, and walked around it, finding where the pickets were stationed, and the best way to get in, so that by the time the men came to him he had his plan all arranged. Promptly at the hour his people came, and dismounting about half of them he placed them under command of "Jack" Dove, Co. A, and William Shehan, Co. B, (than whom braver men never breathed,) with instructions to march directly upon the camp, while, with the mounted men he made a circuit and came in the enemy's rear.

While the vedettes were halting the colonel's party, the dismounted men had gone, unnoticed, into the camp and made their presence known by firing a volley among the tents, which caused a general stampede among all the Yankees who were able to run, and now White's command coming in, the camp was captured with about thirty prisoners and sixty-three horses. The enemy lost about fifteen killed and wounded, but none of the Confederates were injured, and with horses, prisoners and plunder, the raiders retired to their camp at the Trap.

A few days after this, news was received that Gen. Lee's army was advancing towards Washington, and Col. White, with a few men, started on a scout towards Manassas, leaving Capt. Myers in charge of the battalion, who, as soon as he heard that the colonel had reached his scouting ground, marched the command over to join him, and on approaching Thoroughfare Gap, discovered a party of infantry, who seemed disposed to hold the gap, but a dashing charge resulted in their capture, and they were found to be about twenty-five men and a lieutenant from a Vermont regiment, who had been left on picket when their regiment retired.

Passing through the gap the battalion met Col. White at Mt. Zion church, and made several attempts to get among Gen. Meade's wag-

BATTLE OF BRISCOE STATION, 14 OCTOBER, 1863

ons, but he took quite as good care of them in his retreat as he had done on his advance three months before, and the scouting only resulted in the gathering in of a few straggling troopers who wandered too far away from their main army.

The colonel soon branched off again with his little squad, and during his absence Gen. Stuart sent for Capt. Myers and ordered him to get all the men together and report for duty to General Rosser, who was now commanding the Ashby brigade, and shortly afterwards Gen. Lee's army retired to their old lines on the Rappahannock.

The colonel returned and went to work gathering up his men preparatory to going into the regular service again, and with heavy hearts the battalion bade farewell to the fondly-loved border land, about the 25th October, and marched to the camp of the brigade, then near Flint Hill, in Rappahannock County.

14: The Battalion Wins Its Name

The soldiers of Colonel White found their new brigadier to be a handsome, soldierly-looking man, very different in manner, language and appearance from Gen. Jones, though not a whit behind that officer in the maintenance of discipline in his brigade; but it did not take them long to find that he was a genial, warm-hearted gentleman, and they respected and loved him accordingly. For several days there was very little done beyond some scouting along the Rappahannock, and an inspection or two by Gen. Rosser,.

About the middle of November the brigade was ordered to join the division on the historic plains of Brandy Station, where Gen. Stuart purposed holding another of his "spread-eagle" grand reviews, which did no good except to give Yankee spies an opportunity to count the exact number of cavalry attached to the Army of Northern Virginia, and to display the foppishness of Stuart, who rode along his war-torn lines with a multitude of bouquets, which fair hands had presented to him, fastened in his hat and coat.

After the review, Gen. Rosser encamped his brigade at Hamilton's Crossing, on the Richmond, Fredericksburg and Potomac Rail Road, about eight miles from Fredericksburg, where it remained very quietly for several days, except on one occasion, when Gen. Hampton desired to see what the enemy meant by establishing a camp at Stephensburg, a little town in Culpeper, and in order to find out, he took a detail from his several brigades, and crossing the river at Ely's ford with about three hundred men, attacked the camp at daylight, completely routing the enemy and taking a considerable number of prisoners, together with all their tents and baggage. In this affair the 7th regiment led the charge, supported by White's battalion, and the two commands did all the fighting, which was not much, for the enemy fled as soon as they could get away.

On the 27th of November, Gen. Meade's army effected a crossing to the south side of the river at Germania ford, and the cavalry were kept busy, night and day, watching his movements, but Gen. Rosser did not confine himself to watching alone, for on passing Spottsylvania C. H., he sent Lieut. Conrad, with Town H. Vandevanter, "Jack" Dove and Ed. Poland, to find the force and position of the enemy, with orders to report to him at Todd's Tavern, and at the same time put Col. White in front with his battalion, and marched as rapidly as possible towards the plank road.

On arriving at Todd's Tavern, about midnight, and hearing nothing from Conrad, the general sent Capt. Myers out alone on one road, and Sergt. Everhart with a squad on another, telling them to find the Yankees and report as soon as they possibly could. Both of these scouts found the enemy very soon, and returned, and Col. White, in his ranging around through the pines, came upon a large cavalry camp not over a mile from the general's headquarters.

About an hour before day the Yankees were discovered on the road leading from Todd's Tavern to the plank road, and soon after it was ascertained that their wagon train was on the plank road. At daylight all the Yankees moved off towards Chancellorsville, and Gen. Rosser started his brigade for the train, which he cut exactly in two, bringing out eighteen ambulances and about one hundred wagons and teams, besides setting fire to a large number of wagons that had passed the side road too far to turn off, and as it was soon discovered that some of the burning wagons were loaded with ammunition, the raid terminated suddenly.

Lieut. Conrad and his party came in about sunrise, having gotten in among the Yankees and staid there all night, not knowing the country, and were very nearly being captured several times. They fought out of one difficulty with the 1st Jersey Cavalry, and passing on, charged and captured some prisoners from another regiment, finally coming out at the Court-house, where they had started from in the evening. When Conrad came up to Rosser in the morning the general asked him why he didn't report the night before, according to orders, but when

139

the lieutenant explained to him that he had got into a place where he couldn't report to anybody but Gen. Meade's people, he excused him.

On the morning of the 29th, Rosser marched his command to Parker's Store, on the plank road, and found the enemy encamped there, when he at once opened the fight, by charging them, with the 7th regiment, which drove them from their camps, and in the chase many prisoners were taken, but heavy reinforcements came up and the fight was obstinate and severe for two hours. At one time a strong force of the enemy's dismounted men took position on Rosser's left, at a high bank of the Rail Road, with their flanks protected by swamps, heavy timber, and dense undergrowth.

This force General Rosser ordered Col. White to charge, which he did, the battalion going into it in gallant style, and not only driving more than three times their number from the Rail Road, but pressing them through the thick timber until the marsh became too soft for their horses to go farther, when the men were rallied and reformed, and on reaching the plank road the balance of the brigade was found hotly engaged with a greatly superior force, and being forced back over the Rail Road. Here again the battalion charged just in time to save the brigade from rout, and all together drove the Yankees clear of the road.

When the battle was over the colonel reported to Gen. Rosser how he had "unjointed" the Yankees, and the general gave the battalion the name of "Comanches," which stuck to them during the remainder of the war.

On the night of the 30th, Meade went back to his own side of the river so quietly that it was almost daylight before the movement was discovered, but as soon as Gen. Stuart found they were on the move he ordered all his cavalry forward, and harassed their rear-guard severely.

The battalion, with the exception of Co. A, now returned to their old camp near Hamilton's Crossing, and found the quartermaster's department moved for safety towards Richmond, in consequence of which neither rations nor forage was issued for several days, and both men and horses suffered for the necessaries of life.

Company A was detailed to picket on the river at Gold Mine, Ely's, Germania, Banks', and United States fords, and this, too, in the country that had been devastated by the great battle of Chancellorsville, so that they suffered more for supplies than the others, but they opened negotiations with the Yankees on the other side of the river, by which much trading of tobacco for coffee and crackers was effected, and the

GENERAL WARREN'S TROOPS ATTACKING AT THE BATTLE OF MINE RUN, NOV. 27-DEC. 2, 1863

blue and gray pickets would mount their horses and meet in the middle of the river, where they would confer in as friendly a manner as near neighbours generally do.

White's battalion was very poorly prepared for a winter campaign, or even for winter quarters, and seeing that there was not much prospect for improvement the men became very much dissatisfied.

All their tents had been stored near Mount Crawford, in the Valley, at the time of General Jones' march to Brandy Station, and in the preparation for the Pennsylvania campaign, General Lee had cut transportation so low that only one wagon for baggage was allowed to the battalion, in consequence of which, a great quantity of it was stored for safety at Flint Hill, and fully expecting to find that as they had left it, the men had come out from their homes with almost nothing except what they wore; but on reaching Flint Hill they found that the people around that country had appropriated everything of value, only leaving for the depositors a few camp kettles, with the bottoms knocked out, and some scraps of leather that had formerly been valises.

As an evidence that citizens had stolen the property, Lieut. Conrad found one of his shirts on the person of an old citizen, who stoutly swore that the shirt was always his, but the lieutenant proved his claim and made the gentleman "come out of it."

The men clung to the hope that the brigade would be sent to the valley, but after the last advance and retreat of Gen. Meade, their camp appeared to be permanently established and their hope died. The colonel used every means in his power to procure from the government the much-needed supply of clothing, but notwithstanding the battalion had never received anything of the kind from that source, nor even drawn the commutation allowed in lieu thereof, under the law, he only succeeded after many trials in getting about one-fourth the necessary quantity, and as a consequence much discomfort, and in many cases actual suffering prevailed during the cold December of 1863.

Under such circumstances as these, the spirit of discontent culminated in the Loudoun companies, and on the night of the 14th, about sixty of A and C took a regular "French leave" and went home, determined to supply themselves with winter clothing, no matter what might be the consequences of their desertion, and we will there leave them for a time, in order to tell of an event that had a brightening effect upon the heart of every man in the Ashby brigade, which was an order for General Rosser to march his command to the Valley.

6TH CORPS TROOPS AT GERMANNA FORD RETURNING FROM BATTLE OF MINE RUN

On the night of the 18th December, the brigade crossed the Rappahannock at Fredericksburg and moved to Stafford C. H., where it encamped until morning, when the march was resumed, and all day long, through a drenching rain, the Valley men travelled on without a halt until about 11 o'clock at night, when they reached a fortified camp of the enemy at Sangster Station, on the Manassas Gap Rail Road, about twenty miles from Alexandria. Capt. Dan. Hatcher, with his squadron, (1st of 7th Regiment,) immediately charged through a stream of water and over the Rail Road bank, gaining the enemy's rear, but was met by such a heavy force in the breastworks that he was unable to return, and the 11th Regiment dashed forward in a wild, reckless charge, which forced the Yankees to surrender, and released Hatcher and his boys from their perilous position.

The command marched on from Sangster as rapidly as possible, and on reaching Bull Run, about two miles from Centreville, found that stream almost impassable from the continuous rain which had been pouring down for nearly twenty-four hours, and with the greatest difficulty the crossing was effected, but just when the rear guard reached the stream a party of Yankees came down from Centreville, which produced a panic, and in the confusion some of White's men were knocked from their horses into the stream.

The night was excessively dark, and the country totally unknown to the men, and as the head of the column had waited for nothing, but marched quickly on as soon as the swollen stream was passed, the panic was increased by the fast riding of those who got across, and when Col. White got his men over there was no sign of the brigade nor any indication of the route it had taken, while the firing in the rear showed that the Yankees were coming up.

The colonel sent a courier to the general for assistance and on reaching the turnpike found the 12th regiment waiting for him, and order being now restored the command marched quietly on; but the wind had sprung up keen and cold from the northwest, causing the rain to freeze as it fell, and almost depriving the men of the power to keep their saddles, so intense was the cold, but as best they could the dismal march was continued, and at daylight the command reached Middleburg, in Loudoun County, and pushing on to Upperville halted to feed and rest, having travelled over ninety miles during twenty-four hours, with no halt except at Sangster, where one man was killed, and several wounded in the 7th and 11th regiments, and about two hundred Yankees killed, wounded, and captured.

When the brigade reached Upperville the run-away boys from the battalion, who had come by way of Greene County and Luray Valley, were just coming in, and not wishing to risk so much to get home and be met and arrested by their command at the door, they had to go back into the mountain and wait awhile; so that those who came around with the brigade got home earlier than they who had been on the road four days longer.

Many hardships were experienced in reaching the valley, even when so near it, because the Shenandoah was too full to cross with safety, and the general marched to a ford above Swift Run Gap before he could get his people over, and after this came down the valley to Mount Jackson, where he encamped, in the coldest weather, for about a week, when he set out for a raid in the Moorfield Valley and on the B. & O. Railroad, but owing to the extremely bad roads and intensely cold weather his command was unable to execute the general's plans, and he returned to camp with the fruits of some slight successes, including a number of prisoners and a few wagons, captured near Burlington, and with many of his men frost-bitten, some of them badly.

The camp was now at Timberville, in Shenandoah County, and here the colonel exerted himself to induce the deserters from Co.'s A and C to return to the battalion. These men had been told that it was the intention of the officers to arrest and bring them before a general court martial that would certainly sentence some of them to be shot, and when Col. White sent a messenger to them entreating them to return to their duty, they returned for answer that they were willing and anxious to do so, and had no idea of escaping punishment, but that they would never come back if there was a prospect of any of them being shot, and that if the colonel would send Captain Myers to them with an assurance that they should not go before a court martial that had power to inflict the death penalty, they would all return with him.

Accordingly, Capt. M. was detailed to proceed to Loudoun and Fairfax Counties to gather up the deserters, which he did, reaching camp a few days after the brigade had started out on what was familiarly known as the "Patterson's Creek raid."

The facts of this expedition have been principally obtained from Messrs. T. H. Vandevanter, Co. A, White's Battalion, and Jas. T. Robinson, 12th Virginia Cavalry, who were couriers for Gen. Rosser, and from Lieut. Conrad and Sergt. E. L. Bennett, of Co. A.

The command moved from camp to Moorfield about the 25th of January, 1864, where it remained until Gen. Early, with a brigade of infantry and battery of artillery, came over, when it was resolved to attempt the capture of Petersburg, where a strong force of the enemy was reported to be located, and in pursuance of this plan Gen. Early marched up the right bank of the South Branch while Rosser, with his cavalry and one piece of artillery, crossed the river at Moorfield and gained the rear of Petersburg; but on reaching the top of the mountain and getting a view of the road leading to New Creek it was discovered that a long train of wagons, guarded by about 1,000 infantry, was quietly moving along towards Petersburg, and as such game was far more to Rosser's notion than laying siege to a town, he prepared to "come down on it" (to use a familiar expression of the general's).

His first step was to throw a few shells into the head of the train, which brought it to a full stop, and then to charge upon it with his "people," an operation which was entirely successful, and the whole train of ninety wagons and teams was captured, together with about two hundred of the guards, which were all the troopers could catch, as the others made such fast time to the mountain that it was given up to be folly to attempt their capture.

The train was carrying fifteen days' rations to the garrison at Petersburg, but there were also some sutler wagons along filled with the dainties and delicacies that these traveling merchants bartered to the soldiers for their pay, and Rosser's men had a "roaring night" of it.

The first squadron of the battalion, under Lieut. Conrad, was sent forward to drive a party of the enemy from Ridgeville, which was done in the same gallant style that characterized all the performances of Conrad, and the brigade moved forward in the morning to Petersburg, but found that the enemy had evacuated it by a mountain road during the night, and that Gen. Early was gone back to Moorfield, whither the captured wagons and Yankees had been sent, and now Gen. Rosser turned his column towards Patterson's Creek, sending Lieut. Conrad forward with twenty-seven men as advance guard.

On arriving at Franklin, Conrad says, they "took on wood and water," in other words, got a drink or two of whiskey all around, and here "Jim" Robinson came up with an order from Gen. Rosser to Lieut. Conrad, the substance of which was, "Go ahead to Patterson's Creek and run over everything you come to," to which Conrad replied, "All right; I'll do it;" and sending out his advance guard, composed of Robinson, Mobberly, H. C. Sellman, Bicksler, and Douglass, he moved forward briskly on his reckless mission.

Just here it is necessary to briefly call attention to Major Harry

Gilmor's statement of this affair, in his *Four Years in the Saddle,* by way of making a correction. The major says, that by Gen. Rosser's order he commanded White's first squadron in the attack on Patterson's Creek Station, but Lieut. Conrad and his men say that he did no such thing. Conrad says that Gilmor came to him on the road saying that Gen. Rosser had sent him there to get a detail of eight men to go with him to procure artillery horses, and Conrad refused positively to let him have a man until he had got through with his business, which he told him was to whip the Yankees at Patterson's Creek, when Gilmor remarked, "Very well; come on, and I'll lead you;" to which Conrad replied, "No you won't! You nor no other damned man can lead me and my men now;" and ordered his command forward again, and coming in sight of the Station the advance squad was discovered charging the Yankee vedettes, when Conrad ordered his whole party to charge, but Gilmor exclaimed, "Hold on, lieutenant; you don't know what's there!"

"No!" said Conrad, "and we don't care a damn! Forward, boys! Charge them!" and dashing in among the blue-jackets they made quick work of it, killing four, wounding six, and capturing forty-two of the fifty-two infantry soldiers stationed there.

Soon after this, Gen. Rosser rode up and asked hastily, "Where are the Yankees?" To which Conrad's men replied, "Here are the *prisoners.*"

Lieut. Conrad says, that there were desperate attempts on the part of some of the men to burn a large brick water tank at the Station, while others set fire to the Rail Road bridge and tried to learn how often they could ride over it on a hand car before it fell in, but the main body engaged in securing the plunder, of which there was a great quantity.

After damaging the Rail Road as much as possible and securing all the plunder and prisoners, the column turned towards home, but on reaching the graded road from New Creek to Romney, some scouts reported to Gen. Rosser that Kelly was advancing with five regiments of mounted infantry to cut him off, while other scouts reported that Averill, with his command, had reached Burlington.

The situation was not very pleasant now and Rosser turned back, but he soon struck a new mountain road, and ordering White to take the front, pushed rapidly forward, coming out on the grade about four miles east of Burlington, and here Lieut. Conrad and John Stephenson, who had been scouting, reported the road barricaded and campfires in front. Col. White advanced cautiously to the barricade, and finding no enemy there he approached the camp-fires, but they, too, were deserted, and he soon learned that Averill had marched from them only half an hour before, under the impression that Rosser was marching on Cumberland. This left the road clear, and now the raiders moved quietly along once more, and took with them a large drove of cattle, marching until late in the night, when the general halted his people, but had them moving again by dawn.

The Yankees soon learned that their game had slipped them and turned to follow, but all the circumstances in the case showed that they didn't care to overtake them, and Averill's march from Burlington was evidently made to avoid contact with Rosser, for he simply moved out of the road and when the rebel brigade had passed he quietly fell in the rear and made no sign of attack until Rosser reached Moorfield, when he drove in the Confederate pickets, but refused most positively to touch the tempting bait by which General Rosser tried to entice him in reach of Early's infantry, who were still at this place.

Averill's infantry came to the support of his cavalry, but no inducement could make them do anything but skirmish, and finally Rosser ordered Col. White to charge them, but recalled the order just as the battalion was ready to start, and now everything—the ninety wagons, three hundred cattle, and two hundred and fifty prisoners—being safely moving on the road to the Valley, Gen. Rosser wheeled his brigade into marching column, and followed "Old Jubal," leaving White in the rear to amuse Gen. Averill. As soon as he was gone, the Yankees charged into town and chased a few vedettes some distance up the road, but Lieut. Conrad with a party met and drove them back.

While retiring slowly towards the mountain the colonel had his horse killed dead by a sharpshooter, fully one thousand yards distant, and he would have been captured by a party of the enemy that advanced up the road, at the moment, only for the devotion of J. Clendenning, of Co. C, who dismounted and gave him his horse.

This, and the horse of John Stephenson killed in the charge at Patterson's Creek, was all the loss sustained by the battalion during the raid, and I believe not a man in the whole brigade was injured, otherwise than by taking on a little too much "wood and water" occasionally.

The battalion reached camp on the 5th of February, and on the 6th the first squadron, now under Capt. Myers, was ordered to Brock's Gap on picket, where it remained for three weeks, during which time the brigade marched to a camp near Weyer's Cave, where the colonel organised a court-martial for the trial of the deserters, and on the return of the first squadron, Company A, now having about eighty-five men, placed seventy-seven of them under arrest for absence without leave, while Co. C had all her boys, but about a dozen, in the same predicament; but the court worked fast, and soon had them all released on double duty for a month,.

For a few days only two incidents broke the monotony of the camp; the first being a grand horse race, and the second a grand speech from Capt. J. Mort. Kilgour, to the brigade, on the origin and ultimate results of the war; in which he located the origin in the "rule or ruin" spirit that made the Puritans desolate England in the days of Cromwell, and who, on the overthrow of their power there by the death of their leader, emigrated to America; and with prophetic finger he raised the curtain from the future and showed its ultimate results to be the abolition of negro slavery and the Christianisation of Africa.

On the 29th of February a report reached the general, about 9 o'clock at night, that a grand raid on Richmond, under Kilpatrick and Dahlgren, was in progress, and hastily calling out his "people," Rosser marched all night through a freezing rain, over the mountain to Charlottesville, reaching that place about noon, March 1st.

As the part taken by Rosser's brigade in this most intolerable piece of audacious foolishness, on both sides, was of little importance, I shall merely give a brief journal of the marching and counter-marching from the outset.

March 2nd.—Marched from Charlottesville, by Gordonsville, and encamped near Orange Springs about 10 o'clock, p. m. Got corn, per M. G. Hatcher, from Gen. Lee's headquarters.

March 3rd.—Left camp early, and wound around on a very cold trail after Kilpatrick. Halted 8 miles from Spottsylvania C. H., about 3 o'clock, to feed. Mounted at sunset and travelled all night, reaching Hanover Junction at 9 o'clock a. m., March 4th, and at 3 o'clock moved down to 6 miles of Richmond. Raining very hard, and nobody knows where Kilpatrick is.

March 5th.—Lying in camp all day and the rain pouring down. Drew three days rations of corn meal and bacon—about enough for three meals.

March 6th.—Still in camp. Four orders to saddle up and move, and four countermands. Plenty of horse feed, by stealing a little.

149

Monday, March 7th.—Moved out this morning on the road to the Valley, passing up the Rail Road by Beaverdam to Bumpas Station, 16 miles below Louisa C. H., and encamped. Yanks have burned all the Rail Road wood and buildings at Beaverdam, and tore up the rails.

March 8th.—Nothing to eat, and raining fast. Marched to Louisa C. H. and laid over. Still no rations.

March 9th.—Came to Gordonsville and camped. Drew some mule meat and hard-tack about four o'clock—first rations since 7th.

March 10th.—Lying in camp all day near the nastiest and meanest hole in the Southern Confederacy, to wit: Gordonsville. Found a grocery store and bought it out. Cheese, $10 per pound. Butter, $10. Ground Peas, $1.50 per quart. Tobacco, $5 per plug. Lead pencils, $3 each.

March 11th.—Still at this sweet-scented little place waiting for something to turn up, which it did, about 4 p. m., in the shape of an old, long-legged, razor-backed, slab-sided, black sow, poorer than Pharaoh's kine, and the last one left in the county, but we killed and eat her, and the only meat we've had since the mule gave out.

March 12th.—Left camp at sunrise, and marched by Orange Springs to plank road, thence by the old familiar Parker's Store to Chancellorsville, and encamped upon the famous battlefield.

March 13th.—Marched at sunrise, and tonight went into the same old camp at Gordonsville.

March 14th.—In camp at Gordonsville. No rations.

March 15th.—In camp at Gordonsville. More mule.

March 16th.—Marched through Charlottesville and camped. Weather cold as Christmas.

March 17th.—Moved early by Hillsboro', Afton, Brown's Gap, to Waynesborough.

March 18th.—Marched at sunrise through Greenville to camp near Brownsburg, and the Kilpatrick-Dahlgren campaign is ended; the Yankee nation is indelibly disgraced by the objects of the expedition, and Stuart's laurels wilted by his failure to annihilate the whole party.

On the 31st of March the battalion moved its camp, passing Lexington and halting at a superb place for a camp about eight miles from the Natural Bridge, and now the men prepared for winter quarters at last, when the winter was almost over, but as they were always hungry it may well be imagined that their enjoyment was limited. The ration was reduced, by Gen. Lee's order, to a quarter of a pound of meat and one pound of meal per day, and this *always* fell short by our Quartermaster's scales; nor did the horses fare better, for with no hay at all they only got seven ears of corn a day; and the Southern soldiers often seriously doubted if the Revolutionary Fathers could show a record of greater privations than they endured.

If the old Continentals were often without shoes many a barefoot Confederate could say "so am I;" and if the Continentals often suffered for food, the Confederates could point to many harassing scenes when, as Captain Grubb said of Brandy Station, "they fought all day before breakfast and went on picket all night before supper;" and although there were often heard complaints bitter and loud from the poorly-clad, ill-fed, and bad-sheltered soldiers of Dixie, it is doubtful if the Continentals themselves in their dark hours evinced greater fortitude, endurance, and devotion, than they.

And the history of the war that *shall* be written fairly when the clouds of prejudice and passion, that now hide the fame of the Confederates, have blown away, will show before God and the true world a picture of unselfish patriotism as bright as ever crowned victory with glory or lighted the gloom of defeat with honour, but such thoughts as these have no true place in this history, and only show that the clouds are still unbroken.

The month of April, 1864, was passed very pleasantly, notwithstanding the privations that naturally fall to the lot of men who support an impoverished cause; and when, on the 27th, the baggage accumulated during the winter was stored away at Waynesborough, the soldiers felt that in the approaching campaign the question of independence or subjection would be decided, and they prepared for it with hopeful hearts, for they believed their cause was just, and their faith in Gen. Lee was unbounded.

White had moved from his Lexington camp on the 25th, to the Saltpetre works, near Waynesborough, where the battalion remained until the 1st day of May, when the brigade was ordered to cross the mountain and join the army on the Rappahannock, but just before marching Co. D was disbanded and its members became absorbed by the other companies.

The reason of this was that it had no officers and very few men for

151

duty, and all who remained earnestly desired to disband.

The command moved quietly over the Blue Ridge into Greene County, and learned that Gen. Grant's army was crossing the river, and that Gen. Lee was preparing everything for the inevitable meeting with the foe, and strange enough there were no murmurs now, as in all such movements, from the men of Rosser's brigade, about leaving the bright Shenandoah Valley, for they seemed to have learned from the experience that they were soldiers, subject to the powers that be, and whether they approved or not they *must* obey orders.

On the march an incident occurred in Co. F, of the battalion, which, although condemned generally at the time, proved to be highly beneficial in its results. This company had been without an actual commanding officer during almost the whole time of its connection with the battalion, until the promotion of Capt. French, and he had found it an extremely difficult task to bring many of the men into any sort of subjection to discipline.

On the night of the first encampment in Greene County, the captain had given positive orders that no man should leave the camp without permission, but so far from the order being obeyed, it was hardly spoken before some of his men were gone, and remained out all night. In the morning, as they returned, Capt. French met one of them and inquired where he had been, to which the soldier replied, "Out in the country to stay all night."

"Did you not hear my order last night?" asked the captain.

"Yes, but I don't mind orders when I want to go anywhere," was the answer; but it was scarcely given before the captain's sabre came down on his head, and the man fell badly hurt. This created great excitement in the company, and while most of them joined in a petition to the captain to resign, some of them threatened him with personal violence; but when he heard of it he came out among the men alone, and proposed to give any or all of them the satisfaction they required, and awed by his fearless manner, all of them to a man submitted the case without a trial, and ever afterwards Capt. French's orders were law in Co. F, and as has been stated, from being a very inefficient company, he raised it to the position of a first-class one for its numbers, but he never used his sabre on his own men afterwards.

On the evening of May 4th, the "Comanches" encamped in the pines on the Cataupin road, near the right of Gen. Lee's army, and about six miles from Orange C. H.

15: The Laurel Brigade

The morning of May 5th opened calm and still, and there was no sign by which men could judge of the bloody day before them, for literally all was "quiet along the lines," but the quiet of the scene was oppressive in its extreme stillness, and the sun rolled like an immense ball of barely red hot iron, seeming to be almost touching the tops of the pine trees under which lay the "Laurel Brigade," unrefreshed by even the quiet repose of the past night, and many remarks were made about the singular appearance of the Day God as he waded higher and higher through the still, smoke-laden air of that battle-morn, some of the men repeating the Napoleonic exclamation, "*remember the sun of Austerlitz*," and Colonel White declaring that it presaged a bloody day.

Soon after sunrise the command moved slowly down the Cataupin road, and in an hour the dismounted men were skirmishing with the enemy in the dense thickets of pine and undergrowth which closely bordered the road on either side and extended towards the river by Shady Grove and White Hall, but the battalion was not engaged, although rapidly marched from wing to wing, expecting each moment to be thrown upon the Yankee line, and not knowing just where the blue would break through the gray and compel a cavalry charge to drive them back, for the firing each moment grew in volume and intensity until the fight raged fiercely all along the lines.

At this time the battalion was out of ammunition, and although details had been sent to the ordnance trains frequently, they always returned with the same aggravating report that none was to be procured, as the cavalry train had not yet come up, and under the circumstances the men watched with a far deeper interest than usual the progress of the battle. About the middle of the day Capt. Emmett, Rosser's A. A. General, and Jim Robinson, the general's pet courier, came from the front, both badly wounded, and told White's men that the Yankees were reinforcing and they would soon have to charge, but about 2 o'clock General Rosser succeeded in driving the Yankees from their position, and at once pushed his brigade rapidly forward.

Just as the battalion came in range of the enemy's batteries the column halted, and for several minutes the situation was decidedly hot, the shells exploding precisely at that point, and causing the loss of several men and horses; but pretty soon one of the advance regiments drove off the annoying battery, and the whole column moved quickly forward over the Po River, where they struck a considerable force of the enemy, which, after a sharp fight, was completely routed, and Rosser's men followed the retreating Yankees at a gallop, by some plantation roads and swamp paths, far to the left, bringing up at a body of woods on a hill about a mile from the river they had just crossed, and still on the Cataupin road, not far from Todd's Tavern, having made a circuit in the chase of about three miles.

The men had become very much scattered in the rapid ride through such a country, and White's people, being in the rear, were of course worse strung out than any others, in fact when the head of the first squadron (which by the evolutions on the other side of the river had been thrown in rear of the battalion) came up to the woods, where a division of the enemy's cavalry had met and engaged the brigade in a fierce and stubborn fight, there were scarcely a dozen men in sight, and Capt. Myers called a halt in order to allow the others time to close up, as the front of the battalion was hid from view in the thick woods, but Gen. Rosser, who was sitting on his horse near the road, listening to the rapid firing in front of him, called out, excitedly, "Let 'em out, Myers; let 'em out! Old White's in there, knocking them right and left."

And with a wild yell Company A dashed forward, wheeling to the left as it reached the road, the captain supposing he could thus come down upon the right flank of the enemy, but they had scarcely gone one hundred yards when a piece of artillery, hidden in the pines on the road side, blazed a storm of grape into the column, which for a minute checked its progress, and by the time the squadron was ready to charge the masked battery, it was limbered up and moved rapidly away, barely escaping capture. The first squadron then joined the battalion, finding it hotly engaged with fully six times its number, and for want of ammunition being slowly driven back.

The enemy had attempted repeatedly to charge, but was met and repulsed every time, and in this rally and retreat style of fighting, individuals on both sides displayed great skill and courage, but the fight was altogether on horseback, and as in the days when Cavalier and Puritan met in the conflict long ago, so it was now with their descendants, and the superiority of Southern horsemanship gave the advantage to that side, but it was the only one it did possess. Many prisoners were taken by White's men, and the first demand was always for their cartridges and their arms afterwards, and every bullet thus taken from the captured Yankees was soon returned to their comrades, minus the powder however.

After an hour of hard fighting, a flank movement forced them almost to the edge of the woods on the hill before spoken of, and the men, discouraged because of their lack of ammunition, were ready to give up the fight, which the enemy did not show much disposition to press further, but the officers rallied them for another trial.

The battalion was drawn up alongside of the road, and as a regiment of Yankees galloped down in their front, Capt. Myers turned to Col. White, and asked, "Colonel, how can we fight those fellows with no ammunition? We'd as well have rocks as empty pistols."

But the colonel replied so grimly, "What are our sabres for?" that the men drew their blades without any hesitation, and charged square at the Yankee column, which wheeled about and retired faster than it came, closely pursued by the "Comanches," but after going about half a mile a force of the enemy was observed moving through the pines to the right and rear of the battalion, and Capt. Myers, with Jack Dove and Jim Whaley, turned towards them and firing with captured pistols as rapidly as possible, called loudly for "first squadron," "second squadron," &c., to "forward" and "charge," making so much noise in the operation, that the Yankees halted and opened a sharp fire upon what they supposed to be at least a rebel regiment, and shortly after, the colonel returned with the battalion and the enemy retired over the hill.

This ended the fighting for that evening, with the exception of some slight skirmishing as the brigade retired over the Po River to Shady Grove, where it encamped for the night.

The battalion did not number over one hundred and fifty men in the last charge, about twenty having been killed and wounded, and quite a number (as is usually the case) were reported in the list of "missing in action;" but only one was never heard of afterwards, (John J. Clendenning of Co. C,) and it was supposed that he had fallen into the hands of the enemy after being wounded, and died either in hospital or prison.

The hard work for both men and horses, had told grievously on the little band of "Comanches," and they all hoped that they would not be called upon to leave their camp the next day, but by sunrise on the morning of the 6th, the bugles were sounding to horse, and very soon the old Ashby brigade was moving on the same Cataupin road towards Todd's Tavern—names long ago made familiar and famous in the annals of the war.

After crossing again the Po River, on the same crazy, rickety bridge, over that chocolate-coloured stream, which with the "Matt," "Tay," and "Nye" Rivers, form the now celebrated "Mattapony," the column turned to the left, leaving the battle-ground of the preceding evening about half a mile to the right, and when the gates, fields and fences of the Chancellor plantation had been cleared, and the brigade was marching easily and freely through the open pine country bordering on the "Wilderness," General Rosser ordered Col. White to "send his best squadron to the front," when the colonel told Capt. Myers to take his company and report to the general.

As before remarked, Company A was now the first squadron, it being a large and unusually full company, and the small company (D) which formerly with A composed the squadron having been disbanded, and also, besides thus being the easiest handled, was at the head of the column, causing it to be selected to fill the rather invidious order of the general.

As the captain rode forward and reported for special duty, the general gave his order, which was, *verbatim*, "Myers, move your people down this road and run over everything you come to. I'll send a pilot with you." "The people" moved in lively style along the road, which now bore to the right and more in the direction of the previous day's fighting, when they commenced to pass evidences of panic on the part of the "boys in blue," in the shape of gum cloths, blankets, carbines, hats and saddles, and thinking that as Yankee plunder was plenty, the men who left it were out of the way, they moved too fast, and the general sent one of his staff with orders to go slower and not get too far from the brigade.

At length, after crossing a swampy stream and marching quietly along the left of a sedgy old field, in which some Yankees were discovered about a hundred and fifty yards to the right, and who began sending their compliments from Spencer and Sharpe, the squadron found that their road forked at the corner of the field, and not knowing which to take, Myers halted and called for his pilot, but not finding him, Jim Harper, in his peculiar style, reported that "the dam 'scape gallus had picked up a saddle at the branch, and as soon as the first shot was fired in the field had carried it to the rear like the devil."

The men in the field had now stopped firing and gone into the woods, and Myers asked Lieut. Conrad which road he thought they had better take, to which the lieutenant replied "that it didn't make much difference, so they got to the Yankees," when the captain turned the head of the column to the right, and with the command, "Forward, boys; and get ready to fight," marched down the side of the field

156

about a hundred yards, and looking back saw Col. White, with the battalion, moving quietly from the woods at the branch and turning into the field.

Fifty yards further brought the first squadron to a point where the road turned abruptly from the field into the woods, and with a rattling, whizzing blaze of carbines they were received by a squadron of the enemy not twenty steps distant. The fire was instantly returned, and a charge made, when the Yankees broke and as rapidly as possible fell back upon their supporting regiment, which in turn gave way before the dashing charge of the victorious rebels.

Just here the enemy moved forward a heavy line of cavalry, said by prisoners to be two divisions, and Col. White went in with his battalion in his usual "neck or nothing" style, but not being supported, was in a few minutes so roughly handled that it was with great difficulty his people got clear of the swarming masses of Yankees that lined all the space from woods to stream. The colonel's horse was killed, the adjutant's horse was killed, and in trying to save his papers which were fastened on the saddle, that gallant officer was captured.

Several men were killed and wounded in this desperate charge, and the enemy dashed after the retreating Confederates until met by the 11th Regiment, which only checked them and gave way when the 12th and 7th Regiments were, in detail, met and driven back by the overwhelming forces of the Yankees.

But just at this moment the ubiquitous Col. Chew threw his horse artillery into position and poured such a storm of grape and shell into the crowded columns of blue-jackets, that they were in turn forced to retire and let their own artillery come into the fight. The Yankee batteries were posted in a semi-circle, with their right wing thrown forward, and the fiery Capt. Thompson had a red-hot position for his guns, but like the hero he was he held it, and his cannoneers, like smiths at their forges, laboured incessantly in the unequal fight, amid the baleful death-fires that surrounded them. There are two expressions in the military vocabulary that describe situations usually fatal to the party occupying them, the first of which is that terrible word "flanked," and the second "artillery cross-fire," carries with it almost equal dread, and this second is what tried the metal of the boys of Chew and Thompson that day, but they were proof-steel.

However, it is not with the Stuart Horse Artillery that we have to deal now, and to return to the 35th Battalion. As soon as the artillery had checked the enemy, the colonel commenced to rally and form his people in rear of the battery as a support to it, but no one thing in the duty of an officer is harder to accomplish than to form broken troops under such a fire as now swept this same old field of sedge. All the regiments of the brigade were trying it, and with about equal success. General Stuart rode back and forth along the road in the rear, his black plume waving on the death-laden morning air, and his beautiful sword laid across his arm, doing his utmost to stop the fugitives from the terrible field, and induce them to return to their duty.

He was perfectly cool, and his calm but positive words, "You *must* go back, boys, the Yankees can't more than kill you if you fight them—and if you don't go back I'll kill you myself—better be shot by the enemy than your own men—go back, boys!" had a fine effect upon some, but the murderous cross-fire had such a demoralising power that even Gen. Lee himself could not have kept the majority of the runaways on the smoking field; and now, if the enemy had pushed forward one resolute brigade, such as Custer's was said to be, the artillery could have been captured and the victory won, but they didn't know it, and in their ignorance, and Chew's audacity, rested the salvation of Rosser's brigade.

After the cannonade had continued for perhaps half an hour, and the little line of supports to the battery had melted away almost to nothing, composed now of men from the 11th and White's battalion, the colonel resolved to bring such of the men as were lurking to rearward in the woods, into ranks again, and for this purpose ordered Capt. French, of Co. F, to cross the swamp and compel them to return. The captain demurred to the arrangement, however, fearing that those who saw him ride back would imagine he, too, was running from the fight—but no man who ever saw Marcellus French on a battlefield could possibly have entertained such a thought for even a single moment, no matter what might be the surrounding circumstances, or the business in which he might be engaged, for a more stubbornly brave man never drew a sabre, and he was by long odds the coolest man in the battalion, "as cold as ice," was the verdict passed upon him by the lamented Capt. Grubb. After a few moments' consideration, French proceeded to execute the colonel's order, and succeeded in bringing several men back to the command.

White himself was riding around arranging his people, who were all dismounted, and here was the only place he was ever seen to dodge. Shells were plunging and bursting in, around, and over the ranks every moment, and when the business of re-organising the line begun Capt.

158

Myers was placed on the right to rectify the alignment, and stood on a tussock just at the edge of a marsh. When the colonel had arranged matters to his notion he dismounted immediately in front of Myers and springing over the mud stood face to face with him on the tussock, but scarcely was he located than a shell howled wickedly past and very near their heads, when down went the colonel's head in Myers' breast, in such a manner that it was impossible for the latter to bow his acknowledgment to the savage missile, and when, a moment later, the colonel raised his head Myers was as near laughing in his face as the circumstances would permit.

White laughed and shook himself, exclaiming "I golly! I believe I'm demoralised myself," and every man there felt that they would be willing to exchange places with the famous Light Brigade at Balaklava even, for literally the guns volleyed and thundered on the right, left and front of that little band which was standing—and dying—at ease, without an opportunity to strike a blow or shelter themselves from the murderous fire that was literally ploughing the whole field with cannon shot. By-and-bye the fire became so hot that the colonel ordered his men to lie down, and just as a party of them had crowded together in a little hollow that seemed to present the best prospect for shelter, a shell shrieked among them and completely tore the head of young Broy, of Company F, from his shoulders, scattering his blood and brains in the faces of his comrades, and killing a horse by its explosion a moment after.

A considerable number of the horses were struck, and the danger from the wounded steeds was almost as great as from the shells, for a horse, as a general thing, becomes much more frantic from a wound by an exploding shell than by a bullet.

Ed. Oxley's horse was instantly killed, and he walked up to Capt. Myers to report the fact and ask what he must do, when the captain told him to take his rigging from him and go to the rear, which Oxley at once proceeded to do, but on reaching his horse found that one of the 11th regiment had already performed that duty for him, and his saddle and clothes were nowhere to be found, whereupon Oxley became decidedly the most violently excited man in the field, swearing terribly, in his peculiar style, that "any man who would steal at such a time as that ought to be hung."

The Rev. Lieut. Strickler, of Co. E, and Capt. French, both consistent members of the Methodist Church, were standing together conversing on the subject of religion when a party of the enemy's

159

sharpshooters came near enough to add their rifle bullets to the terrible storm of shell that rained around, and during the hottest of it the lieutenant was heard to remark that whatever was foreordained by the Almighty would be accomplished, and if we were intended to be killed there we couldn't help it, while, on the other hand, if our time had not yet been fulfilled according to God's predestined plan, we were safe, although a thousand cannon should open their thunder upon us; and in this comfortable doctrine (under the circumstances) the captain readily acquiesced, greatly to the gratification of Colonel White, who in religious opinion was an Old School Baptist.

About 2 o'clock the firing ceased, and the war-storm lulled to silence, allowing the soldiers a breathing spell and time to inquire for those who were missing from the ranks, and many of the brave boys who had gone gallantly into the battle that morning never came back again, for their names were dropped from the Company rolls to be recorded in the list of heroes who gave their lives for the "Lost Cause," but who made it a glorious one by its bloody baptism.

Henry Moore, one of Company A's best and bravest, and who had been with it from the beginning, had fallen in the front of the fight, shot through the brain. Joseph Hendon, a gallant young soldier, also of Company A, and a native of North Carolina, was killed in the first charge. Samuel W. Crumbaker, Company A, was mortally wounded, and Lieut. Benjamin F. Conrad, who deserved the title of "bravest of the brave," if any man ever did, was terribly wounded in the thigh, (in the first charge, when Co. A was running over "everything she came to,") which made amputation necessary, and he was never able to do duty again. Colour-Sergeant Thos. N. Torreyson, Company C, also lost a leg, and John Douglass and Hugh S. Thompson, Co. C, were killed, as was also Jacob W. Huffman, of Co. E, and quite a large number wounded, whose names, as far as ascertained, will be found at the close of the volume.

The enemy occupied the battle-ground, and of course had the dead of the Confederate cavalry in their lines, but they buried them and marked their graves so their friends could find them.

The cavalry were not the only troops engaged on that bloody day, for at every lull in the battle on the right the muskets of the infantry could be heard along the lines to the left, and during the day the report came that Gen. Longstreet had been badly wounded by his own men, which was soon confirmed, and the thoughts of the soldiers flew back to "Stonewall" Jackson, while many of them cursed the blundering carelessness of the infantry, and the recklessness of the officers, in the same breath.

There was really a vast difference between infantry and cavalry in this respect—the latter, having learned caution from outpost duty, would learn the character of an advancing party before firing, while the former, not being able to travel with the same celerity as the cavalry, nearly always fired first and inquired "Who comes there?" afterwards; a system that cost the Confederate States their independence, for if Jackson had lived, the North would have given up the fight at the close of the Battle of Gettysburg.

In about two hours after the battle ended among the cavalry, the enemy fell back, and Maj. McClellan, of Gen. Stuart's staff, called for Col. White's people to go with him and establish communication with the infantry of Gen. Longstreet on the left, and marching quietly through the blazing Wilderness, their greatest care was to prevent their own men from firing into them.

The dense body of timber through which they had to pass was all on fire, and the dead pine trees were momentarily falling like flaming columns around them, with dark masses of smoke draping the wild scene as if Nature had thrown a funeral pall over the withering tide of desolation which contending armies were sweeping athwart the land, while along the Rail Road to our right, as we marched, we knew the Yankee line of battle was waiting.

As the battalion, with great difficulty, gained the middle of this burning forest, a kind of smothered sound of marching troops was heard, and peering silently through the smoke, we soon discovered a long line of infantry in blue cautiously marching directly towards us from the right, all carrying their muskets at a shoulder arms.

They were not more than fifty yards away, and had not yet discovered us; but the distance was rapidly diminishing, and we knew that if we moved, they would see us. Pretty soon, however, an infantry soldier, in tattered gray, met Col. White and Maj. McClellan, and gave them the welcome information that himself and twenty of his people had scouted near the enemy's line, and getting on the flank of the Yankees, had captured about three hundred of them without firing a shot, and were now taking them back to Longstreet's lines, with all their arms.

In fact, just as they found them; and the Yankees were so impressed with the idea that they were now surrounded by hostile rebels that their whole attention was given to the work of convincing everybody that they were prisoners and didn't mean fight, when, in fact, they were in a gap a mile long, between the right wing and centre of Gen. Lee's army, in which there were no troops but this little force of about one hundred cavalry, who were doing their best to get out of their uncomfortably hot position. Passing on about half a mile we came out on the plank road, and after some difficulty in signalling to the grim old veterans of Longstreet's corps, who held it, that we were all right, they allowed us to come among them.

The next move was to establish vedettes through the Wilderness space we had just passed, and draw the line as near the Rail Road as possible, which was so well done that by dark White's battalion stood on the track for more than half the distance; the enemy having retired a quarter of a mile from it, and about 10 o'clock the infantry extended their lines over the whole ground, relieving the "Comanches," who now retired to their same camp at Shady Grove, and the day's work was done.

It would be useless to proclaim that these men had met the foe unflinchingly, and had braved the iron tempest of this bloody battle day with unbroken front, for this would be at once to pronounce them more than mortal, and like gods, free from all the feelings common to humanity; but we do say, that they had, like men battling for the dearest rights which were given to the race, gone through the fire in the discharge of their duty, and while some had fled in panic from the conflict, the majority had held their ground against a foe that outnumbered them twenty to one, and had only given way when it was absolute suicide to remain longer on that harvest-field of death.

16: The Wilderness

General Rosser ordered the "Comanches" to remain at the Po River bridge during the 7th, and guard it from the attacks of the enemy, who, still posted in the woods where the hard fighting was done on the evening of the 5th, showed a disposition to take the bridge. Here the colonel had some breastworks thrown up, and leaving Capt. Myers with Company A to hold the bridge, he attempted a flank movement to the right with the remainder of his battalion, hoping to capture some horses, but was unsuccessful; and during his absence the Yankees made a demonstration with dismounted cavalry on the little force at the bridge, which, however, held the position, although vigorously shelled for some time. One man was wounded slightly, and on the return of the colonel, with a piece of artillery, they gave it up, and allowed White's men to rest quietly.

On Sunday morning, May 8th, the whole brigade moved early and commenced skirmishing near Todd's Tavern, but the enemy seemed to be shifting, and not quite willing to make a stand anywhere until about 10 o'clock, when we came up with them in force and strongly posted in a heavy body of timber.

Here all the men with long-range guns were dismounted and ordered into the woods, Lieut. Thos. W. White, of Company C, commanding the sharpshooters of the battalion, and pretty soon the firing showed that a sharp fight was going on in the Wilderness.

In a few minutes the mounted men were ordered forward to charge, but the enemy retired beyond the head waters and swamp of the Nye River.

As the battalion moved forward, they met some of the sharpshooters bearing to the rear all that was left of their accomplished commander, Lieut. White, who had been shot dead by a rifleman hid in the woods, as he was arranging that part of the line immediately under his supervision. He was a native of Loudoun county, and as Lieut. Colonel of the militia at the breaking out of the war, had done all that lay in his power to aid Virginia in defending her border against the Northman's ire, but at the time of the evacuation of Manassas and all the lines of defence held in connection with it by the Southern Army, he and Mr. A. M. Vandevanter were engaged in the work of trying to raise a company of volunteer cavalry, and not being posted as to the sudden fall back, was unfortunately left in the hostile lines of Geary before he knew it; but when Capt. Grubb commenced to recruit for his company, Lieut. Col. White was the first to join him, and at the organisation was appointed Orderly Sergeant, discharging his duties faithfully until the death of Capt. Grubb and consequent promotion of the other officers caused his election to the office of Second Lieutenant.

Lieut. White and the colonel were not on entirely friendly terms, for the reason that when the latter was raising his company, the lieutenant caused some opposition, by objecting to the men enlisted by the colonel being excused from duty as militia until the company was organised and in actual service.

This caused a coolness which was not fully dissipated until, in the tremendous Battle of Brandy Station, Lieut. White displayed such conspicuous gallantry that he completely gained the colonel's confidence and good will, and was ever after considered by his commander one of the best officers in the battalion, as he fully deserved to be.

One little incident connected with this, his last day of life on earth, would seem to indicate that he felt a presentiment of his fate, for while riding down to his death, he and Capt. Myers were discussing an order of the general's to the effect that the battalion should be armed with long-range guns, and both agreed that they very much objected, for the reason that they disliked fighting on foot, but the lieutenant remarked that if he should ever be dismounted and sent into that Wilderness country there to fight, that he would certainly be killed, for it would so excite him that he would not understand how to act; and when the order was given for the men to dismount, and he was designated to lead them, he said to the captain as he passed to the front, in allusion to their conversation, "Goodbye, Frank; I am going, and don't expect to see you anymore;" and there we saw for the last time the gay, high-spirited and popular Lieut. Tom White.

From this time until the 21st, the battalion was occupied, with the brigade, in picketing and skirmishing, varied with occasional scouts, in one of which the colonel took a part of his command by the left flank to the rear of Grant's army, visiting three large field hospitals, in which lay thousands of wounded men whose discharges from the service had been issued from the muzzles of Confederate rifles, and on this trip the boys broke up nearly 2,000 stand of arms.

All this while the infantry were passing through that tremendous ordeal of fire which has made the Spottsylvania Wilderness famous for all time in the bloody history which marks the progress of the world from the days of old down to the present, and if ever hard, stubborn fighting deserved success, the army of Lee in those May days of 1864 earned it, for every day the same awful roar of battle rolled along the lines, and every night came the same encouraging reports of the enemy repulsed with heavy slaughter, until it was a given up point that soon Grant would stop his "hammering," for the good reason that the hammer was shivered to atoms on the solid anvil of Southern endurance and grit, but the national butcher kept throwing his doomed legions upon the invincible veterans of Gen. Lee, and supplying, from the teeming millions of Yankeeland and Germany, the places of the slaughtered men in blue, and day after day the hateful gridiron of the Yankee nation floated along the Rappahannock, telling that the war was not over yet.

On the 15th of May, Gen. Rosser marched to Enan Church, near the plank road, where he fought hard for an hour, to find if the enemy had infantry in that neighbourhood, which proved to be the case.

Some of the boys said he only took the brigade down to hold the usual Sunday morning service, as the general had recently joined the Episcopal Church, but others remarked that he made a mistake in the prayer book, as Colt's was not generally used in that church. The night before had been spent by Company A on picket in the Wilderness, and as the author witnessed the performance, it will not be amiss to describe it, showing as it does one part of the soldier's duty, and the manner in which it was performed in that God-forsaken country which is fit for nothing but a battlefield, and the worst one imaginable for that. The company reached the picket line on the Cataupin road about dark, and the night set in rainy, and black as Erebus by the time the posts were established.

There it was necessary to picket all around, and having at length got everything arranged, the reserve lay down on pieces of cracker boxes, an immense number of which were scattered around, for headquarters was established at what had been a field hospital for the 5th and 6th of May.

Nobody was permitted to unsaddle, of course, and without blankets the night was unpleasant enough, but pretty soon firing was heard towards the river, and by the time the pickets came in the company was mounted and ready for action, but no enemy appeared, and soon the line was re-established, only to be broken again in a few minutes, and the same ceremony of preparation for fight gone through with, which ended as before, without it.

This was done several times, and finally two men who never yet experienced the sensation of fear, were placed at the same post, which appeared to be the very centre of the Wilderness. These two men were John W. White and John Chadwell, and pretty soon firing was heard at their post, when all the pickets came in except the two who were supposed to have done the shooting, and after waiting in line of battle for some time, Capt. Myers ordered the corporal, to whose relief they belonged, to ride out and see what was the matter, but that gentleman flatly refused to go, declaring his belief that the Yankees had killed the pickets and were waiting now to shoot whoever went to look for the missing men.

After a little hesitation, the captain concluded to go himself, and riding cautiously along the crooked woods-path soon came up to the two men, who halted him promptly and showed that they were up to their duty, and here the captain found that these two men had captured a squad of the enemy's sharp-shooters, armed with the long-barrelled Sharpe's rifle, and who had been causing all the disturbance during the night by creeping through the thick undergrowth, in the dark and rain, trying to get away from the rebel lines they said, but continually coming in contact with skirmishers, and having to lay quiet, until they were heard by White and Chadwell, who fired on them and then charged, when they surrendered.

The captain asked his men why they didn't come in and report the cause of it, to which White replied, that "there were some more Yankees out there in the woods, and as soon as they caught them, "Chad" was going to take the whole squad in together."

The captain went back and told the company to "go to sleep, for White and Chadwell were on picket," and taking his gum-cloth he spread it down, by feeling, at what he considered a good place for a nap, having a little mound for a pillow; and notwithstanding the offensive smell, went to sleep until daybreak, when, rousing up, he was rather non-plussed at the discovery that his pillow was a pile of amputated legs and arms, and in arm's reach of him lay the swollen, blackened corpse of a Yankee sergeant, whose thigh had been shivered by a shell.

When White and Chadwell came in, they reported total captures, in their two hours on duty, to be fourteen, and were going back to capture a squad quartered for the night in a log-cabin about a mile away, of which some of their prisoners had informed them, and taking with them two or three of the men at the reserve, they did go and capture several more.

On the 19th of May, Gen. Ewell, with part of his corps and Rosser's brigade, made a flank movement, about 4 o'clock in the evening of that rainy day, around the left wing of Grant's line, and had a very severe fight of about half an hour, in which the battalion only engaged as supports to Chew's artillery, and after Ewell had withdrawn, having learned the important fact that Grant was flanking, which was the object of his expedition, the brigade followed slowly and by dark was at its old camp near Shady Grove. The boys used to say that no matter what direction Gen. Rosser moved, during those fighting days in the Wilderness, White's battalion would surely bring up at Shady Grove, and it was true, too, for more than two weeks.

Part of the time, during this warm campaign, "the people" suffered for rations, but were generally better fed than they anticipated, and as a general thing, men under constant and high excitement require less food than at other times; in fact I have frequently seen the soldiers, while listening to details of a battle, apparently forget to eat, although they had fasted for a day; but rations was the first thought which flashed through the minds of White's battalion when the news reached them, about the 10th of May, that Sheridan's cavalry had cut the Virginia Central Rail Road, at Beaverdam Station, and destroyed fifty thousand pounds of bacon.

They had no idea of being whipped in the field, for all thought that no army commanded by "Uncle Bobby" *could* be whipped by fighting, but if starvation came upon them they knew the war must end, and when Gen. Stuart hastily gathered what force he had convenient, to go after the raiders, he had the prayers of every praying man in the Army of Northern Virginia, and the earnest wishes of all the rest, for his success.

About this time the enemy made a heavy movement on the left flank, and General Hampton, with the few cavalry left him by Stuart, had to do his best, and on the evening of the 18th ordered the battalion to support Thompson's battery which, as usual, got into a very hot place. The Cobb Legion was in front along the edge of the pines, dismounted, and the artillery on a hill something like a hundred yards in their rear, while fifty yards to the rear of the guns stood White's people, and when the swarm of Yankee infantry made their appearance the legion retired to their horses without firing a shot, but Thompson opened with grape and canister and for a short time checked the advance, but by this time the musket balls were cutting the wheels of his gun-carriages, and Rosser ordered him to retire, at the same time calling to Colonel White to move everything but one squadron and to leave that with instructions to follow the battery and save it.

The colonel called out to Captain Myers, "hold your squadron there and when the Yankees come on the hill, charge them," and moved the rest of the command to the woods on the left. The enemy's artillery, from the other side of Po River, was now firing rapidly at Thompson, and nearly every shell passed over or through the squadron, while the infantry fire was making the situation very hot, and when at length the battery did move it was found that the tongue of one of the caissons was broken, but Mec Souder, a Loudoun County man and sergeant of the battery, cut a sapling and as rapidly as possible improvised a pole which enabled him to save the caisson.

The 1st squadron then moved off, but none too soon, for as they passed the woods about a hundred yards to the left, the Yankees swarmed upon the hill, cutting General Hampton off from his command, and capturing one man of the battalion. This was looked upon by the men as decidedly the narrowest escape they had ever made, for certainly if they had remained three minutes longer not a man could have escaped, as fully ten thousand infantry would have been within less than fifty yards and the squadron would have stood exactly in the centre of their line.

These were the men who captured General Edward Johnson, of Ewell's Corps, with most of his division that same day, and they were then moving up to make their attack on the Confederate works. The cavalry halted a short distance to the left and waited for the Yankee troopers to appear, but they were all with Sheridan near Richmond.

The battalion had become so much reduced in numbers by the casualties of war that it was now formed in two squadrons, the first composed of Companies A and C, under Captains Myers and Dowdell and Lieut. Sam. Grubb, and the second, of Companies B, E and F, with Capt. French and Lieutenants Strickler, Chiswell and James for officers.

The second squadron was sent on picket to the left of the army, where it remained for some days, and on its return to the command about the 20th, the first was ordered out for a tour of duty of the same kind between Todd's Tavern and the Court House; but about 2 o'clock on the morning of the 21st received an order to join the battalion, then bringing up the rear of the army, which was moving by Spottsylvania Court-house towards the North Anna River.

The march was rather an exciting one, leading as it did over the broad battlefields of the Wilderness, where many hundreds of dead men still lay unburied, and the squadron was obliged to pass directly over them, when, as the hoofs of the horses would strike the corpses, the flesh would strip from the bones, leaving them glistening in the phosphorescent light that played around them, and the weird, ghostly influence of the scene affected the men, in the silence and gloom of that early morning, more than the presence of any number of live Yankees could have done; but the night wore away—very slowly indeed, it seemed—and by an hour after sunrise the battalion united a few miles below the Court-house, when it slowly marched along the Richmond road, still acting as rear guard for the army.

A small party of the men under Lieutenant Samuel Grubb came directly by the Court-house, barely escaping capture by the force of the enemy which occupied the village, as rear guard for Grant's army, and after passing that point they captured about a hundred stragglers, whom the lieutenant and his squad formed in line, and after breaking their guns and "going through them" for watches and greenbacks, paroled the whole party and sent them on their way rejoicing; with a net result of about a dozen brass watches that wouldn't keep time; a hundred pocket-books containing in all, probably five hundred photographs, and two dollars in five cent notes, besides a few sutler tickets.

The battalion crossed the North Anna about sunset and having no horse-feed, rode until 11 o'clock hunting for a grass field, which they at last found near Hanover Junction. For several days the old Fork Church took the place of Shady Grove, to the "Comanches," and although they might be operating along the river—on the Rail Road; or skirmishing on the Telegraph road—yet every day found them in bivouac during some part of it at the church which had stood for more than a century; its bricks having been brought from England during colonial days, and all its surroundings associated with the memory of the boyhood of Henry Clay; indeed the home of the great statesman's mother was scarce half a mile from the church, in the slashes of Hanover, where, as a boy, he cultivated corn and tobacco.

During all these days the rations were scanty, and hard in both senses of the word, but what the commissary department furnished was all that the troops could get, for the country was so impoverished, and the people so naturally shiftless, that they did not live better than the soldiers, and plentiful as were the negroes, none of them made enough to live on without stealing the corn and potatoes of the few white people who did try their best to make a sufficient quantity of provisions to subsist their families.

On the 28th of May the battalion marched with the division in the direction of Mechanicsville, and on arriving near Hawes' Shop, came in contact with a division of the enemy's cavalry. Here Chew's artillery took position on an open field about two hundred yards in front of a heavy pine forest, while the battalion, as usual, formed squadrons in the rear, to support the battery.

Just as this arrangement was completed, Gen. Hampton passed along, and saluting Col. White, exclaimed, "Good morning, colonel, we've got the Yankees where we want them now;" but in about fifteen minutes the battalion concluded that the boot was on the other foot, for the Yankees certainly had them where they didn't want to be. The storm of shot and shell that howled madly over and around them was terrific, and very soon two splendid men, Lieut. Strickler, Co. E, and Jack Howard, Co. A, were wounded, the lieutenant in the knee, and Howard in the face with the big end of an exploded shell, which came bounding along the field. Several horses were also struck, among them that ridden by Capt. Dowdell, and which had been the property of Lieut. Tom White, was killed.

Here the "new issue," a brigade of new recruits from South Carolina and Georgia, which was commanded by the veteran Gen. Butler, of South Carolina, was put, for the first time, under fire, and although their horses were stampeded and their queer bundles of clothes scattered through the pines in every direction, yet the men, fighting on foot with their long guns, stood bravely up to their work and whipped the enemy's cavalry fairly, but when the 6th Corps of Yankee infantry came against them Gen. Hampton was compelled to withdraw them from the position they had held.

The battle had lasted two hours, and when the Confederates withdrew before the heavy lines of infantry the enemy did not follow, clearly showing that they had no taste for Hampton's mode of handling cavalry.

Up to this time the cavalry corps had not learned the style of their new commander, but now they discovered a vast difference between the old and the new, for while General Stuart would attempt his work with whatever force he had at hand, and often seemed to try to accomplish a given result with the smallest possible number of men, Gen. Hampton always endeavoured to carry every available man to his point of operation, and the larger his force the better he liked it.

The advantage of this style of generalship was soon apparent, for while under Stuart stampedes were frequent, with Hampton they were unknown, and the men of his corps soon had the same unwavering confidence in him that the "Stonewall Brigade" entertained for *their* general.

This was the last battle for the month, and the battalion now went on picket until the 1st of June, engaged in frequent skirmishes with the enemy's line of vedettes, but no casualties occurred except the occasional wounding of a horse, which always caused the loss of one man for duty, for no sooner was a horse disabled than his rider applied for and received a detail to go and supply himself with another, and besides the wounded men, the number on horse-detail, as it was called, so reduced the fighting men that the whole battalion now scarcely numbered more than Co. A did at the beginning of the campaign, and officers were scarce in proportion, but on the 1st of June Lieut. Marlow, Co. A, who had been absent since February, reported for duty.

17: Trevillian Station

On the 4th of June an order was received carrying everything to the right; and Rosser's brigade moved out to "Old Church," near the Pamunky, where they found a force of Yankees behind breastworks, which the general ordered White to charge. The order was promptly obeyed without dismounting, and the Yankees fled precipitately from the rather novel scene of horsemen leaping their works, and using both steel and ball in their curious evolution, and the general's wild "Hurrah for the Comanches" was re-echoed from the whole brigade who witnessed the operation.

On the 8th, an order to prepare three day's rations, was sent around to the different commands; and many were the rumours of what Sheridan's cavalry was going to do on the Virginia Central Rail Road. But nothing positive was learned as to the destination or object of the expedition for which Hampton was preparing, but all the Valley brigade concurred in the opinion that anything was better than campaigning in that hateful pine country, where no glimpse of the Blue Ridge could be had.

At daylight on the 9th, the command left the camp at Atlee's Station, and took up the line of march along the Rail Road, encamping that night at Beaver Dam, where they drew four days rations of bacon and "hard tack," making six days on hand, and on the 10th, at dawn, they moved slowly towards Louisa Court-house, where they arrived about 2 o'clock, p. m., and learned that Sheridan was marching with his whole force along the north bank of the North Anna River, and aiming for the junction of the Rail Roads at Gordonsville, where he was going to whip Hampton, and then branch off towards Lynchburg to co-operate with Hunter, who was moving his army from the valley to take that city, and thereby cut off a large portion of Lee's supplies, compelling him to give up Richmond, and either surrender or retreat along the Weldon Rail Road into North Carolina.

How all this information was obtained, nobody could tell, but nearly all the men accepted it as a fair statement of the problem to be worked out, and it will be observed that the success of the whole train of operations depended upon Hampton's receipt of the prescribed whipping at Gordonsville, of which his "people" were extremely doubtful, for "old Wade" had never been whipped yet, nor did they think Sheridan was the man to do it, even though he had command of all the cavalry in the United States.

The night of the 10th Gen. Hampton's own division, now commanded by Gen. Butler, went into camp near Trevillian Station, on the Rail Road, and in the early morning Gen. Rosser moved his brigade up to the road leading off to the left into the Green Spring Valley—the most lovely of all the beautiful Virginia country. Here he made a detail from the several regiments, and sent it, under command of Lieut. Col. Ball, 11th Virginia, towards Gordonsville, while with the brigade he halted very quietly, and waited for whatever duty circumstances might bring him.

It may not be amiss here to give a statement, as the writer understood them in the light of after events, of General Hampton's plans, and his reasons for them, as by this means the reader will better understand the operations about to be described, and which had such a mighty influence in prolonging the defence of the Confederate Capitol. In the first place, then, Gen. Hampton's force was vastly inferior to Sheridan's, not only in point of numbers, but in arms and equipments.

The United States cavalry was splendidly armed with the improved repeating rifles of Spencer and Henry, besides their revolvers, while the Confederates, as a general thing, carried only the ordinary Sharpe's carbine and sabre, and many of them had nothing better than the common infantry musket; in fact, Rosser's brigade was the only one in the division thoroughly armed with revolvers and improved carbines, and these they had captured from the enemy, as the Confederacy was too poor and unskilled in the manufacture of arms to keep pace with their wealthy and ingenious opponents, who also had open ports through which to receive the best supplies of the Old World, and money to buy what they wanted.

In view of all this, it was General Hampton's policy to fight the battle in a position of his own selection, where, in some measure, the superiority of his antagonist could be matched by strategy; and after choosing that position, the next thing was to toll the "blue birds" into his trap, and in order to show how this was done we must go back to Rosser's brigade, which we left above the junction of the Green Spring Valley road with the Rail Road, while Young's Brigade lay some distance below.

The Yankees crossed the river and came down heavily on Young's

Charge of Confederate Cavalry at Trevillian Station

people, capturing a great many and stampeding the remainder with the exception of one regiment which drew up in line some distance from the road and watched the Yankee chase after their comrades. As soon as the attack on Young's men was known, Rosser started his brigade at a gallop to meet them, and arriving at the Green Spring road, found the Yankees loading their prisoners in captured ambulances while all along the road the victorious blue-jackets were chasing and "gobbling up" the scattered Confederates, and right here among the ambulances the *fight* commenced; Rosser's boys going in, as the general said, "very heavy," the Yankees breaking and trying to escape, while Young's men sent up mixed yells of "don't shoot this way," and "hurrah! you 'uns has saved we 'uns agin."

Pretty soon the tide was turned, and in a perfect whirlwind of dust and smoke the "Comanches" pushed hotly after the retreating enemy, many of whom they captured and sent to the rear, and in the chase they passed the regiment before spoken off, still standing quietly in line apparently interested in the view they had of the little "mill" going on around them, but having no inclination to become mixed up with it.

In the chase, many of the Yankees broke into the woods on the right of the road and endeavoured escape, in consequence of which many of White's men made a corresponding movement in order to catch them, so that the battalion was soon very much reduced, and on reaching a hill about a mile down the road and finding, as they supposed, a Confederate battery on the right in full play and apparently unsupported, the colonel resolved to form his men alongside of it, as a large number of the enemy were discovered in the wood below him, and a strong force posted behind a brick-kiln to the left, and with this view, he ordered the plank fence on the right of the road to be broken down; at the same time starting Irish Pat, of Company C, up the road in charge of a wagon and team which had been deserted by somebody just at this point.

The battery was not more than two hundred yards away and the force behind the brick-kiln was every moment growing stronger, all of which made the colonel more impatient for the fence to be opened, but it was a strong one and not easily broken, and while thus engaged, General Hampton galloped over the hill exclaiming, "Colonel White, what are you going to do?"

"Going to support that battery," said the colonel.

"Get away from here, colonel, it's a Yankee battery," replied the general, and immediately the colonel commenced to "get away."

Marching slowly back over the hill we found the brigade forming in a field to the right, and Chew placing his artillery in position
just above them. Farther along, and just where we were to leave the
road to join the brigade, lay a wagon that the Yankees had cut down,
and out of which a barrel of apple-jack had rolled. Three dismounted
men were at work on it trying to fill their canteens, and as the head
of White's column passed it, Captain Myers, who was just at the head,
with Lieutenant Marlow on his right, Orderly Sergeant Bennett on
his left, Will Edwards and Frank Lee immediately behind him and the
bugler just before him, turned to Will Edwards and said, "Will, you'd
better get Frank Lee's canteen and fill it there, hadn't you?"

This was in allusion to Frank's solemn resolution not to drink any
more, caused by some of the boys having fooled him into taking too
much a short time before. The words were scarcely uttered when a
shell from the battery they had just left exploded within a yard of the
captain's head, and leaving him untouched, mortally wounded poor
Will Edwards, terribly mangled Ed Bennett, causing him to lose a leg,
wounded Lieutenant Marlow, and cut Crone Phillips (the bugler) very
severely in the arm and side, besides killing one and wounding badly
two of the dismounted men at the barrel, killing Phillips' horse and
badly damaging that of Sergeant Bennett. Seldom has such execution
been done by a single shell, or such an escape made as Myers.

As may be supposed, the calamity caused great excitement for a
short time, and it was with difficulty that order was maintained under
the incessant fire which now poured in upon them, but pretty soon
the battalion formed her line, Major Ferneyhough displaying great
coolness, as did all the officers and men who were left. The scene was
one of wild confusion, shells and grape-shot whizzing and howling
all around, riderless horses dashing frantically over the field, and ambulances rattling past at a gallop with their freight of wounded men
screaming in agony, while high above all other sounds boomed and
crashed the contending batteries.

Amid all this the major turned to count the men in ranks, and Orderly Sergeant Campbell, of Co. F, who had been severely wounded in
the arm by a grape-shot while assisting to align his company, turned
coolly to Captain French saying, "Captain, I am wounded and would
like to have permission to go to the rear," which was of course readily
granted, but not many waited to ask permission to retire after being
wounded; and this instance shows that panic did not reign entirely

among the "Comanches" even under circumstances most calculated to inspire it.

The whole brigade had by this time retired to a more sheltered position beyond the woods, and now the colonel ordered his battalion to fall back to the woods, which it did very quietly, and just here was the first actual view of flying cannon-shot we had ever *enjoyed*. A heavy battery beyond the Rail Road was throwing solid shot directly across our line of march, one of which, striking the solid ground the eighth of a mile to the right, bounded with a whirling motion just in our front, and so close to the colonel's horse that all who saw it were sure it would strike him, but it did not.

After halting awhile near the woods, and being still in range of the grape, we were ordered to retire to the position of the brigade, where the battalion formed in front of the 12th regiment, and here we witnessed another freak of a round-shot which struck in front of the battalion, bounded over it, and striking again, went over the 12th, and from its third strike made another jump, clearing the led horses as it did so.

The operations of the day were evidently against the Confederates, and the men were blaming Hampton for allowing his men to be beaten in that way, by brigades, but he was working out his problem and baiting his trap for tomorrow, but some of his bait came near being carried off, for the enemy entirely surrounded Col. Chew, who immediately began fighting his guns all around him, and made his position so near "red-hot" that neither friend or foe could reach him, until without difficulty he could limber up and move back to his people again.

Soon after this the enemy occupied the ground from which Chew had retired, and began to advance cautiously upon the woods where Rosser had his dismounted men, and in the fight which ensued the general was severely wounded in the leg and compelled to leave the field.

The command of the brigade now devolved upon Col. Dulaney, of the 7th regiment, and the fighting became stubborn for the possession of the woods; the enemy using artillery sparingly, and the Confederates entirely deprived of the aid of theirs because the situation of the ground would not permit its use without damaging their own men as much as the enemy.

The "Comanches" lay at the mouth of the Green Spring road, dismounted, to avoid the storm of bullets that whistled over them, when

Col. Chew rode past them a short distance to see if he could plant his guns there, and Col. White rode up by his side. Just then the Yankees threw some shells which exploded immediately *at* them, and killed Chew's horse, but the cast-iron artilleryman didn't change his countenance in the least; and Maj. Thompson came prancing up to have a look too, when a shell burst almost in his face, but Thompson only laughed, and giving his hand a flutter in the white cloud of smoke, exclaimed, "Oh! but don't that sound wicked?"

About 5 o'clock Maj. Ferneyhough took the first squadron on a scout up the Rail Road, and on his return found a battery posted at the forks of the road, which, after our previous artillery experience, we proceeded to inspect closely, and it, too, proved to be a Yankee, so branching off to the right, we gave it as wide a berth as the timber would let us.

It was now past sunset, and Sheridan had succeeded, with his whole force, in driving two of Hampton's brigades from their position, and himself occupying, at dark, the same line they held at daylight; but thus far he was successful, and Gen. Hampton knew that he would follow it up tomorrow. But the two generals had very different ideas about the day's work; Sheridan *supposing* the battle was over, and Hampton *knowing* that it had not been fought yet.

About dark the Confederates retired to their camp on the Green Spring road, and rested securely until morning, when, without any hurry at all, they fed their horses, got breakfast, and prepared for the business of this bright and beautiful Sunday morning in June. A shower of rain had fallen during the night, and the stifling dust was nicely laid, so that, with the exception of fighting, whatever they had to do, could be performed in comfort.

Shortly after sunrise White's battalion marched down to the line which Gen. Hampton had fortified, and found the dismounted men quietly lying behind the hastily thrown up piles of rails which stretched along the side of a hill that rose gradually from a creek, both flanks protected by heavy woods with thick undergrowth, and the country in front perfectly clear as far as their rifles would reach. The artillery was posted on the high ground along the road, and could command fully half the circle around them, in fact, it was a splendid position in which to receive an attack; but Sheridan did not seem to be in any hurry to break the glad Sunday quiet of the valley, and hardly any firing was heard until after 12 o'clock.

The "Comanches" had been ordered to the extreme right of the

177

line, on vedette duty, and were occasionally annoyed by Sheridan's sharpshooters, but nothing serious occurred until about 4 o'clock, when the Yankees were discovered advancing in heavy lines, dismounted, on Hampton's left, where all of Butler's big "new issue" regiments were stationed, and almost immediately the artillery opened on them; but that was nothing to the hail-storm of lead that fell upon them from the "new issue." Those raw men didn't know anything at all about being whipped, and had no idea of anything but killing all the Yankees in sight, to which interesting occupation they bent all their energies, and made their rail piles look as if they were on fire, so incessantly did they burn their powder.

In a very short time the first assault was repulsed, and the "new issue" didn't really know they had been fighting; but other attacks followed in quick succession until about dark, when every man in Sheridan's army had been whipped, and his whole force was in full retreat, their ambulances, wagons and demoralised troops rushing pell-mell along the road which ran within one hundred yards of Col. White's position, and every moment the shells would crash from Chew's guns right among the yelling, panic-stricken fugitives, making it a regular "Bull Run" on a small scale.

Col. White and his people moved up as close to them as the shells would permit, and the colonel conceived the idea that with four hundred dismounted men he could capture the whole roadfull, but after sending repeatedly to Col. Dulaney for the required force, that officer finally sent him forty-two men, whom White sent back in disgust and gave up the project.

By nine o'clock everything was quiet along Hampton's lines, and the utterly routed and defeated army of Sheridan was in full retreat towards Grant's headquarters, where he published to the world that he had whipped Hampton's cavalry, driving it to Gordonsville, but finding a heavy force of infantry in the entrenchments at that place had given up the pursuit.

The literal fact in the case was, that Sheridan had been most splendidly outgeneraled, and most terribly beaten by half his number, and not a solitary infantry soldier was engaged in the fight, nor did he get in sight of Gordonsville, but no one blames him for *thinking* that he met infantry, because the "new issue" certainly did *act* infantry up to nature, but they were raw recruits, and had never been under fire but once before, while Sheridan's were all veteran troops. Pollard, in *The Lost Cause*" makes the same unfounded assertion, that Sheridan was "repulsed by infantry in the rifle-pits," but it is probable he drew his information from the official report of that general, instead of the one made by General Hampton.

During the fight of today, Lieut. Nich. Dorsey, of Co. B, who had been a prisoner, closely confined in Fort McHenry for several months, reported to the command for duty, having made his escape by cutting through the slate roof of his prison with a barlow knife, and at once assumed command of his company.

Early on the morning of the 13th, the army of Hampton started in pursuit of the Yankees, and about 3 o'clock came up with their rear guard at the North Anna, when some skirmishing took place, but the enemy moved rapidly, and could not be brought to a stand long enough to make a fight of it, and at night Hampton's men went to the Rail Road, where they drew three double handfuls of corn for their horses, which was the first grain they had eaten since the 8th. In the morning the pursuit was continued through Caroline County, but Sheridan marched rapidly, taking every horse in the country he passed through, and killing his own as fast as they gave out.

It was estimated that in his retreat of one hundred miles his army left, on an average, twelve dead horses to the mile; that besides his losses in horse-flesh at the battle, twelve hundred were shot, by his order, on his retreat; but he took quite that number from the citizens along his route, and in a manner that no other man than a Sheridan or Sherman would have done.

On the 16th, Col. White started with a picked party to intercept a courier with an escort of thirty-eight men, taking dispatches from Sheridan to Grant, but failed to catch them, although he had a brush with a party from the 6th Pa. Cavalry, in which he captured several prisoners and horses, and rejoined the battalion on the 19th, near the White House on the Pamunky.

18: The Cattle Raid

Early on the morning of the 20th we marched for the White House, but before reaching that point met the enemy in heavy force of infantry, cavalry, artillery, and gun-boats, and had a severe fight, which lasted all the afternoon, during which the gun-boats did some of the most magnificent shooting with their heavy guns ever witnessed, exploding their shells at the precise point desired, at nearly two miles. Nothing was accomplished by the fighting except to ascertain that Sheridan was now safe, having reached navigable water, and met strong reinforcements, as well as supplies.

For some days the battalion was on detached duty, scouting in King William County, and trying to catch whatever scattered parties of Yankees that might be ranging in that county, but with no success, for Sheridan did not permit his men to scatter much, knowing the danger of their being caught by the Rebels if they strayed too far from their lines.

On Sunday morning, 26th June, the whole force of Hampton marched quietly down to Drewry's Bluff and crossed the James. Then there was loud and deep complaints and curses heard among the "Comanches," and many prophecies uttered by the various wise men among them that they were going to give up Virginia, all of which combined to make their spirits sink from the hopeful blood-heat, to which their success at Trevillian had raised them, far below the zero of disappointment, in not being allowed to reach the mountain, and their hope of ever again roaming along the Potomac and Shenandoah withered and almost died in the freezing despondency of the hour.

But all this was soon over, for the reason that they were much better fed on this side of the James than while operating on the north bank of it, but still the battalion considered this move very much in the light that Cæsar is supposed to have looked upon the famous crossing of the Rubicon, and felt that the whole thing was reduced to the issue of "victory or death" now, for no live man would be permitted to re-cross the James until the Yankees were whipped, but it was not long until they learned that Hampton's object in coming on this side was to get at the Wilson and Kautz raiders, who had been for some time devastating the "South Side" country and trying to destroy the Rail Roads below and west of Richmond.

As the story of this terrible visitation has already passed into history, together with the (to the raiders) grievous conclusion of it, we will only tell as near as possible the share taken by the "Comanches" in the winding up of the great raid.

On the 27th we passed through Petersburg while the Yankees were shelling the place, and it was really refreshing to see ladies pass coolly along the streets as though nothing unusual was transpiring while the 160-pound shells were howling like hawks of perdition through the smoky air and bursting in the very heart of the city, but they didn't mind it a bit; and even the children would stand and watch, at the sound of the passing shells, to see the explosion, and make funny little speeches about them, as if they had been curious birds flying over their heads. Familiarity with the danger of the bombardment had cured them of all their fears of it, and when it would be told to people on the street, as was frequently the case, that Miss or Mrs. So-and-so was killed in her house by a shell, nobody was horrified at all, but all seemed to take it as a matter of course and to care very little about it.

On the 28th the battalion reached Stony Creek Station, on the Weldon Rail Road, where they drew corn and rations, and about dark took the road to Sapony Church, where they came up with the raiders about 10 o'clock, who had fortified themselves near the Church, and while General Hampton studied out the situation the men lay down to rest for the busy tomorrow which they knew was before them, for if they had hard marching to *find* the Yankees it was evident the work was not to be easy now they were before them.

During the night there was occasional heavy firing between the advanced parties of the two armies, and just before dawn of the 29th, Gen. Butler took White's Battalion through the swamps and thick pines, around the left flank of the raiders, and at daylight the colonel formed "his people" exactly in rear of the fortified line held by the dismounted raiders, whom he charged simultaneously with General Hampton's attack upon their front, when their whole force broke and scampered off through the pines with the yelling "Comanches" after them, but the "race is not always to the swift, nor the battle to the strong," and after White's men had lost time enough with the captured Yankees to give the remainder an opportunity to rally, which they did about two miles from their fortifications, to the number of about two hundred.

It was found to be decidedly hot work capturing a force larger than their own, who availed themselves of every fence, house, swamp and pine forest to form a square and blaze into their pursuers a volley of bullets from their 16-shooting Henry rifles, and the "Comanches" being mounted, in a fight where horses were only an encumbrance, had to watch their points very closely for they had certainly waked up a batch of extremely hard-fighting Yankees.

Two of White's men, John Marlow, Company A, and Aaron Bevans, Company C, were severely wounded, and several of the enemy were killed and wounded, but after reaching the heavy body of timber which spread along the Nottaway River, the brave boys in blue had earned the right to continue their retreat unmolested, and the colonel called off his men and returned to the brigade which he left five or

THE GREAT CATTLE RAID AT HARRISON'S LANDING

six miles behind him.

On reaching the line of retreat followed by the main body of the raiders, it was discovered that through the failure of the Confederates to push forward and seize the bridge over which the Yankees must pass, the most of them had escaped, with the loss of six pieces of artillery and about seven hundred prisoners. The remainder of the day was spent in gathering up the arms and plunder thrown away by the flying raiders, among the latter of which was a large quantity of ladies' clothing which they had stolen from the citizens' houses, and the men would come in with bonnets, shawls, silk dresses, mantles of velvet and many other things, looking, in fact, as if they had broken up all the millinery establishments on the "South Side."

But the most curious scene of all was the troops of negroes of all sizes and ages, from the three-day old baby to the grey-wooled hag of ninety, which were found hid in the woods. They had been persuaded by the Yankees to leave their homes and go with them to their land of "liberty and glory;" and nearly every negro in the country, especially the women and children, had joined them, but now when they had fallen in evil times, and as the Confederates were picking them up, the first thing they would say was to tell the names of masters or mistresses, and beg piteously to be permitted to go home, declaring, "fore God, we neber will beliebe de dam Yankees agin."

For two days the battalion was on picket in this country and during that time the men were constantly picking up the scattered raiders and negroes, who were wandering in the pines almost starved and yet too much afraid of the Rebels to come out of the woods. They had passed through a fiery ordeal during the raid, having been badly whipped by militia at Staunton River, then cut up severely by W. H. F. Lee at Blacks and Whites, and in endeavouring to escape at Reams' had been met by Fitz Lee's cavalry and worse handled than before. While at Stony creek Hampton had completely ruined them, but their generals, Wilson and Kautz, managed to escape with a small portion of their wretched command, and this was their last raid during that campaign on the "South Side."

Up to the 1st of July the colonel had been without an adjutant since the 6th of May, but now Lieutenant Sam Baker, of Frederick County, Va., who had been an officer in the disbanded Company D, came over and took upon himself the responsible duties of that position, which he held until the close of the war, performing all his duties to the entire satisfaction of Colonel White and the whole command.

It was now midsummer, and in the hot climate of that piney, sandy country, where good water was a rarity, many of the men got sick, and the resting days of this month were very gladly accepted by these border men, who had never in their lives known any other than the pure mountain air and water under the shadow of the Blue Ridge; but Col. White was entirely too restless in disposition to let his people lie quietly in camp when there was a chance to operate in his partisan style, so taking with him a detail of 80 men, he left the camp on the evening of the 8th, and marched to the Blackwater, in Sussex County, with the intention of trying a raid on some negro cavalry, who patrolled the road leading from Grant's army, by Cabin Point, to the James River.

Here he halted and made his arrangements, which were not completed until the 13th, when, with about 90 men, the battalion having all moved down in the meantime, he crossed Warwick Swamp and the Blackwater, into Surry county, and marching quietly through the pines reached Cabin Point an hour before day, and halting in the woods a mile beyond the town, on the telegraph road, made his dispositions for the attack, by placing Major Ferneyhough with twenty men armed with double-barrel guns, in ambush along the road, and leaving the remainder, under Capt. Myers, in readiness to charge, while the colonel himself scouted and watched for the enemy to make their appearance.

The usual scouting party consisted of about sixty mounted negroes, and generally passed up a little after sunrise, from a camp of about ten thousand troops of all arms, near the old Surry Court-house, and all the negroes in the country were in the interest of the Yankees and would do anything, short of breaking their necks, to give information of any movement of the Rebels on their side of the Blackwater. So, to render the situation of White's men still more interesting, they had discovered some cabins near them, filled to overflowing, almost, with negroes, and the colonel had posted some men to guard them, but one or two of the small ones had already escaped to the woods with the knowledge that Southern troops were on the road, and under these circumstances it was to be presumed that the patrol would not come as usual, this morning.

But after a while they were discovered quietly advancing, and all thought the affair was to be successful, and prepared themselves for what promised to be genuine sport, but bye-and-bye the colonel discovered that the negroes were only used this time as a bait, and that while about 3,000 infantry were following them, a body of about

1,000 cavalry was moving through the pines to gain his rear and cut him off from the bridges over the Blackwater. These bridges were his only mode of escape, and if the Yankees succeeded, he knew that his raiding would be ended forevermore, unless there should happen to be war in the Elysian fields of glory beyond the Jordan, where all good soldiers hoped to go, but just now the colonel had no intention of crossing that last named river, where it is said boats are used instead of bridges, so hastily leaving the telegraph road, he made a quick march to the Blackwater, and reached it just in time to save his raiders.

The boys, who all fully understood the situation, were perfectly satisfied with their experience by daylight behind Grant's lines, and had no desire to make any further expeditions in that quarter, provided the colonel would be satisfied too; but on their return to camp, and learning that "old Jubal" was thundering at the gates of Washington, every man immediately became possessed of an almost insane desire to desert and go to him, in fact, Co. B did go on the night of the 15th, without leave or license, and left scarcely a man from Maryland to tell the tale of what had become of his companions. They said Companies A and C had done the same thing before and not been punished, and now that Maryland was open and their homes inside of the Confederate lines they intended, if possible, to go to them.

The colonel sympathized deeply with his men and would never enforce the penalties for violations of the army regulations, when it was possible to avoid it, and to this one fact belongs the reason why a Brigadier's stars and wreath never adorned his collar. When he was recommended by the Military Committee of the Confederate Congress, by such men as Gov. Letcher and Judge Brockenborough in private life, and by a multitude of officers in the Ashby Brigade and other portions of the army, Gen. Lee refused to endorse him, simply because his men ran away and went home and the colonel did not punish them; and so, because he had *too much heart*, he was not promoted to a position that no man in the army could fill as well as he after General Rosser was made Major-General; but all this is going too far ahead of the events we are trying to describe, and it is time to go back to the "Comanche" camp on the Nottaway.

This camp was about ten miles from the brigade, and in a really good country, with prime spring water, plenty of fruit, vegetables, and melons, and the people very kind and hospitable, and for the reason that no troops except the Yankee raiders had ever been among them, there was plenty of forage there. Game, such as turkeys and squirrels, was abundant, deer also, but they had to be hunted in large parties, with hounds, while the river had plenty of fish, so that the battalion would have considered itself literally "in clover" only for the tantalising reports of the brilliant success of Gen. Early's operations on the Potomac. This made the boys restless and dissatisfied, and some of them even expressed satisfaction when "Old Jubilee" was compelled to retire to the south bank of the Potomac.

On the morning of the 20th the colonel started with thirty men for Cabin Point again, this time to intercept dispatches on the telegraph, and for this purpose took with him an expert operator.

He succeeded in gaining the desired point before daylight on the morning of the 21st, and his operator at once proceeded to cut the telegraph wire and attach his instruments, so that he was enabled to read every dispatch that passed, and to keep the thing all right he sent them on to their destination as soon as copied; but after carrying on this amusing process for about two hours he became satisfied that from some cause the enemy suspected the line was tapped, from the fact that some ridiculous and foolish dispatches were passed, and communicating his suspicions to Col. White, the latter decided that it was time to be traveling, for he knew that if the enemy really did suspect anything wrong on the line they would soon send an investigating committee, so calling in his pickets he started for the Blackwater.

Before going far, he discovered that a force of infantry was following him, having reached his position on the telegraph road shortly after he started from it, and on reaching the bridge over the Blackwater the colonel halted his party to see if the Yankees would attack. In about half an hour they came up and skirmished with him, but would not advance into the swamp, although they had fully ten times his number. During the skirmishing James Atwood, of Co. E, who was on the bridge to the rear, had his leg broken by a stray ball, and the colonel retired through the swamp, the enemy going back at the same time.

On the 27th the battalion was ordered by Col. Dulaney to report to the brigade, then fifteen miles off, at Freeman's ford, on the Nottaway, and on arriving there was sent to Reams' Station to picket, where we remained until the 1st of August, without any incidents other than the usual routine of such duty, except that on the night of the 30th the Yankees were very active and annoyed the pickets exceedingly all night, and when, just before dawn of day, they grew quiet and allowed the tired men to lie down to rest, the great mine fiasco which Grant had been preparing at Petersburg for a month, broke with a terrible explosion on the morning air, and shook the solid ground for miles, the "Comanches" scrambled up and mounted their horses without a word.

But after a while some of them begun to talk, and wonder "whether it was the day of judgment or an earthquake," but pretty soon, in the distance could be heard the yelling and shouting of the charging columns, as they rolled like a billow upon the Confederate works, and then White's boys dismounted, saying it was "some new-fangled Yankee mill or other that they didn't know anything about, but they *did know* Beaureguard and Uncle Bobby could attend to it."

Capt. Dan. Hatcher, of 7th Regiment, relieved the battalion on the evening of 31st, and on the 1st of August it moved to Stony Creek and encamped, drawing forage by wagon trains from North Carolina, and for several days did nothing but rest, having plenty to eat, and for a rarity, when Col. Dulaney commanded the brigade, no drilling to do.

On Sunday, August 7th, the first sermon the "Comanches" had heard this year was preached in camp, by the Rev. Lieut. Strickler, of Co. E. The religious training of the battalion was very loosely conducted, as a general thing, and yet there were some bright and working Christians in it, especially in Companies C and E, some of whom would engage in prayer before going into battle, and it was remarked by all, that these men made none the worse soldiers for bending the knee to God, and commending their souls and their cause to His keeping, but generally, religion in the ranks was unpopular, and many who had been members of Church endeavoured to hide the fact from their comrades that they ever prayed.

A state of war, and life in camp is always demoralizing; but the soldier always honours the man who bravely stands by his principles, and even though they might jeer and laugh at the one who carried his religion openly, into the camp and on the march, with him, yet in their hearts the most reckless and profane would count him who did it a double hero, in that he both conquered his own pride and lived down—as live down *he would*—the scoffing of his comrades.

On the 8th Maj. Ferneyhough went on a scout into Surry county, to capture some Yankee pickets, but returned without accomplishing anything; and now the command encamped on the Nottaway again, and luxuriated on the many delicacies of the season again, such as watermelons, potatoes, roasting-ears, tomatoes, cucumbers, and last, but not by any means least, the prime spring water, all of which they had in abundance, and the memory of the pleasant days spent on the Nottaway will be a bright one in the hearts of White's Battalion while memory exists; and they were all willing to spend the summer there, and enjoy the good fare and the boating and fishing excursions on the river, but these days couldn't last; and on the 12th the brigade joined the division and took up the line of march for Richmond.

Everybody thought this move had some connection, in some way, with Early's operations on the Shenandoah, and immediately the brigade had dreams of heaven and the valley, which brightened more and more each mile that they advanced, until they were once more on the north bank of the James, and securely booked, as they thought, for over the mountains.

Passing through Richmond, the whole division halted on Main and Broad streets, and from the endless supplies of melons which lined the sidewalks, the men eat, until watermelons and cantaloupes lost their flavour and were no longer fit to it, and then marched to the South Anna and encamped for the night, moving early in the morning to Beaver Dam, on the Rail Road, where three day's rations were issued, and the whole command laid over until next day, when the column took the telegraph road to Ashland, passing that place and going into camp on the Chickahominy, seven miles from Richmond, and still nobody could form an idea of what we had started to do, but there was now considerable doubt, to say the least of it, about going to the valley right away.

The next morning the division again marched through Richmond and passed out on the Charles City road to Malvern Hill, where General W. H. F. Lee was fighting the enemy, and here the "Comanches" were ordered forward to cut off some Yankee pickets to the left, but they left so quick we had no chance at them at all.

After this the brigade moved over to the Williamsburg road, and encamped at Savage Station on York River Rail Road, leaving White's men on picket at the Chickahominy, where they remained until the 19th, when they again marched to the Charles City road and encamped until the 22nd, when it was found that the Yankees, who had caused all this trouble by trying to *steal* Richmond, had gone across the James, after losing about one thousand of their men; and at midnight Hampton moved his people over to the "South Side" again, and kept on to Reams' Station, where, on the 23rd, he met the Yankees and commenced to fight in earnest about 4 o'clock in the afternoon.

Here the battalion was divided, Captain Myers being sent with the first squadron to report to General Butler on the right, while the colonel with the remainder moved to the left with Rosser, who, today, resumed the command of his brigade. The first order of General Butler to Myers was to "find the Yankees in his front and tell him how many there were," and in order to do this the captain took five men—Jim Oneale, Frank Lee, John White, Billy Lee, and Lum Wenner—and deployed them at the edge of the woods, from where they rode out into a field covered with tall sedge grass and small pine bushes, in which a thousand Yankees could have lain in line, without being perceived, but they had not advanced far when a long blue line raised up and commenced firing.

This was enough and the captain rode up to the general with the report that he had found about twelve hundred Yankees on the left of the road. "Very well," said Gen. Butler, "I *know* what's on the right," and ordering forward a brigade of dismounted men, this wooden-legged general led them in a furious attack upon the enemy, galloping along full fifty yards in front of his line, and exposed to the fire of both friends and foes. This settled the question on that part of the field, for the Yankees ran, and Butler followed them half a mile, when they met reinforcements and made a stubborn resistance for some time, but General Rosser came in on the left and they were again forced back.

The battalion now united again, and formed, by General Butler's order, on a hill in the road, prepared to charge when the enemy attempted to advance, and here from six o'clock until dark they stood exposed to a hot fire from the Yankee line below them, but fortunately not a man was injured, although seven horses were struck and killed. About dark Hancock's corps of infantry moved up from the Rail Road and joined in the fight, when General Butler, who was sitting on his horse a short distance from the battalion, and under a very hot fire, called for a courier to go to his line of dismounted men below and order them to retire.

The man who was sent to him displayed evident signs of much perturbation under the storm of bullets that whistled around, and the general said to him, "Young man, you're scared; go back to Captain Myers and tell him to send me a *courier!*" upon which the fellow returned *instanter*, and the captain sent Sergeant Everhart, whom the general asked if he could carry a dispatch down to the dismounted men; to which Everhart replied, "I God! I'll *start!* don't know so much about *going*," when the general replied "you'll do," sent the order, and withdrew his line from the fight.

189

It was evident that Grant had made a heavy lodgement on the Rail Road at Reams', and that General Hampton couldn't make him give it up with his cavalry, but the latter was compelled to send wagons to Stony Creek to get forage, which was twenty miles further away than Reams', soon the morning of the 24th, before day, Captain Myers was ordered to mount his squadron and escort the battalion train to that place, where they arrived about 11 o'clock.

Here they found big, luscious watermelons from North Carolina by the car-load, which they enjoyed to their utmost until late in the evening, when they pushed on after the wagons which had loaded and started back by two o'clock, and having overtaken them, the squadron moved with them over the dangerous part of the road, and it being now midnight and the trains safe, the escort bivouacked in the pines while the wagons drove on to camp.

An hour before daylight Col. White, with a few men, came down the road, and halting with the 1st squadron informed Capt. Myers that A. P. Hill was coming down during the day to drive the Yankees away from Reams'; that Hampton was going to draw their attention and amuse them until Hill could get his position; that the colonel was going on a scout for Hampton, and would be gone all day, and that Myers was to take charge of the battalion for that length of time.

About sunrise Gen. Hampton came along, and putting White's men in front ordered them to go to Wyatt's Crossing, about a mile from Reams', and wait further orders.

Gen. Rosser was now at the head of the Laurel Brigade, and he soon came up and remarked to Myers that he wanted "his people" for advance guard again today, to which the captain replied that he "didn't mind the *hanging* half as much as he did the being told of it so long beforehand." On reaching the Crossing they found some Yankee pickets who retired towards Reams', and with the exception of an occasional shot, everything was quiet until 9 o'clock, when the enemy opened fire with artillery upon Rosser's men, and pretty soon Chew commenced to reply, but no advance was attempted on either side.

During the cannonade Generals Rosser and Butler sat on their horses just in front of White's Battalion, which, as a matter of course, stood by Chew's artillery, and once, when the shells flew low over their heads, and some of the men dodged, Gen. Butler remarked, "They are disposed to be rather familiar this morning," to which Rosser replied, "Yes, politeness is in order this morning, but don't bow too low, boys, it isn't becoming;" but Henry Simpson exclaimed, "Yes it is; it's *becom-*

ing a little too dam hot here, if that's what you mean," and most of the boys were of Henry's opinion.

The day passed in constant marching and counter-marching; sometimes the "Comanches" would be dismounted and ordered to pile up rails for breastworks, and then ordered to mount quick and charge; but no fighting was done until about 3 o'clock in the evening, when the heavy firing on the left showed that Hampton had "amused" the Yankees long enough, and now A. P. Hill was at them.

The Yankees were strongly fortified at the Station, and in their front had an abattis of trees felled with their tops from the works, and all the branches trimmed sharp, so that it was almost impossible for Hill's infantry to get through at all, and in fact two brigades were repulsed with heavy loss, but when Gen. Mahone, the builder and president of the Rail Road, came up with his brigade; he took his people through and up to the breastworks, but the enemy was still there, and now both parties lay along the works, so that neither could fight or retreat.

But pretty soon Mahone's men out-Yankeed the Yankees, and taking up some heavy cross-ties and rail-bars that were convenient they threw them high over the fortifications, causing them to fall with telling effect upon the heads of the Yankees, forcing them to leave their defences, and as they retired Mahone's men, with the works now completely turned upon them, raised up and poured a terribly destructive fire upon the retreating enemy, causing tremendous slaughter, and at the same moment Gen. Hampton charged them in flank, capturing four guns and many prisoners.

Gen. Hill's infantry took twelve pieces in the works, making sixteen guns captured, and about three thousand prisoners, besides five hundred killed and many wounded, making their loss in this day's fight certainly reach very near five thousand in all, while the Confederates lost about seven hundred, killed, wounded and missing.

At dark, Gen. Rosser ordered Capt. Sipe, commanding the 12th regiment, and Capt. Myers, of White's Battalion, to report to Gen. Hampton, who instructed them to move their commands to Reams' and relieve the infantry in the fortifications, which they did about midnight, in the most terrible storm of rain, thunder and lightning it is possible to imagine. The vivid streams, not flashes, of lightning danced and glanced along the Rail Road track and over the captured guns, which still stood there, while every moment the crashing thunder just overhead pealed out as if the inky sky was being torn to splinters, and in sheets and torrents the floods of rain poured down, while through the thick blackness of the storm and night could be heard all around the shrieks and groans of the wounded and dying Federals, who, totally unable to help themselves, were gasping out their lives in agony, without one friend to shelter them from the raging of the fierce tempest or stop the ebbing life-tide that poured from their mangled bodies, and in the morning light there lay many corpses along the ground at Reams' whose souls had gone up to the judgment-throne amid the bursting storm and thunder of that horrible night.

Among those who survived was a captain of infantry, who had cause to bless the genius of Freemasonry, for by aid of its mystic signs he found a brother in the ranks of his foes, who helped him as only a brother would have done and gave him back to life again.

There was no attempt on the part of the enemy to come back to Reams', but they established their vedette lines along the pines and old fields of tossing sedge to the right of the Rail Road, towards Petersburg, and on the 26th Col. White placed his battalion on picket in front of them and scarcely three hundred yards from their lines, but there was no firing, and both sides, in fact, agreed to the childish proposition of "I'll let you alone if you'll let me alone."

It was now apparent that Gen. Hampton's style of fighting was a decided success, for he had so invariably whipped the enemy's cavalry that they were afraid to come from behind their infantry lines, and as a consequence his own people had much less duty to perform than at any time during the long and arduous campaign.

On the 11th of September the general became impatient to hear the news from the Presidential Conventions in the North, and as the Southern papers were deficient, he took a detail from the "Laurel Brigade" and made a raid to the rear of Grant's lines at Petersburg for Yankee newspapers, in which he attacked and whipped a brigade of cavalry from their camp, with considerable loss in killed, wounded, and prisoners, to them, but none whatever to himself, and brought out enough papers to supply his camps for a month with reading matter.

Major Ferneyhough, who commanded the detail of White's Battalion on the expedition, incurred Gen. Hampton's displeasure because of a misconception of orders, in consequence of which he resigned on the 13th, and a few days after Capt. Myers, of Co. A, was selected by Colonel White, and by Generals Rosser and Hampton, to fill the vacancy.

On the 14th of September General Hampton marched with a division of his cavalry in the direction of Grant's left wing, and succeeded in gaining, unobserved, the rear of his army, an operation which was comparatively easy, from the character of the country, which was low and flat, with many swamps and vast bodies of dense pine forest, through which an army might have marched without being discovered, except by accident, as there were few inhabitants in that region, they having been compelled, from the proximity of the two armies, to refugee or starve.

About daylight, on the 16th, when the raiders had reached a point about one mile from the James River, and not more than six miles in rear of the main line of the Federal Army, a strong party of dismounted cavalry was discovered behind some barricades, near an old church, and the 7th and 11th Regiments, of Rosser's brigade, which was in front, were dismounted and sent forward to dislodge the enemy, which they did after a severe fight, and now the general ordered the battalion forward at a brisk trot, which soon brought them in full view of an immense drove of beef cattle, guarded by a Federal brigade, one regiment of which, the 1st D. C. Cavalry, was mounted near the cattle pens. Gen. Rosser sent a flag of truce demanding the surrender of this force, but the officer commanding, returned for answer, "Come and get us, if you want us," and at the same time told the truce-bearer that if he came there any more with "that damned thing," (the flag) he would shoot him.

The general at once turned to the battalion, and in his short, solid tone, that always had something of the wicked ring of a Whitworth in it, when he meant fight, exclaimed, "Come down on them, White!" and the "Comanches" did it with such splendid effect, that the Yankees were scattered in wild flight, in less than five minutes, pursued in every direction by the men of the battalion.

Some prisoners were taken, and a large quantity of camp equipage and arms, among the latter quite a number of the "Henry rifles" or "sixteen-shooters," fell into the hands of the "Comanches," but what pleased them most and really made this one of the grandest raids of the war, was the capture of the immense herd of broad-horned Western beeves, averaging over fifteen hundred pounds, and numbering two thousand five hundred and thirty-five head, all of which were brought safely out.

On the return, Col. White was sent with a portion of his command to Sycamore Church, on the Jerusalem plank road, to guard that point until the cattle could be driven over the Blackwater, but on reaching his position he was assailed by a force of the enemy numbering about five thousand cavalry and artillery, and after a stubborn engagement, was forced to retire a mile from the plank road, but by strategy in keeping his men concealed, and by moving his flag from one point to another, he succeeded in deceiving the enemy and holding them in check until the arrival of Gen. Rosser with the remainder of the brigade, some two hours after his first meeting with them.

While contesting the Yankee advance the colonel caused his men to throw up rail fortifications at Monk's Neck bridge, and here the enemy used artillery upon them severely, by which two men of Company A were killed, *viz.*: Samuel T. Presgraves, of Loudoun, and William Brown, a native of North Carolina, both excellent soldiers.

After holding the Yankees here until the safety of the cattle was assured, the brigade flanked them and quietly returned to camp near Reams', highly elated with the splendid success of the expedition, and more than ever convinced of the ability and generalship of their great commander, General Hampton.

19: Swamp Dragoons

Everything was very quiet in camp after the "cattle raid" until the 27th of September, when the eager longing of the "Ash by Brigade" to go home was gratified, and General Rosser, in a beautifully touching general order, in which he reviewed the past campaign and paid eloquent tributes to the fallen members of the command, announced that he was ordered to proceed immediately to the Valley, and the brigade marched out for the "promised land" again.

Colonel White had obtained a furlough, or rather a sick leave, and Captain Myers commanded the "Comanches." The season was the most pleasant of the whole year, and the line of march was through a beautiful (in part, a grandly magnificent) country, and notwithstanding the unfavourable news from General Early's department, the "Laurel Brigade" moved with joyous hearts towards "their own country."

A journal of the march will tell best of its pleasures, and it is inserted for the benefit of the men who made it.

Tuesday, September 27th.—Bade (we hope) a long farewell to the "Old Virginia lowlands, low," and turned our faces towards the grand old mountain-bound Valley of the Shenandoah, and everybody is glad.

September 28th.—Passed Blacks-and-Whites and Burksville Junction; camped sixty miles from Lynchburg.

September 29th.—Marched through Prince Edward by the C. H. and camped in Charlotte County, thirty miles from Lynchburg. The people down here reckon all distances "from Lynchburg."

September 30th.—Marched at 9½ a. m. into Campbell County, and camped three miles from Lynchburg among the bushes; weather delightful and news from valley more so, for *they say* Early has whipped the Yankees.

October 1st.—Passed the great "Tobacco city," a dingy old town; crossed the James on a dilapidated bridge and took the road to Lexington; raining all day.

October 2nd.—Marching all day through the mountains, along the James River and canal, and it is worth a whole year of life to ride for the first time through this wildly picturesque country, but for the men who love the mountains as we do, and have not so much as seen them for five months, it is *more* than glorious to find ourselves in their very heart.

October 3rd.—Still in the blessed old Blue Ridge, but passed Lexington about 1 o'clock p. m. and camped near Fairfield; raining very hard.

October 4th.—Passed Fairfield, Midway and Greenville; camped on the famous Valley pike, seven miles from Staunton.

October 5.—Marched through Staunton to Augusta Church and turned to the left; encamped near Bridgewater; General Rosser is a major general, with Wickham's, Lomax's and the old Ashby brigades; says he is going to "run over everything in the Valley." This country is very different from the "land o' cakes and brither Scots" we used to find it; for since we were here it has been roughly handled, but we get plenty of good water and pure air, and see the mountains just as they have stood from the beginning, and that is satisfaction enough.

On the 6th of October, before daylight, it was ascertained that Sheridan was retreating and Gen. Rosser immediately started with his division in pursuit, pressing as rapidly as possible to the front, but the scene was horrifying, for with the infernal instincts of his worse than savage nature, the merciless fiend, Sheridan, was disgracing the humanity of any age and visiting the Valley with a baptism of fire, in which was swept away the bread of the old men and women and children of that weeping land.

On every side, from mountain to mountain, the flames from all the barns, mills, grain and hay stacks, and in very many instances from dwellings, too, were blazing skyward, leaving a smoky trail of desolation to mark the footsteps of the devil's inspector-general, and show in a fiery record, that will last as long as the war is remembered, that the United States, under the government of Satan and Lincoln, sent Phil. Sheridan to campaign in the Valley of Virginia.

Rosser's men tried hard to overtake them, and did capture a few, who lingered to make sure work of a mill near New Market, but they were instantly shot, and when night came the troops encamped near Brock's Gap, in a position where, all through the dark, they could see the work of the "journeymen of desolation" still progressing.

Early next morning the advance was continued, and about 2 o'clock the fire-fiends were overtaken at Mount Clifton, on Mill Creek, above Mount Jackson, and so strongly posted at the fords, that Rosser ordered Col. Dulaney to cross the creek some distance to the right, and with Hatcher's squadron of the 7th Va. Cavalry and White's battalion, attack them in flank, in order that they might be forced to uncover the ford.

The crossing was effected without difficulty, but after marching up the stream about half a mile, Capt. Hatcher met a force of the Yankees coming down, and with his usual game he charged and drove them in confusion towards Cedar Creek, and shortly after, the battalion reached the top of a hill overlooking the ford and open fields adjoining, where the Yankees were prepared to dispute Rosser's progress until they could get their wagons, and great droves of cattle and sheep which they were driving with them down the valley, clear.

Col. Dulaney halted the battalion on the crest of the hill, and the Yankees, perceiving it, commenced a brisk fire with Spencer and Henry rifles, and at the same moment, what was afterward found to be Custer's brigade, began to form on a hill just opposite, in a field that sloped gradually down to the road in which White's men were standing.

The fire became too hot for comfort, and Capt. Myers rode up to Col. Dulaney, who was coolly watching the Yankees, and said to him, "Colonel, give us orders, and let us do something quick;" but the colonel only replied, "Be cautious;" and the captain thinking that he had not been understood, as the colonel was somewhat deaf, repeated his request for orders, but received the same reply, and knowing that his men could not remain in that position a minute longer, Myers gave the order to charge, which was performed in the most brilliant style.

There was a plank fence to open before getting into the field, and here the long-range guns, which had been forced upon the men some time before, were thrown away, and the "Comanches," numbering now less than two hundred, passed the fence, and were within one hundred yards of three of Custer's regiments, one of which was in line and the other two rapidly forming; but no halt was intended or attempted, and in a very brief space the battalion was among the Yankees, neutralising their superiority in numbers and carbines by a very free use of their pistols and sabres.

The enemy stood quiet until their assailants had gotten in ten steps, when they broke up in great confusion; and Gen. Rosser, at the moment, rushed the 11th and 12th, regiments over, which completed the business, and the Yankees fled in utter rout, losing many men killed, wounded and captured, and all their trains and stock. The battalion had several men wounded, among them Captain Myers, but none were killed or very badly hurt.

Captain Hatcher had fought heavily on the right and also lost heavily, but he pushed the retreating Yankees until dark.

The command of White's Battalion now fell upon Lieutenant Nich. Dorsey, Company B, and moved with the brigade to a position on the "middle road," at a stream known as Tom's brook, where the division halted on the evening of the 8th, and Lieutenant Dorsey was ordered on picket with his battalion during the night. Very early in the morning (9th) the Yankee sharpshooters made their appearance and some very sharp skirmishing was engaged in, the men with carbines being sent to the front under command of Lieutenant Chiswell, who, with forty men, held a line more than a quarter of a mile in length for more than an hour,.

Finally the 12th regiment on his right was driven back, at the same moment a column of the enemy charged up a road to the left, and being thus outflanked on both wings, Lieutenant Chiswell and his men had to make a run for it on foot, barely escaping capture by the Yankees, who pressed them very hotly, and but for a gallant charge of the mounted men, led by Captain Dowdell, who had just arrived and taken command a few minutes before, these sharpshooters would have been captured.

The Yankee force in the road was driven back for two hundred yards, but the flank firing compelled the battalion to retire, and now the whole Confederate line, from the Valley pike to the back road, gave way, and what had before been a boasting advance of Rosser's men, turned into a shameful rout and stampede which continued for several miles, although only a comparatively small force of the enemy pursued. The battalion lost severely in wounded, among whom was Orderly Sergeant Thomas S. Grubb, of Company A, who was mortally wounded, and died one week afterwards.

He was one of the first to join the old company and no more faithful soldier, or honest, conscientious Christian gentleman ever lived to defend the stars and bars, or died to consecrate its memory.

When the lines commenced to give way the artillery of Captain Thompson was firing rapidly upon the advancing columns of the enemy, and made desperate efforts to check the Yankees long enough to give Rosser a chance to rally his people, but nothing could bring anything like order out of the confused mass of fugitives that fled so wildly from the field. They had been flanked, and without seeing more than the skirmish line of the enemy, gave way to a panic that increased each moment, and unaccountable as such things were, every soldier knows that it only requires a shout in the rear to keep a stampeded force on the run, and it was so now, for the author saw fully six hundred veteran Confederate troops flying madly along the "back road" with no pursuers but about thirty Yankees who were afraid to ride closer than a mile to the demoralised crowd in their front, and in this miserable retreat the gallant Thompson lost his guns, but he held them until the main body of the enemy was around him.

Every wagon and ambulance that Rosser had brought down with him, and every piece of artillery, fell into the Yankees' hands. And on this subject General Imboden got off a rather sharp specimen of satire at the expense of Gen. Rosser. At the opening of the campaign in the Wilderness in May, the brigade of Rosser had been highly complimented by Generals Lee and Stuart for its desperately gallant fighting, and General Rosser had christened it the "Laurel Brigade," in a general order, which prescribed that the battle-flags should be trimmed with laurel and the members should wear a badge of three or five leaves of laurel.

The brigade of Gen. Imboden had made a very poor reputation for fighting, simply because it had not been in a situation where much could be accomplished, as the enemy's cavalry in the valley was all the time in vastly superior force, and well handled.

When Rosser's men were going down the valley they flourished

The Laurel Brigade originally the Ashby Cavalry of the Army of Northern Virginia

their laurels proudly, and declared they were going to whip the Yankees and then chase Imboden's brigade to the mountains.

On the day of the stampede, when Rosser lost all his artillery, the Yankees made an advance on Imboden in the Page Valley, who drove them back and captured two guns, after which he sent his compliments to Gen. Rosser, with a polite request to know how he would "trade laurels for artillery." The "Laurel Brigade" shouted "Bully for Imboden," and they never said any more about "chasing him into the mountains."

After the stampede, the Yankees went back towards Winchester, and for ten days nothing was done but picket and scout, but on the 19th Gen. Early made his advance on the enemy, in which he surprised and routed Sheridan's army, capturing a great quantity of artillery, arms and camp equipage, with many prisoners; and was himself surprised, his army routed, his artillery captured, and his wagon train destroyed, all in one and the same day, constituting one of the most remarkable cases on record, and the only one that ever occurred in the war, where a Yankee Army, after being routed, returned the same day and inflicted a loss on its foe.

In this affair Gen. Rosser operated along the "back road," to Early's left, and succeeded in whipping the Yankee cavalry there, with small loss in men to himself.

White's Battalion was engaged in skirmishing, but the enemy did not press their right wing forward until Early had been driven on the turnpike, and when that was known, Rosser retired also.

The battalion was engaged in no special service of much consequence, for some time after the battle, and it was, in fact, hardly a good squadron, so many of the men being absent, some on detail to procure fresh horses, some on furlough, and many on sick leave, while others again were absent without leave; but they were the lucky ones who always avoided the fights, kept clear of camp duty and court-martial, and yet had a reputation as soldiers, were doted on by the ladies, and could make eloquent parlour speeches about their devotion to the "Sunny South," and tell of daring deeds performed by themselves, which, like themselves, possessed but one thing upon which the listener could rely, and that one thing was falsehood.

About the 1st of November Col. White took his battalion to Loudoun, and for several days was engaged in collecting cattle and sending them to the army, an operation which he also performed in the counties of Fauquier and Rappahannock, by which means the scarcity in the Valley was counterbalanced and the troops furnished with meat.

The brigade was now commanded by Col. O. R. Funsten, of the 11th, Col. Dulaney having been severely wounded in the stampede on the 9th, and there was great interest taken in the question as to who was to be brigadier, many of the men expressing their preference for Col. White, but, as before stated, he was not enough of a disciplinarian for Gen. Lee.

The following letter of recommendation to President Davis, in his favour, shows that his merit was appreciated by the great men of Virginia:

To his Excellency Jefferson Davis:
We take great pleasure in recommending Colonel Elijah V. White as a most fit successor to the gallant Gen. Thomas L. Rosser to the command of the 'Laurel Brigade.'
We are well aware that but little weight is generally attached to a recommendation, by mere civilians, of military men for promotion; yet we are so strongly impressed with the conviction of Col. White's peculiar fitness for the command of this distinguished brigade that we cannot forbear to place our estimate of his qualifications on record.
The chivalric courage and dashing gallantry of this battle-scarred hero, combined, as we are persuaded, with quickness of apprehension and coolness in action, inspiring perfect and enthusiastic confidence in the troops under his command, seem to point him out as a worthy successor of the noble Rosser.
Respectfully submitted,

John Letcher,
John W. Brockenborough.

The battalion arrived in camp, eight miles above New Market, on the 19th, and the next day marched down the pike with the brigade to meet the enemy, who had advanced in force as far as Rood's Hill, but only staid long enough for a slight skirmish with the Confederates, and retired to Strasburg, after which White's "people" were ordered on picket, and remained at this duty until the 24th, when they returned to camp only to prepare for a raid into the mountains.

On the morning of the 26th of November Gen. Rosser marched with two brigades, his own and Gen. Paine's, towards West Virginia, passing through Brock's Gap, and camping at Matthias', on Lost River, a place well-remembered as being the first night's bivouac of every expedition to that country, and the next morning the march was continued all day and night, when about 9 o'clock a. m. of the 28th the column advanced upon the forts at New Creek Station on the Baltimore and Ohio Rail Road.

There was a strong force, of all arms, at this place, but the general conducted everything so rapidly that almost before they knew it, he had surprised the fort where the infantry were stationed, making prisoners of the garrison, and capturing all the artillery. A charge was then made upon the station, and all the horses of the cavalry and artillery taken at the first dash, besides a number of prisoners, but the greater portion of the Yankees, who were outside of the fort, crossed the Rail Road bridge and escaped into the mountains.

A large quantity of stores of all kinds fell into the hands of the raiders, and they were busily employed in securing them when a tremendous firing was heard nearby, causing almost a panic, but it was soon learned that the depot building had been set on fire and the flames had reached about fifteen thousand rounds of fixed ammunition for artillery that had been stored there, which caused a sound very much like as if a heavy cannonade had opened in that quarter.

As soon as everything was attended to the division set out for the valley again, having destroyed the Rail Road for some distance, captured about six hundred prisoners, seven pieces of artillery, over a thousand horses and mules, and secured a large quantity of plunder of all sorts, making it a highly successful raid, without the loss of a man on the Confederate side, as the enemy were pushed so close that they did not fire a gun.

The return was effected without difficulty, and the camp reached on the 2nd of December, where all remained quiet until the 15th, when Colonel White started with the battalion for an independent raid among the Swamp-Dragons of Western Virginia.

The weather was very cold, the ground covered with snow, and both men and horses were badly prepared for such an expedition, nor could anybody form an idea of what it was intended to accomplish, and as a consequence the "Comanches" were rather savage at the prospect of a useless winter campaign among the mountains, and in order to *get any* the company officers were obliged to take *all* the men in camp, who had horses fit to travel at all, which broke seriously into the wagon-train *escort*, and left Co. "Q" with a small force.

Marching by Moorfield the colonel halted opposite Petersburg, where he was joined by the Company of the famous Capt. McNeill, of the Moorfield Valley, and by Captains Woodson and Kirkendall, with their companies, from the brigade, but all did not make his force more than three hundred men.

The 18th was a rainy day, and the colonel permitted the regiment to lie in camp, but the camp was not more comfortable than the march. About noon Henry Simpson, sometimes called the "reckless babe," started with three or four men to visit a shooting-match which some citizens had told him of, and where it was supposed that some of the "Swamps" could be found, but getting lost in the mountains they brought up at a cabin where some of the aforesaid "Swamps" were visiting. Henry and his party forced them to surrender, after which, by blowing a horn, yelling, firing, and other equally characteristic operations, they induced the people in the neighbourhood to believe that they were the crazy advance guard of an army of lunatics about to be turned loose upon the country, and securing whatever of rations they wanted, the scouts returned with their prisoners to camp without being molested by the "Dragons," a performance which no other man than Henry Simpson could have accomplished.

The command marched out the next morning on the Franklin grade, and during the day were fired at frequently, but at too great a distance to do any harm; however, about noon a party of them came too near, and were attacked by Mobberly, who killed one and chased the others into the mountains, as he said, "as far as the devil went," and being asked how far that was, he replied, "as far as he could get for the rocks."

These "Swamp Dragons" were a different people from the "bushwhackers," the latter being only citizens armed with their sporting guns, while the former were a sort of home organisation, armed by the United States, and who operated just as the Highland outlaws of Scotland, in former days did, by coming in forays upon the citizens in the low country, and appropriating whatever of their property they pleased to their own use, supplying themselves and families with bacon, beef, corn and flour from the defenceless inhabitants, and if the latter objected to this blackmail proceeding or attempted to follow their plunderers, they were unhesitatingly shot by the "Swamp Dragons." Whether or not they were in the pay of the government for such work as this, I do not know, but there is no question of the fact that the United States furnished them uniforms, arms and ammunition.

The road led by the house of a man named Bond, who was a captain among the Dragons, and on approaching it, the Confederates discovered his company on the side of the mountain, about a mile distant, and from their appearance, the colonel judged that they would attack him, but after waiting on them awhile, he gave Mobberly permission to make another charge, and the Dragons scattered, soon disappearing entirely, when the command moved forward once more; but Captain Bond had no reason to complain that the Scripture law of "*What measure ye mete it shall be measured to you again*," had not been fulfilled, for White's people took everything about the premises they wanted, and if the whole truth must be told, a good many that they didn't want, as they passed his residence.

The command halted for the night near the town of Franklin, and in the morning the extra companies left the battalion; McNeil to return to Moorfield, and Woodson and Kirkendall to go on toward the valley, by way of Monterey, while White, with his people, turned short to the right, and climbed into the Alleghany mountains, at a point where a tributary stream, to the South Branch of Potomac, cut close along the base of the main mountain, and leaving only a narrow path, up a perpendicular wall of rock that rose a hundred yards in height from the water.

Along the right bank of the stream was a little cove of flat land, completely hemmed in by the mountain, and where the colonel decided to make some investigation of the business of the Swamp Dragons, sending Capt. Myers with a party, at the same time, up this mule path, to gain the overhanging mountain top and keep the "Swamps" from getting the position on him, for if one hundred men had been stationed on the top of the precipice, they could, with stones, have whipped a thousand down in the cove.

On reaching the top, Myers sent Jack Dove, Henry Simpson, John Stephenson, and two or three others, down a road towards some houses, while with half a dozen others he struck out for a scout to the southward, and after going about two miles, came to some cabins where there were only women, but they told the scouts that their husbands, brothers, sweethearts and all, were out with the "Dragons."

Here one of the men roused the ire of a lady, by attempting to take a coverlet, to such an extent that she made an attack on him with stones, and pressed him so close and hot, cursing him roundly all the while, that Richards, unable to mount his mule, surrendered the property, and soon after a rapid firing was heard in the direction of the party over on the road, which compelled the captain to return to their assistance, and on approaching their position they were found warmly engaged with a party of the Dragons, and it was with great difficulty that Simpson and Stephenson, who were completely cut off, rejoined their comrades.

The Dragons could now be seen skulking and creeping among the rocks and trees, on the mountain side, in considerable numbers, and Myers judged it best to keep his party well together and ready for emergencies, until the colonel should get through with his arrangements in the cove and come to his assistance, which he did soon after, and the command moved down the mountain to the west, through what the citizens called "Smoke Hole," a narrow gorge with the great walls of mountains on either side.

Arrived at a cabin, with greased paper for windows, and everything else in keeping, a yearling colt and an enormous deer hound volunteered to take service in the battalion, and followed the column, which marched along a narrow path on the side of one mountain for a half mile further, when suddenly, from the top of the opposite one, the "Swamp Dragons," in considerable force, opened a hot fire, but as good luck would have it, they fired too high. The command was very much scattered, marching by file, and the head of the column halted as it came out of the gorge below, which forced the rear and centre to stand still under the fire, but the colonel, with about half a dozen men, charged instantly up the steep side of the mountain, on which the "Swamps" were posted, gallantly led by the colt and dog, who dashed into the foremost fire, and as soon as the enemy found that they had waked up fighting people in earnest they ran off; but one man, an old citizen with a sporting rifle, resolved to kill somebody, and creeping through the bushes, had levelled his gun on the colonel, at ten steps, when Nich. Dorsey saw him and warned White, who instantly fired on him with his pistol, wounding him in the hip, and at the same moment Alonzo Sellman shot him in the side, and the old man rolled over with the load still in his rifle.

The other "Swamps" all made their escape, although they had nearly equal force with the "Comanches," and had all advantages possible in position, with the latter so hemmed in that not one-fourth of them could move. The old citizen was placed behind John Walker, and carried down the mountain, but he soon died, and was left at a cabin on the road where his son lived, and with no further attention than to lay him on the ground, (except that the dog licked his face in passing,) the battalion marched on, looking out for more trouble with the Dragons. On approaching a house in a less wild and broken country, a woman, mounted man-fashion, on a horse, met the command, proclaiming that she was a rebel, and being shown the rifle of the old citizen, who had been shot, she exclaimed, "It's daddy's gun; I know it; he's a damned old Yankee, and I hope you have killed him."

Col. White made no halt at her house, although his boys had cleaned out pretty generally all the houses they had passed, but marched quietly on and camped at the first hay stacks they had seen in the mountains, in fact the only long forage found all day was buckwheat straw in little round stacks, and a few fodder blades.

On the morning of the 21st, the "Comanches" waked up finding a foot of snow on their blankets and more of it coming down, but they had slept warm and sound beneath this extra covering, and soon as possible the march was resumed for Petersburg, but it was a very disagreeable one, the weather being excessively cold and the "people" were forced to ford the South branch six times in deep water, which told bitterly on the horses, and at the last one, which was at Petersburg, some of the weak ones fell and the men had to wade out, but an early camp with plenty of feed and good attention made everything all ready for the mountain march in the morning.

The weather continued freezing cold, and the colonel halted for two nights and a day in the South Fork Valley, but on Christmas day the battalion passed Brock's Gap—the gateway to the valley—and if there was a sober man in the battalion, outside of Company E, I did not see him; was with the command all day too.

The great business was now to get permission for the "Comanches" to disband. The escaped convict from the devil's penitentiary, Sheridan, had made the destruction of forage in the Valley complete; the snow lay deep upon the blue grass field, making it impossible for the starving horses to glean the shadow of a subsistence from them; and the worn-out Rail Road, with its rickety rolling stock, was scarcely capable of carrying supplies to Early's men at Staunton, while the cavalry division, in camp at Swope's Depot, six miles west of that place, only had an allowance of six pounds of wheat straw a day for the horses, and no grain at all, all of which made White's battalion swear that they would not winter in the valley,.

But all the exertions of the colonel seemed to be fruitless, for General Early declined to permit them to shift for themselves; and now Company F, following the examples set by Companies A, B and C, deserted in a body on the night of the 27th December, leaving Company E the banner Company, as being the only one that did not stain its reputation with the shame of desertion.

The colonel was in Staunton trying to get permission to take his battalion to Loudoun, and when Captain Myers called for the morning reports on the 28th, they showed a force in camp all told of forty-three men and three officers, viz: Company A, 18 men, 1 officer; Company B, 16 men, 1 officer; Company C, 3 men; Company E, 6 men, 1 officer; and when the colonel came in on the 30th and learned of the desertion of Company F, he was so much troubled and excited over it that he declared he would not try to do anything more for the "Comanches," and would never command them again, but the Loudoun boys gathered around their chief like children around a father, beseeching him to think better of it, and not cast them away from his care entirely, and he recalled his bitter words, promising to try again to have them disbanded for this winter, as portions of General Fitz Lee's division had been done the preceding one; and on the last day of the year he started again for Staunton, telling Captain Myers he would dispatch to him the next day at Harrisonburg, telling him what to do, and when on Sunday morning, January 1st, 1865, the captain entered the telegraph office at that place, he found the welcome dispatch:

Move out as soon as you like; take my horses with you to Semper's.

E. V. White, Lieut. Colonel.

There was no time lost; but Myers had taken time by the forelock, and before leaving camp in the morning, had ordered the border companies to move out for Loudoun, and Company E to go home, so that he, being sixteen miles behind, did not overtake them until they reached Front Royal.

A violent snowstorm was raging as they passed through Manassa Gap, but it was no hindrance to them now; in fact, they were glad of it, for it served to prevent scouting parties of Yankees from coming out, and also shut other avenues through which news of them might have been communicated to the enemy; and the little band of "Comanches" felt very much like fugitives, for what they had seen and experienced in the valley, had impressed upon them, to a considerable extent, the belief that the "starry cross" was being enveloped in the gloom of annihilation, and the fact that their government was unable to support them, had tamed their spirits wonderfully.

When they entered their paradise, for such Loudoun county seemed to them, they found that the fire-fiends had been to work there too, but not to the same extent they had practiced their inhuman desolation on the Shenandoah; and now they were glad that the "Quaker settlements" and "Dutch corner" of this county, were full of men loyal to Yankee land, for, as the burning devils began their work among the Union men first, it brought such influential remonstrances to the powers that were, that the destruction was partially averted; and then the gallant Mosby, with his partisans in the mountains, had a most salutary effect in preventing the burners from wandering too far from their line of march and too near the mountains which run through this region.

So that badly damaged though they were, the people of Loudoun were far more removed from the want of provisions that fell heavily upon their neighbours over the Blue Ridge, and the soldiers, whose homes were here, found themselves in the midst of what seemed to them an endless abundance.

The men whose homes were in Albemarle, were far the most fortunate though, for, with an abundance of rations and forage, they were entirely free from any fear of the enemy's raiding parties, while Company E, in Page and Shenandoah and Warren, were not only in a destitute country, but in nightly danger of being "gobbled up" by the scouting bands sent out by Sheridan's army in the "lower Valley," but they betook themselves to the mountains and the "Little Foot Valley," or Powell's Foot, as it is sometimes called, and enjoyed themselves as only men can do who have continual danger to add zest to their enjoyment of home and rest.

Of how the winter passed away, each individual had a different story to tell, and it would be impossible to give them all in the history of the battalion; but of two or three incidents that kept the men from forgetting they were still soldiers, we must tell the history.

The three Companies, A, B and C, were scattered through Loudoun and Fairfax counties, nominally under the command of Captain Myers, Co. A, who held weekly meetings of his squadron at various points, but apart from the meetings the men were under no restrictions or control except such as the necessity for watching the Yankees and keeping out of the way of their scouting parties imposed.

Company B staid, for the most part, in the mountain near Hughesville and Leesburg, but Lieut. Chiswell had his headquarters near the Potomac, and learning of a Yankee camp on the Maryland side, at Edwards' Ferry, he concluded to attempt a raid on their horses, and early in February he got twenty-two of his men together, started from

Mrs. Mavin's mill about 8 o'clock at night, leaving their horses on the Virginia side. They crossed the river on the ice, about three-quarters of a mile below the Ferry, and coming out on the road made as good time as possible for the camp, but when within one hundred yards of it were called upon by two vedettes to halt. This brought on some firing, and without waiting a moment for the Yankees to get ready, the lieutenant and his men, giving the customary yell, and keeping it up, charged at a double-quick into the camp.

The Yankees had not yet gone to bed, and rushed to see what was coming, but one glance was sufficient for them it seems, for Lieut. Chiswell says they could not have disappeared any quicker than they did if the ground had opened beneath them and swallowed them, but there was one exception, for one man (a soldier he was) tried his utmost to fire his carbine, but it refused to go off, and he was captured in the attempt to defend his camp; he and one other were wounded, and one prisoner taken, and as soon as the camp was cleared Lieut. Chiswell and some of his men hunted up and secured fourteen good horses and rigging, the property of the 1st Delaware Cavalry. While this was being done another party paid a visit to a store nearby, and Lieut. C. says, that considering the fact of their having no light, he thinks they made a very fair selection of goods.

After arranging matters to their notion the raiders returned to the Virginia side with their spoils, bringing their one prisoner along, but as soon as they got over the question arose "What will we do with him?" and as none of the party was willing to escort the gentleman to Richmond, which was the only place they could take him, they proposed to him that if he would trade shoes with one of the captors, who was bad off in that line, they would release him unconditionally, a proposition which he eagerly accepted, and lost no time in consummating the trade.

About Christmas a Federal brigade, commanded by General Deven, had established itself in winter quarters near Lovettsville, in Loudoun county, with its right wing protected by the Short Hill and its left resting on the turnpike, near the Berlin Ferry on the Potomac; and during the time they were there these troops had treated the inhabitants of the country through which they scouted and foraged with far more courtesy and consideration than was the custom of Federal soldiers south of the Potomac.

It is true that buildings in the vicinity of their camps were in many instances stripped of their planking to be used for the more comfortable fitting up of the soldiers quarters, but as a general thing Deven showed that his warfare was not upon helpless citizens, whose persons and property were entirely at his mercy, and in this respect proved himself an exception to the majority of commanding officers in the abolition crusade upon the South, who only limited their license to the extent of their power.

And this forbearance on the part of Gen. Deven was all the more remarkable from the fact that the indomitable Mobberly, in company with a few others whose homes and sweethearts were in the Federal lines, made almost nightly attacks upon the pickets, and some nights this rough-riding scout with his little band would commence at one end of the chain and make the entire circuit of the camps, driving in every picket on the line, and keeping the regiments under arms the whole night. It is easy to imagine what a visitation of wrath this would have brought upon the citizens in his power, from Sir "Headquarters-in-the-Saddle," although they were as innocent of any complicity in or knowledge of these forays as the silent tenants of the graveyard, and because Gen. Deven looked upon them with the judgment of the true soldier in an enemy's country, and acted like a soldier and not a barbarian, the people respected him; but when his scouting parties went through the country piloted by Means' men, hen-roosts, milk-houses and ladies' wardrobes were invaded in the most approved style of genuine Yankee warfare, as was invariably the case when the "Independent Loudoun Rangers" went out on the war-path, and no dread of Mosby or White sharpened their consciences.

This much for General Deven and his men.

In February, 1865, Colonel White came to Loudoun and taking a view of the situation, resolved to try a raid into the Federal camp.

Mobberly, Lum Wenner and others who knew the Lovettsville country almost as well as if they had made it, scouted for him and with great difficulty obtained the information that the 6th New York Cavalry was encamped nearest the Short Hill and had about two hundred and fifty men in camp.

On the evening of the 17th, the colonel quietly collected what force he could in that part of the county, and at Woodgrove found he had about eighty men all told, including Colonel R. P. Chew, of the famous "Horse Artillery," and a few of Mosby's men, and about 9 o'clock the little squadron moved from the rendezvous, and passing Neersville, crossed the Short Hill by a narrow path near St. Paul's.

On clearing the mountain, a small advance guard, led by Mobberly, was sent out to capture the pickets, but very soon firing was heard, and dashing rapidly forward the colonel found that Mobberly and Frank Curry had been compelled to shoot some of the enemy at the reserve of the post, and knowing that success depended on surprising the camp, he continued the charge.

On reaching the place the unwelcome discovery was made that instead of two hundred and fifty—which was considered about as many as White's eighty men wanted—the enemy's force had been increased that day by the addition of over three hundred new men, making fully six hundred, and it had something the appearance of fool-hardiness to attack them, especially as a large portion were in strong log huts; however, a good part of the new men were in tents along the side of the camp where the attack was to be made, and their canvas walls were not much protection against the bullets that White's charging command began to pour into them as soon as they became fairly headed for them.

Great confusion was the result of the attack, and fully one hundred and fifty prisoners, and as many horses, were captured at the first onset, and if the colonel had now been content to retire, he would have had as much as he ought to have expected, but still ignorant of the new force, he judged from the confusion that he was in a fair way to become master of the camp, when, in fact, he had only captured the outskirts, and had not reached the real camp, which, as stated, was composed of huts, and under this wrong impression he remained too long, for a veteran officer, Capt. Bell, coolly proceeded to rally such of his men as were not too much demoralised, and in a very brief space had about two hundred of them in line on the opposite side of the extensive ground, with whom he advanced very unexpectedly upon the raiders, who were compelled to retire very precipitately, only bringing out about fifty horses and a dozen prisoners; but the colonel had lost nothing, only one of his men being wounded, and he very slightly, so that all he got was clear gain to his command.

On reaching Woodgrove again the command disbanded and prepared to "lie low" until the inevitable scouring of the country by parties from Deven's camp was accomplished, which sunrise would be the signal for commencing, and this was the last blow struck by the famous battalion against the enemy in Old Loudoun, whose hills and valleys were still darkened by the smoke of the burning barns and grain of her people, which had been fired by the vandal foe whom the 35th battalion was organised to protect the Loudoun border against.

20: Sheridan's March and the End

During the month following the foray into Deven's camp, the "Comanches" devoted themselves to the duty of recruiting their horses and preparing for the return to the army whenever their chief should call them from their winter quarters to perform their part in what all felt and believed was to be the final campaign of the war.

The long rest and freedom from discipline had not been beneficial to the "morale" of the command, and in fact a great deal of the energy and fire that had formerly characterized White's Battalion, had been chilled and worn out by the privations and blood of the many trying campaigns through which they had passed, and which had been productive of no result, so far as they could see, except to make each succeeding one more desperate and bloody.

The isolated raids, skirmishes and picket fights, which had once been their delight and pride, had now lost the peculiar charm to them, for all the men saw that in the magnitude to which the war had grown, such affairs were of no importance at all, and they all felt that to attain the liberty for which so much blood had already been spilled, there must be great and decisive battles fought, in which superior generalship and stubborn courage on the part of the South should overmatch the swarming legions of Northmen, who, bought by the Federal bounty, were constantly swelling the ranks of Grant's army.

Very few of the Southern soldiers doubted the ultimate success of the cause which had stood such terrible storms, and all believed that the last day of the war was very near, when, with a second Waterloo, the stars on the Southern Cross would blaze grandly in a glorious triumph or sink beneath an ocean of blood into the dark, but still glorious, gloom of defeat; and with a faith that might shame the Christian in his trust in his God the soldiers trusted in Gen. Lee, willing to give their lives to his keeping, and if *not* willing to die for their cause they *were* willing and ready to follow their great commander with unquestioning confidence wherever he might lead them.

On the 17th of March, 1865, Col. White's order for his men to join him was put into the hands of his company officers, and as it was his last general order to an organised battalion, I append it in full; and the reader will bear in mind that it was written the day after the Yankee Sheridan, whose name will ever be synonymous with infamy, had marched with fifteen thousand cavalry up the Shenandoah Valley;

Headquarters, 35th Battalion,
March 6th, 1865.

General Order, No. 1.

Soldiers of the renowned 35th: Your chief calls you again from your pleasant homes and loved ones to the field of battle! You will not be slow to answer his call.

The invading foe has penetrated to the very heart of your beloved Virginia, and proud spirits like yours cannot tamely rest while upon every breeze is borne the wailing of helpless women and children!

Come, my gallant boys! and we will throw the weight of our sabres in the scale with our brethren in arms against the dastard hordes of the North, who thus, without mercy or justice, pollute the sacred altars of our bleeding land.

E. V. White,
Lieutenant-Colonel Commanding.

After several attempts, which failed because of the scattered condition of his command, Captain Myers got about sixty men of Companies A, B and C, together on the night of the 20th, at the Semper's Mill rendezvous, and on the morning of the 21st started for Richmond, leaving Boyd Barrett and Sam White in Loudoun, with instructions to gather up the remaining "Comanches," who were not yet ready to march, and bring them out in ten days.

The line of march was by Madison C. H. and Gordonsville, through the country that Sheridan's army had just passed over, and it would have taken a man with a nicely balanced mind for calculation to figure out anything in the way of destruction that might be added to what had been accomplished by these fire-brands of Satan or *Stanton*; but what affected the military situation was the ruin to the Rail Road, for there was literally not a rail or even a cross-tie left upon it for miles, and everything that bore the faintest resemblance to a bridge.

Though it was only a foot-plank over a ditch, had been taken up and destroyed, but the injury which this destruction was intended to inflict upon the army of Gen. Lee was scarcely felt by it now, from the fact that the road ran through an already impoverished country, and there were no supplies in the valley to be brought over it, while the necessity for sending rations from Richmond to Gen. Early's forces at Staunton was ended by the annihilation of that command by Sheridan before he struck the Rail Road at all, and consequently the raiding on the road was, in a military point of view, utterly useless.

The Loudoun detachment marched by Hanover Junction, over the well-remembered fighting-ground of Cold Harbor and Mechanicsville, and joined the brigade, on the night of the 25th, near Atlee's Station, six miles north of Richmond, where it encamped for the night, and on the morning of the 26th passed through the city, crossing on Mayo's bridge to the south side of the James.

General Rosser's division was composed now of two brigades, one commanded by Brig. General McCausland, and the other—his own old brigade—by Brig. General Dearing, an accomplished young officer, who had highly distinguished himself under General Hoke at the capture of Plymouth, N. C., and also on the Petersburg lines during the long campaign of 1864, and although a total stranger to the valley brigade, his genial, affable disposition and soldierly appearance, together with the brilliant reputation which had preceded him, soon rendered him a great favourite with the troops who had followed the lead of such men as Ashby, Jones and Rosser.

The division passed Petersburg on the 27th, and on the 28th united with General W. H. F. Lee's division near Stony Creek Station, and encamped on the Nottaway River. The two divisions had less than three thousand men in them, that of Rosser not numbering over twelve hundred, when if all its men out of prison and capable of duty had been present the brigade of Dearing alone would have had certainly not less than twenty-five hundred in ranks; but what was true of one part of the army was also true of the balance of it, and General Lee had only a remnant of what had been the A. N.V. to meet Grant's hundred and sixty thousand men.

The weather was most unfavourable, as rain fell almost continually; the ground was as full of water as a sponge, so that it was difficult and dangerous to ride a horse off the roads, which were themselves almost knee-deep in mire and mud, while the streams were swollen to the brim, and many of them the troopers had to cross by swimming their horses, to the great damage of ammunition and such rations as they had.

On the 39th the command was ordered towards Dinwiddie Courthouse, where Sheridan was pressing the Confederates in his attempt to reach the South Side Rail Road, which, if cut, would completely destroy all outside communication with Richmond and Petersburg, and here Gen. Fitz. Lee, who now commanded the Cavalry Corps A. N.V., was combining all his energies to save the road and the right wing of Lee's army.

On the 31st of March the battalion took part in the battle of Five Forks, and on the 1st of April was engaged all day in fighting, scouting and picketing, in the vicinity of Hatcher's run; two names rendered famous in the history of the war by the desperate fighting of the cavalry corps, and of the glorious infantry division of General Pickett; and from now to the end, the battalion was closely connected with the operations of the army, in the last brief and gloomy, but forever glorious campaign, which crushed the hopes that had sustained the hearts of Lee's veterans through four weary years of suffering and blood, and we cannot separate the history of the "Comanches" from that of the corps to which they belonged, and in which they performed all the duties allotted to them.

The night of April 1st was a sleepless one, for the horribly incessant thundering of the artillery at Petersburg, and the rattling of the muskets over Hatcher's run, told to the troopers that the moment when they must take to their saddles and engage in the fray might be at hand; but no move was made until the morning of the 2nd, when the enemy on the right succeeded in flanking the divisions of Fitz. and W. H. Lee and Pickett, routing and driving them from their position, and the retreat began, not towards Petersburg, for that, too, had fallen, but along the Rail Road towards the West.

Here Col. White, with his battalion of eighty men, was placed in the rear, and until 3 o'clock kept back the harassing forces of the enemy which pressed close on flanks and rear, threatening to ride over the "Comanches" at almost every step of the march, which was clogged and hindered continually by the trains of wagons that the worn-out teams were dragging through the mud at what seemed almost a snail's pace.

In the evening it became necessary to halt, in order to protect the trains, and Fitz. Lee's division wheeled to the rear, where temporary breastworks were thrown up, and the Yankees checked for a time; but the battalion lost the services of two of its best officers in Lieut. Chiswell, of Company B, and Lieut. Strickler, Company E, who were both severely wounded, and also of Sergeant Alonzo Sellman, Company B, who, though shot in the head and given up for dead, survived and finally recovered.

The division of General Johnson (infantry) moved also to the rear, and by aid of the cavalry repulsed every attack of the Yankees until midnight, when the whole force again crossed Hatcher's run and halted until daylight, when the toilsome retreat was continued, the wagons still dragging along slower and slower, requiring the cavalry to dispute the passage of every stream with the enemy, and halt on every hill-top to offer battle to their pressing columns, which, flushed with success, and brave because of their numbers, grew more and more determined in their dogging attacks upon the rear, while the Confederates, worn-out, hungry and disheartened, still plodded on through rain and mud, and still faintly hoped that General Lee would stop, in some way, the advancing foe, and bring success out of the cloud of disaster that now overwhelmed them.

The quartermasters said that there were plenty of rations for the army at Amelia C. H., and the prospect kept the men up, and on the evening of the 4th they reached that place, only to meet the bitterest disappointment, for not an ounce of rations was there, and now it really did seem that famine would accomplish what all of Grant's bayonets could not effect and compel the veteran army of Lee to surrender; but *that* alternative impressed the men as worse than starvation, and plucking the buds and twigs of the trees as they passed along, these men of iron nerves and lion hearts essayed to quiet the cravings of hunger by eating them.

A short rest was permitted at the Court-house, as the enemy's cavalry had not pressed them so closely today as before, and the reason for this was discovered on the 5th, when near Amelia Springs, a strong force of them dashed in from the flank upon the wagon-train and destroyed more than a hundred wagons, causing such a stampede among the Quartermasters, teamsters and stragglers, as only those who had been in the valley with Gen. Early could imagine, and leaving the road blocked up with the smoking wrecks.

As soon as Gen. Rosser learned this, he started the brigade of Dearing forward, and as rapidly as possible they came up with the Yankees at the Springs and attacked them furiously, the 11th Virginia, under Lieut. Col. M. D. Ball, leading most gallantly, and being supported by the remainder of the division, and by a portion of Gen. Fitz. Lee's division, they whipped the enemy's cavalry handsomely, killing and wounding nearly as many as were engaged on the Confederate side, and driving the remainder back upon their infantry.

This affair did more to revive the drooping spirits of the cavalry corps than anything else could, but it is doubtful if they would have fought so fiercely if they had not been so hungry, and the first demand, on taking a prisoner, was "hand me your haversack, quick, or

I'll blow your brains out."

They camped that night at the Springs, and after this the cavalry fared much better than the infantry, for they were kept constantly riding on the flanks, from rear to front, and back again, having thereby an opportunity to obtain something to eat at the houses of citizens off from the line of march pursued by the main army, but it was saddening to see the despairing looks cast by the inhabitants of the country as they would say farewell to the boys in gray after they had willingly fed them with the best they had and saw them ride away, for they dreaded what was to come after them more than if all the plagues of old Egypt's King had been turned loose in their land and were approaching their plantations,

On one occasion, when the "Comanches" were riding past a house, some beautiful young ladies came out, and closing the gate in front of the column, said, "You are going the wrong way; please don't leave us to Sheridan's mercy; go back and whip the Yankees for our sakes;" but noticing the bitterness which their act and words added to the already heart-crushing sadness of retreat and defeat, they opened the gate, saying, "Go on; we know you can't help it; but we will pray for you, and hope that you will soon be back to drive them away; don't forget us when you meet the Yankees."

There is no doubt that the citizens of the South were subjugated long before the armies were reduced to the extremity of surrendering, but the noble-souled, true-hearted women of the sunny Southern land were not, nor ever have been, willing to surrender their faith in the justice of the "Lost Cause," or to give up their hope of a final triumph of the principles they so fondly loved and cherished, and

Though long deferred their hope hath been,
Yet it shall come at last.

The Southern women were the "power behind the throne" during the whole existence of the Confederate States, and were so acknowledged by Seward, the Yankee Secretary of State; by Butler, "the Beast;" and by Sherman, the prince of "bummers" and thieves, in their bitter persecution of them, for they knew that the steady, unchanging influence of the mothers, sisters, wives and sweethearts of the South did more to fill the ranks of the Confederate Army than all the edicts of its Congress or acts of its Conscript Bureau. And nobly and bravely did the ladies meet their persecution. Up to the day of Lee's surrender their voices were still for war, and their tongues, sharper than sabre-blades, turned against deserters and skulkers from the army and "bomb-proof" officers in it.

They equalled the women of Poland in their enthusiasm and devotion, and excelled them in persistent opposition to, and hatred of, those whom they regarded as the oppressors of their country. Many a poor fellow whom the surrender caught in a Northern prison, hesitated to take the oath of allegiance which would have procured his release, although he knew there was no longer a "Dixie" banner to be true to, because he did not know "what the women at home would say to it;" and when they *did* take the oath and go home the women sometimes blamed them, sometimes said nothing, and sometimes only remarked, "Yes, you did right, 'needs must when the devil drives,' and if ever he held the reins on earth he does today."

A Federal officer in North Carolina asked a lady "Are you not sorry you ever used your influence in support of this rebellion, when you see the misery which has followed it?"

"No, sir," she replied, "we have done what we could, and my sorrow is not for the effort we made, but for its failure. Better, ten thousand times better, the present sufferings than the degradation of submitting tamely without a struggle. We feel that we were right and that is a great thing, let the conviction cost us what it may."

But it is time to go back into the forlorn death-march of Lee's army.

Early in the morning of the 6th the enemy advanced on the pickets at Amelia Springs, who were from the second squadron of White's Battalion, commanded by Captain French, who, after a firm resistance, was compelled to retire upon the infantry, who at the same time were being warmly pressed by the main body of Grant's army in the rear, and the retreat was resumed and continued during the day with constant fighting.

On arriving near Rice's Station, a heavy force of the enemy's cavalry made an attack upon Rosser's division, but the general wheeled his regiments and threw them in fierce and desperate charges upon the foe, routing and driving him back upon his infantry.

The old brigade seemed inspired with the fiery valour which had in other days given it the proud title of the "Laurel," and impelled its men to follow the battle-flag of Dixie through blood to victory, on many a well-fought field, and never in all the years of the war, had it acted more gallantly.

When this affair opened the "Laurel Brigade" was near the High

218

Bridge, and was forced to charge the enemy's infantry, which in strong force was posted in the edge of a body of timber, and here the Yankee line was driven back, but pretty soon Gen. Dearing ordered his people to retire, and riding up to Col. White, the general informed him that the enemy had surrounded them, and asked his advice, saying, "We must cut through or surrender." The colonel only replied, by saying, "You know best what to do;" and Dearing then said, "We *must* whip that infantry, and if you and I lead the charge, it *can* be done," which Col. White at once agreed to, and the regiment were again ordered forward, the battalion in front, with Col. White and Gen. Dearing leading it.

By this time the Yankees had returned and taken position some fifteen yards in front of the woods, from which they opened a terrible fire, but the "Comanches" swept onward, supported by the brigade, and the enemy was again driven in great confusion over the hill.

Here Gen. Dearing was mortally wounded, and carried from the field, and Federal Gen. Read, who commanded the Yankee forces, was also mortally wounded, and fell into the hands of the Confederates.

On reaching the top of the hill, and finding himself in command of the brigade, Col. White halted, to reform his scattered line, preparatory to charging again upon the Yankees, who were rallying at a corner of woods about a quarter of a mile away, but while thus engaged, a small party of the enemy's cavalry, from towards Rice's, appeared, and two of them attacked the gallant Maj. Breathed, of the Stuart Horse Artillery, who had ridden alone, some distance beyond the Confederate line, and a desperate conflict took place, in full view of both parties, wherein nothing but the sabre was used.

In a short time, the major knocked one of his foes from his horse, and was almost instantly knocked down himself by the remaining one, but just as the Yankee had wheeled his horse, and was leaning over with his sabre in *tierce* to despatch the prostrate major, one of White's men approached, and with a pistol shot brought the Yankee to the ground, when Breathed sprang up with his sabre still in his hand, exclaiming, "Oh! damn you! I've got you now," and killed him.

This seemed to convince the Yankees that they could do nothing with such men, and they again retreated; but now a force of cavalry was discovered advancing rapidly upon the right of the brigade, and White turned to meet them, as they advanced bravely to the charge, led by as gallant an officer as ever graced a battlefield, but brave as was the commander, and promptly supported by his men as he was, the

"Comanches" had their fighting blood on fire, with the excitement of victory, and in a few minutes broke the Yankee line and captured their colonel, using their sabres with such desperate courage, that no troops could have stood long before this little band of men who had been starved and harassed into very devils of war and blood.

The battle-tide was again turned against the enemy's legions, and the cavalry driven back upon their infantry, who, in heavy force had taken position on the crest of a steep, rocky hill, and here for a moment they checked the Confederate advance, but General Munford had now arrived with his division, and Gen. McCausland ordered Capt. Myers to go to a regiment of dismounted men and take them to the top of the hill. This regiment proved to be the 6th Virginia Cavalry, commanded by Major Grimsley, who moved his men forward at once, and Col. Boston, the commander of Paine's Brigade, rode to the head of the regiment to lead it, but was shot through the brain.

The 6th, however, kept on, and now Colonel White led his men through a perfect storm of bullets, up the bluff, and again the Yankees fled, pursued fiercely by the "Comanches," who captured many prisoners in the chase to the river, and on reaching the bank, near the High Bridge, their infantry, to the number of over seven hundred, threw down their arms and surrendered to White's Battalion.

In this last charge, as Maj. Thompson, who had left his battery to help the cavalry fight, was riding recklessly down upon the enemy, whirling his sabre around his head and shouting to the "Comanches" to "charge the devils," that he "wanted to go in with White's Battalion," &c., a Yankee fired upon him with fatal aim, sending a bullet through his head, and the brave young officer leaped from his saddle a corpse, and thus the light of that gallant spirit, which for four years had revelled unscathed, amid the most appalling dangers, went out in blood upon the field of victory to the men whom he had so often seen following the lead of his loved friend and commander, Turner Ashby; that friend who, on the bloody field at Harrisonburg, breathed out his noble life in Jamie Thompson's arms, but his eyes' last glance rested on a beaten foe, and the last sounds that fell upon his ear were the wild triumphant yells of the "Comanches."

The battalion took four regimental standards and about eight hundred prisoners, while the total of prisoners amounted to about eleven hundred, greatly exceeding the whole Confederate force engaged, and their loss in killed and wounded was certainly not less than four hundred, including many officers, and six flags were displayed as trophies of the fight.

General Dearing had been carried to a house near the field, and after the battle Colonel White went to see him, finding him unable to speak above a whisper, and in fact, dying. Gen. Rosser was seated on one side, and as White came in, the wounded general took his hand, and pointing with the other to the brigadier's stars on his own collar, turned his face to General Rosser and whispered, "I want these to be put on his coat."

Among the wounded in the battalion was Benjamin F. Leslie, Company A, who had been remarkable for his unwavering faith in the success of the South, through all the gloomy retreat, even when every heart was despondent, and who while fighting desperately at the bridge was mortally wounded.

He, too, was at the house, and when the colonel went in to see him found him suffering greatly from the bullet wound through his body and lying with his knees almost drawn up to his chin. The colonel asked him if he was badly hurt, and he replied, "Yes, colonel, I am mortally wounded."

"Oh!" said the colonel, "I hope not. Ben, you must cheer up."

"No, sir," said Ben, "there's do hope for me; I asked the doctor and he says I must die," and then raising his head, with the light of faith in and devotion to his cherished country's cause beaming from his eye, he exclaimed, "But there are men enough left to gain our independence."

The gallant commander of the 12th Virginia Cavalry, Major Nott, was killed in the charge upon the infantry early in the engagement, and the scene was full of sad and solemn meaning as the soldiers buried their dead comrades on the hill near the house, just before leaving the ground to the enemy, but many felt that the hero blood of the Southland had not been spilled in vain when they saw so many of their foes laid beneath the same sod, and knew they had lost so many more, but the enemy had fought bravely and well, and the Confederate loss was very severe, the battalion alone losing eighteen killed and wounded out of about forty engaged.

Only the first squadron was present at the opening of the fight, as Capt. French with his squadron had been left on picket at Amelia Springs in the morning, and all day long was bringing up the rear closely pressed by the enemy, and compelled to turn and fight at every hill and wood and stream along the route, so that he did not reach the ground until towards the close of the battle.

About dark the command of White reached the main army, which was still wearily plodding along the muddy road towards Lynchburg, and now the brigade lay in line of battle until midnight, waiting for the slow-moving train to pass, while less than a mile away the camp-fires of Grant's army shone brightly through the gloom of that dismal night.

Two hours after the last wagon had passed, the old Valley brigade marched silently along in rear of the whole army, but it was as slow as ever, for the rain was again falling, and the bottom of the road sinking deeper and deeper beneath the mud, so that, although the enemy had rested during the hours of darkness, their advance was up with the Confederates by 9 o'clock on the morning of the 7th, and the latter, who had toiled on through all the weary night, were forced to renew and continue the same old story of turning at bay on every hill along the route.

About noon the rear-guard reached Farmville, in Prince Edward County, and so stubbornly did Rosser hang on in his bull-dog style to the favourable positions around that place, that the pursuit was checked, and the enemy compelled to resort to a flank movement, which their great force rendered easy, but which came to grief from being performed too near the view of Gen. Rosser.

During the operations on the hills of Farmville a Federal brigade approached White's people, and the commander, mistaking them for a part of his own force, sent a courier forward to order them not to advance too far ahead of their supports, but Col. White, not wishing to be so supported, made no attempt to obey the Yankee's order, and only pointed his pistol at the courier's head with a demand for his surrender, which was of course complied with.

After destroying the bridges, the brigade of White retired, and the battalion, being the rear guard, was very hotly pressed, many of the men being forced to swim the river in effecting their escape, as the enemy advanced their whole force the moment the Confederates commenced to fall back, and Captain Dowdell's Company, together with a portion of Co. A, under Lieut. Marlow, were very near being taken.

After getting clear of Farmville the men found some oat stacks, and of course helped themselves to what they could carry, intending to feed their horses at the first halt, and as Col. White was riding along with Capt. Myers, who was in command of the battalion, each of them carrying a sheaf of oats before him, while the battalion was scattered for a mile (there being no thought of danger now as the enemy had halted at Farmville), a sudden commotion was observed in the woods through which the route of the main army lay, and in a few moments Gen. Rosser appeared, almost alone, with the Yankees charging after him.

Col. White instantly ordered his people forward, and hastily throwing away their oats, the men went in again, driving the enemy back upon their main body, which proved to be the flanking force before spoken of, and numbered about four thousand cavalry commanded by Gen. Gregg, who had been sent over the river to fall upon the wagon train while the affair was enacting at Farmville, but although they reached to within fifty yards of the train they did not reach it from the fact that the very men whom they had left confronting Sheridan at Farmville, were here between them and the wagons.

The few men of Rosser's division held the whole force of the enemy in check until Gen. Fitz. Lee's division came up, and the two together attacked so vigorously that Gregg's command was driven back in confusion before scarcely a third of its number, and Gen. Gregg himself was captured as he was gallantly attempting to rally his fugitive troops, he having made the same mistake as the courier to Col. White, and tried to prevail on a body of Confederates, who were chasing the Yankees, to "halt and form."

After this, the Southern troops destroyed about one hundred of their wagons, as it was evident they could not take them much farther, and putting their teams to the other wagons attempted to make up in speed for the time lost already; and tonight the colonel halted his brigade in line of battle again to watch the rear, and about two o'clock in the morning followed on after the army, leaving the battalion to act as rear guard for him, with instructions not to approach nearer than one mile to the brigade unless *forced* back, and it was fully understood by the "Comanches" that they were not to consider themselves *forced* without a fight.

About sunrise the enemy became very troublesome and as not more than one mile could be marched without a halt to wait for the wagons to be pulled out of the mud, which in many places was hub-deep, the position of the rear guard became a very exciting one, especially as it was found that the enemy's infantry had left the road and was outmarching them through the fields and open pine woods to the left.

During one of the halts, about nine o'clock, as the battalion was, as usual, drawn up in line facing the left, and Capt. Myers, with a few pickets, was a half mile from his people down a road that led towards the enemy, a party of four Yankees were seen approaching through the woods, and as they came very confidently along making no sign to the two Confederates, who were standing in full view, it was decided best to halt them with a shot from a Sharpe's rifle, which resulted in the killing of the foremost Yankee, and in falling he displayed a white flag, which, until that moment, had not been seen, because of the pines.

Both parties hastily retired, and it being now discovered that the army was moving again, the battalion also marched quietly, but in the distance of two miles another halt was called, and now the country being open the thousands of men in blue could be seen, drawing close along the flank and rear, but what puzzled the Confederates was the total absence of cavalry, in any force, with Grant's army.

While standing here, a mounted Yankee was observed galloping along the road waving a white flag, and being met by one of the battalion, he presented a letter addressed to General Lee, but Capt. Myers refused to forward it unless the line of infantry, now within half a mile, would halt, which the bearer of the flag communicated to the enemy's officers, and a halt was immediately ordered, the command being distinctly heard by the Confederate rear-guard.

The letter was now sent forward to Gen. Lee, and in half an hour an answer, directed to Gen. Grant, was returned, with a request from Gen. Lee that one or two of the *best dressed* officers in the battalion be sent in company with the truce-bearer to the enemy's line, and this mission fell upon Capt. French and Lieut. James, who rode back to Grant's headquarters and met with his Chief-of-Staff, Gen. Williams, who treated them handsomely, gave them a drink of whiskey, and talked, as James said, "exactly like a gentleman."

He asked them a number of questions, and informed them that they (the Yankees) had taken thirty-two thousand prisoners since the capture of Petersburg. Capt. French asked him the meaning of the correspondence between the generals, to which he replied that Gen. Custis Lee had been taken prisoner, and his father, Gen. Lee, had merely inquired if he was killed or wounded, and that Gen. Grant had replied, telling him that his son was unhurt.

Another letter was dispatched to Gen. Lee, and the *well-dressed* Confederates returned to their own lines, with no idea that they were aiding the negotiations for the surrender of Lee's army by carrying the letters on the subject back and forth, and as the wagons were again out of the mud the rear-guard resumed its march, as also did the Federal

224

army. About 3 o'clock the battalion was relieved from its perilous position in the rear by a portion of Gen. W. H. F. Lee's division, and soon after the division of Rosser was ordered to the front.

The scene which presented itself to the view of the rear-guard as it passed the army on the way was distressing in the extreme. The few men who still carried their muskets had hardly the appearance of soldiers as they wearily moved along the toilsome route, their clothes all tattered and covered with mud, their eyes sunken and lustreless, and their faces peaked and pinched from their ceaseless march, through storm and sunshine, without food or sleep, through all that dire retreat, when in fact they were worn-out, from excessive duty in the trenches at Petersburg, before the retreat begun.

Many of the men who had thrown away their arms and knapsacks were lying prone on the ground along the road-side, too much exhausted to march further, and only waiting for the enemy to come and pick them up as prisoners, while at short intervals there were wagons mired down, their teams of horses and mules lying in the mud, from which they had struggled to extricate themselves until complete exhaustion had forced them to be still and wait for death to glaze their wildly starting eyes, and still their quick gasping and panting for the breath which could scarcely reach some of them through the mud that almost closed their nostrils; but through all this a part of the army still trudged on, with their faith still strong, and only waiting for General Lee to say where they were to face about and fight, for they knew that the enemy would be whipped, and that every day brought nearer the last decisive battlefield, where the hosts of the North would be overthrown and the final success of the Confederate States assured.

About sunset of the 8th the cavalry, now entirely clear of the army, went into a pleasant bivouac in a body of timber, where they were permitted to build fires and remove the saddles from the horses' backs, upon which they had constantly been since the fifth, and the tired troopers felt good at the prospect of an all-night rest, but in less than two hours the bugles sounded "to horse," and the march was again taken up, and slowly followed until about two o'clock in the morning, when the division of Rosser, which was in front, halted at Appomattox C. H.

After waiting awhile to see if anything further was to be done, the men made fires of the fences, and sat down, each man holding his bridle rein and wondering what would come with daylight, but about an hour before dawn a battery exactly in front opened fire, and now the absence of cavalry in the rear during all of the day before was explained, as was also the reason why the Confederate cavalry had been brought forward, for right here, exactly before them, stood Sheridan's whole command, cutting off the retreat of the army from Lynchburg.

Soon after the battery opened, Colonel White moved his brigade forward a short distance and formed on a hill near some timber that extended to the head of a swamp, and here it remained until after sunrise, when the colonel rode out to the battalion, which was on the right of the line, and informed Captain Myers that the army was about to surrender and Rosser was arranging to take his cavalry out. There was no time to arrive at a full realization of the meaning contained in this simple announcement, for the enemy was now pressing vigorously in front and Sheridan's cannon were throwing their shells among the Confederates with great rapidity.

General Rosser moved forward about half a mile and halted to wait for a demonstration which General Gordon, who now commanded all that was left of "Stonewall" Jackson's old corps, had arranged to make with his infantry, in order to draw Sheridan's force towards the left, and about 7 o'clock the signal was given in the rattling rifles of Gordon's men, who had followed Lee and Jackson through victory after victory, from Manassas, where they had made "Stonewall" immortal, to fire their last shot and lay down their arms in surrender at Appomattox Court-house.

Rosser now put White's brigade in front and moved promptly upon the enemy, who appeared not to understand exactly what was expected of them, and as White took a position on a hill in an open field about four or five hundred yards from a division of Federal cavalry, the latter only looked, but made no hostile movement, and now Rosser, finding the way open to gain the Lynchburg road, pushed forward with the brigades of Munford and McCausland, leaving Colonel White to guard the rear and the old brigade to be the sacrifice, if necessary, to secure the safety of the balance.

After looking at the little line of Confederates for a little while a party of about four hundred marched from the division and commenced to form on the same hill with the little remnant of the "Laurel Brigade," but this was too much for White, and he ordered Capt. Hatcher, of the 7th regiment, to charge, and Capt. Myers, of the battalion to support him. The enemy soon broke and retreated upon their reserve, which in turn gave way, and the whole force fled, panic-stricken, before the little party of about one hundred Rebels, who were within an hour of surrendering, and again, but for the last time, the avenging sabres of the Ashby boys glanced fiercely over the Yankee cavalry.

Many of the enemy fell killed or wounded, but no prisoners were taken, and when the chase had continued about two miles the colonel again called a halt, and the boys had to dismount and skirmish with the Yankee infantry for a short time, and when the great firing of guns and sky-rending shouts of Grant's army away off to the front and right announced that 9 o'clock had passed, and that General Lee, with his troops had surrendered, Colonel White withdrew his men and took the way to Lynchburg, overtaking Rosser about seven miles from that place, and on reaching the city everything was in confusion, nobody knew what to do and all thought it pretty certain that the Yankees would soon be up.

About dark Gen. Rosser ordered the division to move to the Fair Grounds, near the town, and wait for orders, but shortly after a rumour was circulated to the effect that the Yankees were advancing, and that Gen. Grant had sent a summons to the mayor ordering that the place be surrendered by 9 o'clock that night, which produced a panic, and the regiments moved out across the river, where Colonels White and Ball, the only two field officers in the whole brigade, addressed them, urging the men to still keep their faith bright and trust in the God who "gives not the battle to the strong;" and about midnight the Laurel Brigade was disbanded, never to meet again, the men going to their homes to wait for orders (which were never received) to follow Gen. Rosser and Col. White to the army of Johnson.

After this, the men who were not captured went by twos and threes to the Federal officers and were paroled, and by the 1st of May the "Comanches" could scarcely be recognised in the men who were in their fields holding the plough-handles, or behind the counter, but they hoped against hope for many months that they would be called upon to rally again around the stars and bars and draw their sabres for "Dixie" and Freedom.

Hope died at last though, and the world saw a nation of soldiers transformed, as suddenly as the night vanishes before the rising sun, into a nation of quiet, law-abiding citizens.

The war was over; the Confederacy was dead; and her soldiers accepted the terms granted by their conquerors, in good faith, and began to hope that peace would bring them back the blessings which the sword had driven from them, and that the country might be united, although they were conscientious in the conviction that the Southern States had the *right* to separate from the compact styled the Federal Constitution, and that it was vastly to their interests to do so; and thus the Southern Confederacy, in her brief but brilliant career, followed the footsteps of nations gone before, and like them, passed through all the chances and changes of triumph and defeat that in this weak human life follow each other so closely from sunshine to the sunless land.

Lists of Killed and Wounded in White's Battalion

The list of killed and wounded is incomplete, in consequence of the loss of all the muster-rolls, which were in the wagons, and at the surrender of the army, fell into the hands of the enemy; and the author will esteem it a favor on the part of any one who will furnish him with the names of any who are omitted.

KILLED AND DIED OF WOUNDS.

" On fame's eternal camping ground,
Their silent tents are spread ;
And glory guards with solemn round
The bivouac of the dead."

COMPANY A.

Brook Hays, Waterford, August 27th, 1862.

Peter J. Kabrich, mortally wounded, August 27th, 1862, and died at Waterford, September 6th, 1862.

Lycurgus W. Bussard, killed, Glenmore, October 21st, 1862.

Samuel Jenkins, killed, Poolsville, December, 1862.

Daniel L. Prince, killed, Brandy Station, June 9th, 1863.

Henry O. Hummer, killed, Parker's Store, Nov. 29th, 1863.

Henry R. Moore, killed, Wilderness, May 6th, 1864.

Joseph Hendon, killed, Wilderness, May 6th, 1864.

Samuel W. Crumbaker, Wilderness, May 6th, 1864, mortally wounded, and died May 16th, 1864.

Thomas E. Tippett, killed, Wilderness, May 12th, 1864.

William Edwards, killed, Trevillian, June 11th, 1864.

Samuel T. Presgraves, killed, Monk's Neck, Sept. 16th, 1864.

William Brown, killed, Monk's Neck, September 16th, 1864.

Orderly-Sergeant Thomas S. Grubb, mortally wounded at Tom's Brook, October 9th, 1864, and died Oct. 16th, 1864.

229

EDWIN DRISH, killed in Leesburg, July, 1864, after he had su
  rendered to Means' Company.
JAMES R. DOUGLASS, killed at Neersville, February, 1865.
BENJAMIN F. LESLIE, killed at High Bridge, April 6th, 1865.
JOHN W. MOBBERLY, murdered in Loudoun, April, 1865.

COMPANY B.

EDWARD WELCH, killed, Brandy Station, June 9th, 1863.
— McCORMACK, killed, Mount Clifton, October 7th, 1864.

COMPANY C.

Capt. R. B. GRUBB, killed, Waterford, August 7th, 1863.
Lieut. THOMAS W. WHITE, killed, Wilderness, May 8th, 1864.
JOHN C. GRUBB, killed, Waterford, August 7th, 1863.
— WILSON, killed, Maryland, September, 1863.
JOHN J. CLENDENING, killed, Wilderness, May 5th, 1864.
JOHN DOUGLASS, killed, Wilderness, May 6th, 1864.
WILLIAM D. GOODING, killed, Hillsboro', January, 1865.

COMPANY E.

ISAAC N. BRUMBACK, killed, Brandy Station, June 9th, 1863.
MARCUS McINTURFF, killed, Brandy Station, June 9th, 1863.
PHILIP A. HOCKMAN, killed, Wilderness, May 6th, 1864.
GEORGE BENNETT, killed, Wilderness, May 20th, 1864.
— ROGERS, killed, Wilderness, May, 1864.

COMPANY F.

— GROGAN, killed, Greenland Gap, April 25th, 1863.
— BROY, killed, Wilderness, May 6th, 1864.
— RHODES, killed, Hawes' Shop.
CHARLES SINCLAIR, killed, Tom's Brook, October 9th, 1864.
Lieut. WATTS, killed at Brandy Station, June 9th, 1863.

WOUNDED IN THE BATTALION.

COMPANY A.

Sergt. JOHN DOVE, Waterford, August 27th, 1862.
JACOB H. ROBERTSON, Glenmore, October 21st, 1862.
JOHN STEPHENSON, Snicker's Gap, November 1st, 1862.
FENTON FOLEY, Greenland Gap, April 25, 1863.
THOMAS SPATES,   "   "   "   "
Lieut. W. F. BARRETT, Brandy Station, June 9th, 1863.
EDWARD S. WRIGHT,   "   "   "   "
PHILIP W. CARPER,   "   "   "   "
WILLIAM P. KYLE,   "   "   "   "
H. C. McFARLAND,   "   "   "   "
JAMES T. FREEMAN,   "   "   "   "
CHARLES F. GALLAWAY,   "   "   "   "
ROBERT F. JONES, Edward's Ferry, September 2d, 1863.
Corp. D. C. PETTINGALL, Thornton's Mill, October 10th, 1863.
CHARLES L. MYERS,   "   "   "   "
Sergt. THOMAS S. GRUBB, Wilderness, May 5th, 1864.
  "   GEO. F. EVERHART,   "   "   "
C. BOYD BARRETT,   "   "   "
J. FRANK BICKSLER,   "   "   "
JOHN KEPHART,   "   "   "
W. W. McDONOUGH,   "   "   "
Lieut. BENJ. F. CONRAD,   "   May 6th, 1864.
Sergt. WILLIAM SNOOTS,   "   "   "
WILLIAM O. HOUSHOLDER,   "   "   "
JOHN HOWARD, Enan Church, May 28th, 1864.
Lieut. R. C. MARLOW, Trevillian, June 11th, 1864.
Sergt. EDWARD L. BENNETT, Trevillian, June 11th, 1864.
JOHN H. MARLOW, Sapony Church, June 29th, 1864.
Capt. F. M. MYERS, Mount Clifton, October 7th, 1864.
JAMES GOARD,   "   "   "   "
Corp. E. H. TAVENNER, Tom's Brook, October 9th, 1864.
WILLIAM TITUS,   "   "   "   "

O. M. BUSSARD, Fairfax, February, 1865.
GEORGE CRAIG, High Bridge, April 6th, 1865.
GEORGE LEE, High Bridge, April 6th, 1865.
JOHN W. FLETCHER, High Bridge, April 6th, 1865.
JOHN W. WHITE, High Bridge, April 6th, 1865.

COMPANY B,

FRANK WILLIAMS, Greenland Gap, April 25th, 1863.
Orderly-Sergeant HENRY C. SELLMAN, Brandy Station, June 9th, 1863.
Capt. GEORGE W. CHISWELL, Brandy Station, June 9th, 1863, badly.
Lieut. J. R. CROWN, Brandy Station, June 9th, 1863.
WILLIAM HERBERT,   "   "   "   "
PINKNEY MARTIN,   "   "   "   "
— PETERS,   "   "   "   "
ELIAS PRICE, Parker's Store, November 29th, 1863.
DANIEL KEY,   "   "   "   "
CHARLES SMITH, Moorfield, January, 1864.
ALONZO SELLMAN, Wilderness, May 5th, 1864.
FRANK WILLIAMS,   "   "   "
WILLIAM SHEHAN,   "   "   "
ROBERT DADE,   "   "   "
MARTIN TAYLOR,   "   May 6th,   "
ELIJAH VIERS,   "   "   "
— ODEN,   "   "   "
CRONE PHILLIPS, (bugler,) Trevillian, June 11th, 1864.
Lieut. E. J. CHISWELL, Tom's Brook, October 9th, 1864.
Sergt. ALONZO SELLMAN, "   "   "   "
"   CHARLES GREEN, "   "   "   "
HENRY ORME,   "   "   "   "
BYRON THOMAS,   "   "   "   "
AB. GAMAR, Lovettsville, February 25, 1865.
Lieut. E. J. CHISWELL, Hatcher's Run, April 3d, 1865.
Sergt. ALONZO SELLMAN,   "   "   "   "
LEWIS NEEDHAMMER, High Bridge, April 6th, 1865.
CHARLES SCOLL, Monk's Neck, September 16th, 1864.

COMPANY C.

JAMES HOOD, Glenmore, October 21st, 1862.
JOHN J. WHITE,   "   "   "
WILLIAM FRITZ,   "   "   "
Corp. JAMES M. FOSTER, Greenland Gap, February 25th, 1863.
SYDNOR FOUCHE,   "   "   "   "
Sergt. SILAS COPELAND, Brandy Station, June 9th, 1863.
JOHN W. HAMMERLY,   "   "   "   "
JOSEPH S. HART,   "   "   "   "
JOHN MILBOURN,   "   "   "   "
WILLIAM D. GOODING,   "   "   "   "
— WILSON, Waterford, August 7th, 1863.
MAITLAND TAYLOR, Wilderness, May 5th, 1864.
RICHARD FOLLEN,   "   "   "
MANLY TRIPLETT,   "   "   "
Color-Sergt. T. N. TORREYSON, Wilderness, May 6th, 1864.
WILLIAM T. CLENDENING,   "   "   "
HUGH S. THOMPSON, (mortally,)   "   "   "
AARON T. BEANS, Sapony Church, June 29th, 1864.
Sergt. EBEN SIMPSON, Tom's Brook, October 9th, 1864.
THOMAS ELGIN,   "   "   "   "
ELWOOD BEANS,   "   "   "   "
Lieut. SAM. E. GRUBB, Hillsboro', January, 1865.
GEORGE CHAMBLIN, Neersville, February, 1865.
Color-Sergt. RODNEY MATTHEWS, High Bridge, April 6th, 1865.
JOHN W. DAVISSON,   "   "   "   "

COMPANY E.

Lieut. H. M. STRICKLER, Payne's Church, April 2d, 1865.
     "   A. C. GRUBBS, Parker's Store, November 29th, 1863.
WILLIAM T. WARREN, Wilderness, May 6th, 1864.
JACOB HUFFMAN,   "   "   "
JAMES ATWOOD, Cabin Point, August 20th, 1864.
CHARLES B. FRISTOE, Brandy Station, June 9th, 1863.

RECAPITULATION.

	Killed.	Wounded.	Total.
Company A	18	37	55
" B	2	28	30
" C	7	25	32
" E	5	6	11
" F	4	1 at Brandy Stat'n.	5
" D	—	3 " "	3
	26	100	136

Service With the Laurel Brigade

William N. McDonald

The cavalry being not only the eyes and ears of the army, but also foragers for it, it was not in the nature of things that Fitz Lee's force, being now augmented by the arrival of Rosser's brigade, could long remain idle in camp. An expedition west of the mountains was ordered by Early to secure cattle for the use of Lee's army, and at the same time to capture detached bodies of the enemy and do such damage to his communications on the Baltimore and Ohio Railroad as might be found practicable.

The expedition under General Fitz Lee started in the latter days of December. The citizens of the Moorefield and South Branch valleys were loyal, with few exceptions, to the Confederacy, and most of them zealous in its cause, and had consequently suffered, both in their persons and substance, from the frequent predatory visits of the Federals.

When it was known that the expedition was made for the purpose of procuring beef for Lee's army, it was not long before droves of well-fed steers were on their way to "Dixie."

Upon arriving at Moorefield, Fitz Lee learned that a Federal force, eight or nine hundred strong, was at Petersburg and strongly fortified behind entrenchments and abattis. For the want of artillery and because much of the small-arms ammunition had been ruined in the storm, he decided not to attack Petersburg, but to move upon the enemy's line of communication on the Baltimore and Ohio Railroad.

On the morning of January, the 2nd, he marched down the South Branch, and began to cross the Branch Mountain at Mills Gap. Rosser's brigade led the advance, with the Eleventh Virginia in front, followed by the Seventh.

Upon nearing the top of the mountain, the road was found to be blockaded with fallen trees, and a way had to be opened by axemen. While engaged in this, scouts reported that a Federal wagon train, moving in the direction of New Creek, was approaching the point where the road on which Rosser was marching forked with the Petersburg and New Creek road.

Rosser at once hurried up his foremost regiments, and the men at many places leaped their horses over the fallen trees in their eagerness to get to the front.

After passing the top of the gap and rounding a curve in the road, they came in sight of the train, which was moving slowly and in careless security, attended by a small guard of soldiers. There were about forty wagons, six mules to each, loaded, as was afterwards found, with ammunition, hides, and sutlers' stores.

Rosser ordered the Eleventh, commanded by Maj. E. H. McDonald, to charge the train, and the Seventh, commanded by Colonel Dulany, to follow closely in support. The column emerged from cover of the woods, and with loud shouts galloped down the mountainside. The train quickened its snail-like pace into a run, and then rushed along at a furious speed. In their eagerness to escape, the faster teams tried to pass the slower ones, and then followed upsets and collisions, mules entangled, kicking to free themselves from harness, and great confusion. It seemed at first an easy capture, the guard in sight making off to the woods.

But as the train halted, about seventy-five infantrymen leaped out of the wagons, and running up the hillside beyond the road, began to fire upon the nearest horsemen. They were soon charged by a small portion of the Eleventh, under Major McDonald, and most of them compelled to surrender. Among the captured sutlers' stores were canned goods of every description, which were much enjoyed by the victors.

Fitz Lee now moved down Patterson's Creek with foragers on the flanks gathering cattle and sheep. At Burlington more sutlers' stores were captured, and a blockhouse abandoned by the enemy was destroyed.

After a short delay at Burlington the column moved on to Ridgeville and pitched camp. This place was six miles from New Creek, against which Fitz Lee intended to advance the following day. But a severe snowstorm set in during the night, and next morning Fitz Lee withdrew and returned to the Valley, going by way of Romney and Brock's Gap to Harrisonburg. He took back with him 400 cattle and no prisoners.

Very soon after his return Fitz Lee with his command rejoined the Army of Northern Virginia. Rosser's brigade, however, remained with Early, then in command of the Valley district.

After a short rest the brigade participated in another cattle expedition across the mountain that proved quite successful, and the fruitful results of which were due in a great measure to Rosser's skilful handling of his command.

On January 28th, 1864, General Early, with Rosser's brigade, Thomas' brigade of infantry, all the effective men of Gilmore's and McNeil's Partisan Rangers, and four pieces of McClannahan's Battery, moved from New Market to Moorefield.

On the 29th Rosser, with the cavalry and artillery, accompanied by Early, reached Moorefield somewhat in advance of the infantry. Scouts having reported that a large train was on its way from New Creek to Petersburg, Rosser was ordered to cross over the Branch Mountain and capture it.

Accordingly, on the morning of the 30th, he marched from Moorefield, having besides his own brigade one or two pieces of McClannahan's Battery.

Moving by way of the Moorefield and Alleghany turn pike, when nearing the top of the mountain, he found the road to be blocked with fallen trees, and the gap held by a regiment of Federal infantry. Rosser, dismounting the Twelfth Regiment, made a vigorous attack, and soon forced his way through, driving the enemy before him, who retired in the direction of Medley to meet the train which was then coming up towards Petersburg.

Upon discovering Rosser's approach, the Federals parked their train of ninety-five wagons at Medley, and prepared to defend it. The guard consisted of about 800 infantry and a small body of cavalry, which seemed amply sufficient to keep off an inferior number of Confederate cavalrymen. Rosser at once determined to attack, though having all told not more than 400 men. The Twelfth Regiment, under Colonel Massie, was ordered to go around and fall upon the enemy's rear, and the other regiments, partly dismounted, were advanced upon his front and flank.

The attempt was a bold one. The Federals were in a defensive position, superior in numbers, and at that time dismounted cavalrymen were hardly considered a match for disciplined infantry.

Encouraged, however, by the confidence of their leader and stimulated by the sight of the rich prize, the Confederates moved forward with spirit to the assault. The Federals stood firm and repulsed the first onset, inflicting some loss. Rosser determined to attack again, as by this time a piece of artillery had reached the field, which he ordered to immediately open upon them, and the sight of its bursting shells spreading panic among the teamsters, was exhilarating to the Confederates.

After one or two salutes from his gun, Rosser renewed the attack. The dismounted men advanced on the enemy's left, while the cavalry, led by Major Meyers, charged in front. The Federals broke and fled in disorder, leaving all their wagons and forty-two prisoners in the hands of the victors. With the retreating Federals the teamsters carried off mules belonging to nearly forty wagons, which escape was owing greatly to the fact, as stated by General Rosser, that the Twelfth Regiment, from some misunderstanding, had failed to get in position in the rear before the retreat began. The wagons were loaded with bacon, sugar, coffee, and other army supplies, and proved to be a very valuable capture.

In the engagement Rosser lost in killed and wounded twenty-five men. The enemy's loss was greater. Their dead and wounded were left on the field, but the number is not reported.

On the morning of the 1st of February Rosser, now reinforced by Thomas' brigade of infantry, moved against Petersburg. Upon arriving there, it was found that the Federal force was gone, having abandoned in their haste a considerable quantity of ammunition and commissary stores.

From Petersburg Rosser, in obedience to orders from Early, moved down Patterson's Creek to collect cattle, and do what damage he could to the Federal communications on the line of the Baltimore and Ohio Railroad.

After sending Colonel Marshall with the Seventh Regiment to hold the gap at Mechanicsburg against General Averill, who was expected from Martinsburg, Rosser marched down Patterson's Creek to its mouth, sending parties out to bring in cattle and sheep. Upon reaching the line of the Baltimore and Ohio Railroad at the mouth of the creek, he captured one guard there, and destroyed the railroad bridges over the Potomac, Patterson's Creek, and the canal. With his prisoners and cattle, he now retraced his steps, moving cautiously to avoid Averill, who, he learned, had forced the gap at Mechanicsburg and gotten in his rear.

By taking by-roads at different points, Rosser succeeded in eluding Averill, who, mistaking his purpose, or fearing to come up with him, adroitly kept out of his way while pretending to pursue him.

Rosser with all his prisoners, about 1,200 cattle, and other captures reached Moorefield unmolested by the enemy.

Captain John McNeil also arrived, bringing from beyond the Alleghany 300 cattle.

General Averill, disappointed on all sides, now approached Moorefield and menaced it. Early recalled Thomas' brigade, which had started for the Valley, and ordered Rosser to withdraw through Moorefield as if in retreat. He thought to draw Averill into the clutches of his infantry, but the wily Federal, whose caution now served him a good turn, refused the bait and halted. Early, after waiting a few hours, set out for the Valley, taking with him fifty of the captured wagons, 1,500 cattle, and 500 sheep.

Stuart's appreciation of what was done by Rosser and his command on this expedition, is shown in the following endorsement of Rosser's report:

> The bold and successful enterprise herein reported furnishes additional proof of General Rosser's merit as a commander, and adds fresh laurels to that veteran brigade, so signalised for valour already.

Upon its return to the Valley the brigade went into camp near Weyer's Cave. Many of the sutlers' stores found in the captured wagon train, had been appropriated by the soldiers, and for several days the new camp was the scene of festive mirth. Brandied cherries, pickled oysters, boned turkey, and other delicious canned edibles, formed a part of the menu, while Boston gingerbread and Goshen cheese were served *ad libitum*.

The weather was bright and cool. There were daily visits to Weyer's Cave, not a few picnics, and an occasional horse-race. The luxuries disappeared rapidly, and when the sugar and coffee had been exhausted, the troopers began to yearn for another raid.

The opportunity soon came. On the evening of the 29th of February, the command was again in saddle, and started across the Blue Ridge.

Kilpatrick and Dahlgren were then making their notorious raid on Richmond. Rosser marched rapidly to take part in the pursuit. At the outset the weather was fine, and many of the men not dreaming of a

long march, left their overcoats in camp. By night the clouds thick-
ened, the moon and the stars were hid, and a drizzling rain began to
fall. By and by a stiff northeaster blew, and before midnight it began to
sleet. The falling drops freezing as soon as they touched horse or man,
enveloped each in a sheet of ice. The moon from behind the clouds
furnished enough light to make objects visible, and the appearance of
the moving horsemen was weird and ghostlike. Hat, coat, equipments,
hair, and beard covered with ice, furnished a complete disguise. The
horses, too, were masked in glistening white, and shivering with cold
the men moved on in profound silence, nothing being heard but the
steady tramp of the column.

After an all-night ride Charlottesville was reached. There a short
rest was taken, and thence by forced marches the command proceeded,
sometimes marching all night, until they went into camp within six
miles of Richmond. Kilpatrick was, however, not overtaken, though
so closely were his heels clogged, that frequently in the night, the
country people insisted that Rosser's men were a part of the enemy.
After marching and counter-marching for two weeks in vain pursuit
of the doubling Federals, a rest of two days was taken at Gordonsville,
which was greatly enjoyed in spite of the scarcity of food and forage.

March the 16th the brigade started back to the Valley, making short
marches until by the 31st it was settled in comfortable quarters near
Lexington, Virginia. Though the section of country in which the new
camp was pitched was rich and as yet untouched by the devastating
hand of the enemy, its abundant supplies had been much exhausted
to feed Lee's half-starved veterans. The army ration was reduced to a
quarter of a pound of meat and one pound of meal a day.

The soldiers submitted, though they reserved the right to grumble,
and seldom failed when opportunity offered, to supplement the defi-
ciency at the tables of the hospitable farmers in the vicinity. Although
food was scarce the air and water were fine, and among a people full
of patriotic zeal, ardour for the cause was rekindled.

Indeed, it was a period of happiness for many, who far away from
scenes of war, with reviews and dress parades, enjoyed its pomp and
circumstance, while giving full range to the enjoyment of the charms
of peace.

It was a season, too, of growth for the brigade. New recruits were
added, fresh horses brought in, and the old ones rested, if not fattened.

With the approach of spring, came rumours of the moving of
Grant's vast multitude. Lee had appealed to the mothers of Virginia to

send all the laggards to the field, to help him in the desperate struggle he felt was approaching. In response to this, recruits poured in, and the brigade got its share of what was called the "new issue." Many of the sick and wounded had recovered and rejoined their regiments, so that the brigade was now much stronger both in quantity and quality of material than it had been since its active campaigns.

When the flowers of April foretokened, alas, the return of war and a leave-taking from the new-found friends, there was no hanging back now, as formerly, at the prospect of quitting the Valley. The trumpet call of Lee had stirred the depths of the Confederate heart. Like the slogan of the Highlands, "Lee needs help!" was the word passed from house to house, and from mountain and plain came the sons of Virginia in response.

The Valley men were behind none in their eagerness to take part in the decisive struggle; and when on a bright May morning the column descended the slopes of the Blue Ridge and turned towards the banks of the Rappahannock, there was a look of firm resolve in the faces of the gallant troopers, which said that they would do their best for Lee and their country.

May the 4th, 1864, Grant crossed the Rapidan and the Wilderness campaign began.

After breaking camp at Wolf Town, Madison County, May the 4th, Rosser's brigade moved up and joined Lee's army, passing the infantry in breastworks at Mine Run and encamping on Lee's right.

From all appearances the morrow promised to be a busy day.

That night a prisoner captured by some of the Eleventh Regiment was brought into Rosser's camp. Many questions were put to him by some of the soldiers, as to what was thought of Grant, the new commander of the Army of the Potomac. His answers indicated that there was great confidence in Grant's luck and energy.

"Where is your pontoon train?" said one.

To the surprise of all he responded, "Grant has no pontoon train."

"How, then, are you going to get back over the river?" asked another.

"Grant says," answered the Federal quietly, "that all of his men who go back over the river can cross on a log."

This, with other trifling incidents that soldiers eagerly seized upon, showed that the Federal Army under its new leader, confiding in numbers and Grant's luck, meant serious work.

Next day, the 5th, the sun rose hot and lurid. The heat of the night had been oppressive and the men poorly refreshed by broken slumbers, were called early into the saddle.

The command moved down the Catharpin Road, which led to Todd's Tavern. A short distance west of the River Po, a strong force of the enemy was encountered. On both sides of the road, it was heavily wooded, and the fight began between dismounted men on the flanks. At first these lines were strengthened, and for some time the battle was of an infantry character. It continued to increase in intensity, the enemy using his artillery with considerable effect. Soon the enemy began to yield to the impetuosity of the attack.

But a Federal battery on a hill sorely annoyed Rosser, who now became impatient to get to close quarters. There was no charging practicable except by fours in the road, and that which was in front and to be overcome was an unknown quantity. Had Rosser been aware that a Federal division, Wilson's, was confronting him, he might have been more cautious. Under the circumstances, there seemed nothing else to do but go forward, and the whole brigade was ordered to advance by fours. The Twelfth was in front under Col. Thomas Massie; next came the Seventh, followed by the Eleventh, with White's Battalion bringing up the rear.

The Twelfth, with the "Rebel yell," dashed at the solid ranks of the enemy over a barricade of abattis. For a while they stood firm and received the charge. Now it was man to man and hand to hand. Pistol and sabre were busy in slaughter, while the shrieks of the stricken and the shouts of the victors mingled with the roar of battle.

The fierce onset of the Confederates did not slacken. On pressed the whole brigade, crowding to the front. The Federals gave way and retreated across the River Po. On the other side they made a gallant stand, but the Confederates, now flushed with victory, pressed forward, and again drove them, in spite of the efforts of the officers to hold the men in line.

With great coolness, the enemy kept selecting new positions for their artillery, which enabled him to shell the advancing column, but nothing could keep back the horse men in the road.

The Federal retreat, however, was orderly, and at every favourable point the enemy again made efforts to rally. Although the attempts were ineffectual, they were successful enough to allow their artillery to withdraw and escape capture. Finally, a good position was reached, where there was little timber, and posting squadrons with supporting squadrons on both sides of the road, the Federals poured a deadly fire from carbines into Rosser's advancing column. Most bravely did the Twelfth charge, rally and charge again, but the Federals stood like a rock.

Rosser now ordered the Seventh and Eleventh to charge. Says Lieutenant Vandiver, who commanded Company F of the Seventh, that day:

At length we reached a point where the enemy had evidently made a stand. Coming to an old field grown up in scattering pines and sumac, we found the Federal cavalry formed. General Rosser stood on a slight eminence to our left, and as the organised supporting column emerged from the timber, he ordered the charge. My company came up in good shape. It seemed to me that the enemy was then weakening, and in spite of efforts of brave officers to hold them in line, were breaking up. About that time, the Eleventh Regiment, which followed us, came into the open ground, and Maj. E. H. McDonald led it into action, heading the charge. Our boys joined in, and the body went like a solid shot into the ranks of the Federals, who now broke and ran. Many of them were captured in the pursuit, which was continued for several miles.

During this retreat the Federals made several attempts to rally, selecting new positions for their guns, and stationing fresh squadrons of carbineers on the flanks to annoy the oncoming Confederates.

But the Confederates only halted to reform, and charging the flanking parties drove them away.

Rosser's men had begun the fight with a scant supply of ammunition, the ordnance train in the march from the Valley not having kept up with the column. As prisoners were taken their ammunition was eagerly seized, but this was not sufficient, and after several hours of fighting some of the men became discouraged.

White's Battalion was drawn up on one side of the road, and as a regiment of Yankees galloped down in their front Captain Meyers, commanding Company A, turned to Colonel White and asked, "Colonel, how can we fight those fellows with no ammunition? We'd as well have rocks as empty pistols."

But the colonel replied so grimly, "What are our sabres for?" that the men drew their blades without further hesitation, and charged square at the Yankee column, which wheeled about and retired faster than it came.

White's Battalion had been christened by Rosser "The Comanches" on account of the wild and reckless dash with which they usually bore down upon the enemy.

After pursuing the Federals to the vicinity of Todd's Tavern, Rosser halted and began to retrace his steps.

Meantime Wilson, reinforced by Gregg's division, assumed the offensive and began to harass Rosser's rear. The skirmishing was slight, but continued until the Confederates had crossed the river Po. In this fight Rosser's loss was considerable, but not nearly so great as it was the next day; yet it seems to be remembered with greater pride. It was a sort of duel between a Confederate brigade and a Federal division, in which the former had come out victorious. The superiority of the enemy in numbers, clearly seen by the men. instead of dispiriting only roused them to more energetic action. There was, too, a good deal of dis order on both sides, and more than once the scales of victory were turned by the prowess of a few.

Whether Gregg came up before Wilson had retired, does not appear.

General Grant, in his *memoirs*, says:

During the afternoon, Sheridan sent Gregg's division of cavalry to Todd's Tavern in search of Wilson. This was fortunate. He found Wilson engaged with a superior force under General Rosser supported by infantry, and falling back before it. Together, they were strong enough to turn the tables upon the enemy and themselves become aggressive. They soon drove the Rebel cavalry back beyond Corbin's bridge.

Grant was evidently misinformed and, if we are to compute the historical value of all the *Personal Memoirs* by the measure of truth in this statement, it would amount to very little. There was no infantry with Rosser and his force was greatly inferior to that of Wilson. It was not known for a long time afterwards, by the men at least, that Gregg had reinforced Wilson, or they would have been still more proud of the work done that day.

The general impression among the survivors is that then for the first time the command assumed the name of the Laurel Brigade. Whether, as some say, it was due to the fact that several soldiers conspicuous on the field wore laurel on their hats, or that Rosser, proud of his victory, dubbed the command the "Laurel Brigade," does not appear. Certain it is that from and after that date the name of "Laurel" was first used by the men themselves.

★★★★★★★★★★

Quite a number of survivors of the brigade insist that the name was given by General Rosser, at an earlier date, in the Valley, which is probably true; the name, however, was not immediately adopted by the men.

★★★★★★★★★★

General Wilson, in his official report of this fight on May 5th, says:

By eight a. m. the Second Brigade, with the First Vermont Cavalry, Colonel Preston commanding, in advance, had arrived at Craig's Meeting-House. Just beyond they encountered the enemy's cavalry, Rosser's brigade, and after a very sharp fight and several handsome charges, drove it rapidly back a distance of two miles, taking some prisoners. About noon Chapman's ammunition became exhausted, and, fearing to press the pursuit too far, I directed him to hold the position he then occupied and observe closely the movements of the enemy's troops. Having observed the menacing disposition of the enemy in front of Chapman's brigade, I directed him to collect his dis mounted men and be prepared to fall back if the enemy should press him too severely.

Soon after this, having received reinforcements, the enemy advanced and compelled Chapman to retire. It was now apparent that the Rebel force was consider ably superior to ours, and, being short of ammunition, I directed Chapman to fall back rapidly beyond the Meeting-House, and reform in rear of the First Brigade. My headquarters having been located at Mrs. Faulkner's house, when the Rebels arrived at that place my escort, composed of about fifty men of the Eighth Illinois Cavalry, commanded by Lieutenant Long, Third Indiana Cavalry, gave them a severe check, and in conjunction with a heavy fire from Pennington's and Fitzhugh's batteries, enabled everything to withdraw from the main road to the position occupied by the First Brigade.

I had scarcely arrived there, however, when I was informed by Colonel Bryan that the enemy had made his appearance, at an early hour in the forenoon, in his rear, on the road to Parker's Store, and that none of my couriers to General Meade had succeeded in getting through. Surprised at this, and fearing for the safety of my command, I immediately determined to withdraw by a blind road by Todd's Tavern to Chancellorsville.

I had scarcely taken this resolution, when I perceived that the enemy was pushing rapidly down the Catharpin Road in the same direction. The march was begun at once; the Second Brigade in advance, followed by the batteries and the First Brigade. The Eighteenth Pennsylvania Cavalry, Lieut. -Col. W. P. Brinton commanding, was left to cover the rear. The main column crossed the river Po near its head, and struck the Catharpin Road just beyond Corbin's Bridge.

It had scarcely got upon the road when the Rebels made their appearance on the hill west of the bridge. I succeeded in reaching the road with my escort just in time to prevent being cut off. The rear guard found the road occupied by the enemy, but Colonel Brinton made three brilliant and determined charges, breaking the enemy's cavalry; but finding he could not succeed in getting through without heavy loss, he struck off to the left and joined the division late in the evening.

At Todd's Tavern I found Brigadier-General Gregg, with his division, and passing behind him, formed my command to assist in holding the place. Gregg moved promptly out, attacked the enemy, and after a sharp fight repulsed him.

General Davies of Gregg's division, in his report, says:

On the morning of the 5th we marched to Todd's Tavern, and on arriving there relieved the Third Division. We fought until dark and succeeded in driving the enemy. Lost sixty-one men, mostly from the First New Jersey and First Massachusetts Cavalry.

Col. John W. Kester, of First New Jersey Cavalry, reports:

When we arrived at a village called Todd's Tavern, we met the Third Cavalry Division, commanded by General Wilson, rapidly retreating before the enemy's cavalry in a very disordered state. General Davies' brigade was immediately thrown forward, and having rapidly moved a half mile, we met the advance of the enemy's cavalry pressing forward on the rear of General Wilson. Captain Hart, with the First Squadron, was ordered to charge, which he did with such impetuosity that the enemy in turn was routed, and the gallant First Squadron pressed them back on their main body, until they in turn were met by the charge of a Rebel regiment, which again turned the tide of battle.

At this critical juncture, I hastened to his support with three squadrons of my regiment, the remaining two being sent on the flanks. Hastily forming these squadrons in line of battle, the whole line moved forward and gave the enemy such a sharp volley, followed by a rapid fire at will, that they desisted from their charge and endeavoured to keep back the advancing line of my regiment, but without success. Forward we moved as steadily as a parade, the Rebels endeavouring to check us with showers of canister, but with no avail; and they hastily limbered up their guns, and fell back just in time to prevent their capture.

From the foregoing official reports of the Federal officers in command of the opposed forces, it will be seen that the Laurel Brigade, consisting of three regiments, one battalion, and Chew's Battery, had repulsed the whole of Wilson's division, and driven it beyond the Po River, compelling Wilson to seek shelter and reform his command in the rear of Gregg's division, which had been sent to his support. It was not until the Laurel Brigade was assailed by the combined forces of Wilson and Gregg, numbering seventeen regiments of cavalry and six batteries, that it was forced to fall back beyond the Po River.

General Lee, in his report to the Secretary of War, says:

A large force of cavalry and artillery on our right flank was driven back by Rosser's brigade.

The brigade, in this all-day conflict, had more than sustained its previous reputation, and earned the name of "Laurel," by which it was thereafter known. It had opened the ball of the Wilderness campaign, the most noted in the annals of modern warfare, the campaign in which, more than in any other, the marvellous generalship of Robert E. Lee was demonstrated, and had protected the right flank of his army against an overwhelming force of Federal cavalry.

Its loss in killed, wounded, and missing was 114, the larger part in killed and wounded. It had inflicted upon its antagonist, as admitted by Federal reports, three officers and ninety-four men killed, twenty-seven officers and 389 men wounded, and 187 men missing.

Weary with the hard day's work and the excitement of battle, the men slept an unbroken sleep, little dreaming that the morrow would prove for them the bloodiest day of the war.

At break of day on the 6th all was astir, and by sunrise the bugle called to horse. The sun was just glinting through the pine-tree tops as

MAJ. JOHN W. EMMETT

Maj. John W. Emmett, assistant adjutant-general on staff of Genl. Thos. L. Rosser. This gallant gentleman and officer, so well and favourably known to the men and officers of the Laurel Brigade, was severely wounded in the body in the Battle of the Wilderness, on the 5th of May, 1864, and again was wounded in the foot in one of the battles with Sheridan in the Valley of Virginia, by which he was disabled for the rest of the war.

the column marched out to its place in the battle line.

Lee's infantry was already engaged, and on the right could be distinctly heard the ceaseless roll of musketry, which rose and fell like the distant roar of a mighty torrent.

White with his battalion led the advance, with Company A, commanded by Captain Myers, in front. After crossing the river Po, and passing the Chancellor plantation, the brigade entered the open pine country bordering the Wilderness. Rosser sent orders to White to run over everything he came to.

"How far must I go?" inquired White. To this the officer bearing the order could not well reply, and at White's suggestion went back for more explicit instructions.

"Tell him," said Rosser, "to drive them as far as he can."

In obedience to which, White immediately closed up his ranks and moved briskly forward. Soon the enemy's pickets were encountered and driven rapidly back upon their reserve. White pushed them all before him, the whole brigade following at a gallop. Above the rush of the column could be heard the shouts of the "Comanches" as they dashed upon the flying Federals.

White, in the ardour of the pursuit, which carried his command some distance in advance of any support, came suddenly upon Federal infantry and dismounted cavalry in a pine forest, who promptly opened upon him with volleys of musketry and carbines, inflicting some loss among the "Comanches."

He would probably have been pursued by the mounted cavalry, which had reformed, had not Rosser quickly put in the Eleventh to cover his retreat.

The Eleventh, under Major McDonald, now charged in fine style, and again the pines resounded with the "shout of the captains" and the roar of battle.

The Federals were now better prepared, and the rattle of the musketry grew louder. The Eleventh pressed on into the pines and turned back the advancing column of Federals, driving them through the pines until it came suddenly upon Grant's entrenched infantry. Though the Eleventh had delivered a staggering blow, yet it quailed before the tremendous fire then poured into it, and began to retire.

Now the Twelfth, under Colonel Massie, tried it, closely followed by the Seventh under Colonel Dulany. Into the pines, murky with the smoke of battle, they charged. Every step forward revealed new bodies of the enemy. The timid recoiled, but a few of the bravest pushed on until forced to retire to avoid capture.

Rosser now ordered a piece of artillery, which was the first of Thompson's Battery to reach the field, and was commanded by Lieutenant Carter, to open. Carter hastily pulling down a rail fence, brought his piece at a gallop into the field, and planted it on the rising ground before mentioned. He delivered his fire into the pines over the heads of the few struggling Confederates who—at the edge of the woods, still faced the foe. The enemy did not advance. Not a bluecoat rode out of the pines. For a brief space, the broken regiments attempted a stand on the hill upon which Carter's piece was planted. But the Federals had now quickly placed in position to the left of the pines, on a slight eminence opposite to Carter, five or six guns.

These swept the hills with a terrible fire. Before it went down men and horses, and the ground was strewn with the dead and dying. The horsemen now fell back into a woods behind Carter's piece in much confusion. There they halted and began to reform. Rosser hastily strengthened his left with about 150 dismounted men under Maj. E. H. McDonald.

The enemy lined the ridge-like eminence opposite with infantry or dismounted men, whose continuous volleys, uniting with those of their well-served artillery, swept every part of the Confederate position. A little to the right and rear of Carter's piece, White had gathered about thirty of his men, and a little further to the right was a small portion of the Eleventh, probably a dozen men, under Lieut. Isaac Parsons, still facing the foe. Carter stood his ground, answering with great rapidity the Federal shots. Now and then the enemy concentrated his fire on Carter, raining bombs around him. But he and his men, like salamanders, seemed to revel amidst the fire. Enveloped in the smoke of bursting shells the brave gunners worked their pieces, Carter encouraging them with cheering words and with shouts of triumph as he saw his well-aimed shots take effect.

The truth is that the Federal artillery was making great havoc, though the foe could not see it. Most of the bombs aimed at Carter's gun passed over him, so close was he to the enemy, and burst in the woods where the Confederate cavalry regiments were attempting to reform, falling right among them, killing and wounding a great many.

The care of the dead and dying, and the plunging of the wounded and frightened horses, created unavoidable confusion. Under the circumstances, it seemed impossible to form column. Stuart was there, riding among the men and officers, and calling upon them to be steady. The ordeal was a terrible one for cavalry, and though apparently deaf to orders amidst the thunder of bursting shells, yet most of the men stood firm. The number of killed and wounded was considerable.

Meantime Rosser sat on his horse near Carter's gun, expecting every moment to see a regiment of Federal horse burst over the crest of the opposite hill. None came, however, and it was evident that the splendid and well-maintained charges of the Laurel Brigade, together with the incomparable service of the horse artillery, which had charged with the cavalry, and discharged canister into large bodies of the enemy at close range, had severely punished the Federal cavalry and dampened the ardour of Wilson.

On the 7th, there was little fighting along any part of Lee's line. White's Battalion had a light skirmish at the bridge over the River Po, in which it defeated an attempt of the Federals to take and hold it.

Towards evening General Hampton met a reconnoitring force of the enemy, and drove it back. In this engagement the brigade participated to some extent.

On the night of the 7th, Grant began his movement by the left flank towards Spottsylvania Court House, and on the 8th, Lee's infantry began a movement to the right.

On the morning of May, the 8th, Rosser with the Laurel Brigade joined Genl. Wade Hampton at Shady Grove, and from that time to the 1st of September, the brigade formed a part of Hampton's division.

When Stuart fell and Hampton was put in command of the cavalry corps, his division was commanded by General Butler of South Carolina.

The enemy now appeared, May 8th, in full force in front of Hampton's division, then consisting of Young's and Rosser's brigades. By means of the artillery's well-directed fire his advance was soon checked.

Receiving orders from Lee to attack the enemy vigorously, in order to co-operate with Early, who was about to attack their left at Todd's Tavern, Hampton sent Rosser to attack their right and rear, while he with Young's brigade pressed their front. Both movements were executed handsomely and vigorously, and the attack was a complete success. The enemy fell back rapidly, abandoning his camp and newly-issued rations.

The fighting had been mostly against the enemy's infantry, little or no cavalry having been seen since the 6th.

This was the first engagement of the Laurel Brigade under Genl. Wade Hampton, and was fought mainly by dismounted men. It was

Hampton's favourite method, to use cavalry as mounted infantry and carbineers, wherever the nature of the country, such as that of the Wilderness, made it practicable; the horses being of use primarily for quickness of movement from one point to another, the fighting being done on foot with carbines. By adopting this use of cavalry, Hampton had by several decades anticipated the universal modern use of mounted soldiers. The introduction of the long-range repeating carbine having rendered the cavalry charge with sabre and pistol almost entirely impracticable and obsolete.

The cavalrymen realising the usual success of Hampton's method, especially where there was to be long-maintained opposition to the enemy's infantry, were willing to dismount and accepted the use of carbines, which many of them had heretofore despised, preferring to dash in upon the enemy with sabre and pistol.

The fighting on the 8th being mainly skirmishing with the infantry, most of whom were behind breastworks and abattis, the day was destitute of incidents worthy of mention.

Next day the enemy drove in Hampton's pickets and after a sharp fight obtained possession of the main road leading from Shady Grove to Spottsylvania Court House, and also held the bridge over the River Po.

On the 10th Early was sent to dislodge them. In this attack, which was successful, Hampton's division participated.

On May the 12th, the great and bloody Battle of Spottsylvania Court House was fought. Hampton took position on Lee's left, with his sharpshooters in the trenches, and his artillery posted so as to seriously annoy the right flank of the Federals.

On the 15th, Rosser made a forced reconnaissance as far as the Poor House, in the direction of Fredericksburg, driving in all the cavalry he met, and developing the position of Grant's right flank. In this movement the Eleventh was in front and suffered some losses. Among the wounded was Lieut. B. Funsten, adjutant of the regiment.

On the 16th, news came of the fight at Yellow Tavern and the fall of Gen. J. E. B. Stuart. The effect of the news, at first, was greatly to depress the men of the Laurel Brigade, who had followed the plume of Stuart on many a hard-fought field, and had been extricated by his genius and daring, from frequent situations of imminent peril. But recognising such fatalities as the inevitable and looked-for incidents of war, they steeled themselves to the performance of present duty for sake of the cause, which, with the noble example of Stuart, still

GENL. J. E. B. STUART

remained.

Grant was now moving rapidly towards Spottsylvania Court House, and Lee's infantry, in order to confront him, moved speedily in the same direction, leaving the Laurel Brigade to protect the left wing of Lee's army.

Sheridan with his cavalry corps continued his march towards Richmond, and on the 9th had gone around Lee's right with a heavy force of cavalry, and on the 11th, was confronted at Yellow Tavern by Stuart with greatly inferior numbers. Sheridan pressed his whole front vigorously, while he sent one brigade to make a dash upon Stuart's left. To this point, as the one of greatest danger, Stuart rode. Before he got there, nearly the whole left had given way, but he found a few men still holding the ground, and these he joined. With these men he fired into the enemy's flank and rear as they passed and repassed him, for they were driven back by the First Virginia Cavalry. As the Federals retired "one man who had been dismounted in the charge, and was running out on foot, turned as he passed the general and discharging his pistol, inflicted the fatal wound." (McClellan's *Stuart and His Campaigns*.)

While a few still held the enemy in check Stuart was borne from the field in an ambulance. When he noticed the disorganised ranks of his men he cried out: "Go back, go back and do your duty as I have done mine, and our country will be safe. Go back! Go back! I had rather die than be whipped." (McClellan). These were his last words on the battlefield. On the evening of the following day, he died.

Few, if any, of Lee's great captains had won more fame than Stuart, and none was more beloved by the cavalrymen. Perhaps, his most distinguishing characteristic, and the one which endeared him most to the rank and file, was his self-contained and buoyant manner in the presence of the greatest danger, and his personal courage and dash. The brilliant and successful charge, being in the nature of what he expected, often seemed unnoticed by him; but if there was a repulse or a threatening of disaster, right in the deadly breach was to be seen the waving plume of Stuart, where with burning words and flashing sword he strove to wrest victory from defeat.

In the bloom of manhood and the noontide of his fame, this brilliant soldier, superb cavalier, and Christian patriot gave to his State the libation of his blood, and his life a noble sacrifice on the altar of his country.

www.ingramcontent.com/pod-product-compliance
Lightning Source LLC
Chambersburg PA
CBHW032041080426
42733CB00006B/155